Mandatory Minimum Penalties for Drug Offenses in the Federal Criminal Justice System

William H. Pryor, Jr.
Acting Chair

Rachel E. Barkow
Commissioner

Charles R. Breyer
Commissioner

Danny C. Reeves
Commissioner

J. Patricia Wilson Smoot
Ex Officio

Zachary Bolitho
Ex Officio

Kenneth P. Cohen
Staff Director

October 2017

TABLE OF CONTENTS

1 Introduction

Introduction

In July 2017, the Commission published its *Overview of Mandatory Minimum Penalties in the Federal Criminal Justice System* (2017 *Overview Publication*),[1] which was the first in a series of publications on mandatory minimum penalties.[2] The 2017 *Overview Publication* built on the Commission's 2011 *Report to the Congress: Mandatory Minimum Penalties in the Federal Criminal Justice System* (2011 *Mandatory Minimum Report*).[3] The 2011 report, which was submitted pursuant to a Congressional directive,[4] provided detailed historical analyses of the evolution of federal mandatory minimums, scientific literature on the topic, and extensive analysis of the Commission's own data, public comment, and expert testimony. It further analyzed data related to each of the primary offenses carrying mandatory minimum penalties, and, in the chapter devoted to drug offenses, provided information about drug mandatory minimums overall and separately by drug type.

The 2017 *Overview Publication* highlighted recent trends in the charging of offenses carrying mandatory minimum penalties and provided updated sentencing data demonstrating the impact of those penalties, supplementing the analysis presented in the 2011 *Mandatory Minimum Report*. This publication, the second in the series, focuses on the application of mandatory minimum penalties specifically to drug offenses,[5] which are the most common offenses carrying mandatory minimum penalties in the federal system. As reflected in the 2017 *Overview Publication*, drug offenses have accounted for approximately two-thirds of the offenses carrying a mandatory minimum penalty in recent years, significantly higher than the next largest class of offenses.[6]

Using fiscal year 2016 data, this publication includes analysis similar to that provided in the 2017 *Overview Publication*, providing sentencing data on offenses carrying drug mandatory minimums, the impact on the Federal Bureau of Prisons (BOP) population, and differences observed when analyzing each of five main drug types. Where appropriate, the publication highlights changes and trends since the Commission's 2011 *Mandatory Minimum Report*. Because drug offenses are the most common offenses carrying mandatory minimum penalties, many of the trends in this publication mirror the trends seen in the 2017 *Overview Publication*.

In addition to reporting general data regarding the use of drug mandatory minimum penalties, the Commission also analyzed the functions performed by drug offenders as part of their offenses.[7] This function analysis provides a more complete profile of federal drug offenders and examines the use and impact of mandatory minimum penalties on offenders with differing levels of culpability.

2 Key Findings

Key Findings

Building directly on its previous reports and the analyses set forth in the 2017 *Overview Publication*, this publication examines the use and impact of mandatory minimum penalties for drug offenses. As part of this analysis, the Commission makes the following key findings:

Key Findings

1. Drug mandatory minimum penalties continued to result in long sentences in the federal system.

- In fiscal year 2016, over half (52.8%) of offenders convicted of an offense carrying a drug mandatory minimum penalty faced a mandatory minimum penalty of ten years or greater.

- In fiscal year 2016, the average sentence for offenders who were convicted of an offense carrying a drug mandatory minimum penalty was 94 months of imprisonment, more than double the average sentence (42 months) for drug offenders not convicted of an offense carrying a mandatory minimum penalty.

- Offenders who qualified for relief received significantly lower sentences (64 months) than those offenders who remained subject to a mandatory minimum penalty at sentencing (126 months). Even when offenders received relief from a mandatory minimum penalty, the average sentence (64 months) was still one and half times greater than the average sentence for those not convicted of an offense carrying a drug mandatory minimum.

- The guidelines also contributed to the sentence length as nearly three-quarters of offenders who remained subject to a drug mandatory minimum penalty (72.6%) had a guideline minimum that exceeded the statutorily required minimum, and the majority of offenders (58.8%) who remained subject to a drug mandatory minimum penalty received a sentence above the statutorily required minimum.

2. Mandatory minimum penalties continued to have a significant impact on the size and composition of the federal prison population.

- As of September 30, 2016, 49.1 percent of federal inmates were drug offenders.

- Among drug offenders in federal prison as of September 30, 2016, almost three-quarters (72.3%) were convicted of an offense carrying a mandatory minimum penalty, and more than half (50.4%) remained subject to that penalty at sentencing.

Key Findings

3.   Offenses carrying a drug mandatory minimum penalty were used less often, as the number and percentage of offenders convicted of an offense carrying a mandatory minimum penalty has decreased since fiscal year 2010.

- Less than half (44.7%) of all drug offenders sentenced in fiscal year 2016 were convicted of an offense carrying a mandatory minimum penalty, which was a significant decrease from fiscal year 2010 when approximately two-thirds (66.1%) of drug offenders were convicted of such an offense. In fact, the number of offenders convicted of a drug mandatory minimum penalty has decreased by 44.7 percent since fiscal year 2010, falling from 15,831 offenders to 8,760 such offenders in fiscal year 2016.

- The downward trend in the prevalence of offenders convicted of such penalties occurred across all drug types, but the largest decrease occurred in the context of crack cocaine offenders. Following the passage of the Fair Sentencing Act of 2010, the percent of crack cocaine offenders convicted of an offense carrying a mandatory minimum penalty has fallen from 80.1 percent in fiscal year 2010 to 46.6 percent in fiscal year 2016.

4.   While fewer offenders were convicted of an offense carrying a mandatory minimum penalty in recent years, those who were tended to be more serious.

- Convictions for offenses carrying a drug mandatory minimum penalty were more likely to involve the use of a weapon, as evidenced by the application of a guideline enhancement for having a weapon involved in the offense (17.4% in fiscal year 2016 compared to 12.5% in fiscal year 2010) or a conviction for a firearms offense carrying a mandatory minimum (5.4% in fiscal year 2016 compared to 5.1% in fiscal year 2010). Similarly, convictions for offenses carrying a drug mandatory minimum penalty were also more likely to have resulted in bodily injury (4.1% in fiscal year 2016 compared to 1.9% in fiscal year 2010).

- Offenders convicted of such offenses were also more likely to have played a leadership role, as evidenced by application of a guideline adjustment for aggravating role (11.9% in fiscal year 2016 compared to 7.7% in fiscal year 2010), and were less likely to receive a mitigating role adjustment (12.1% compared to 16.3%).

- Consistent with increased likelihood of the above aggravating factors, the rate at which offenders convicted of an offense carrying a drug mandatory minimum penalty received relief through the statutory safety valve decreased from 35.1 percent in fiscal year 2010 to 30.0 percent in fiscal year 2016.

Key Findings

5.   Drug mandatory minimum penalties applied more broadly than Congress may have anticipated.

- While some legislative history leading up to passage of the Anti-Drug Abuse Act of 1986 suggests that "major" traffickers would be subject to the ten-year drug mandatory minimum penalty and "serious" traffickers would be subject to the five-year penalty, they often apply to offenders who perform relatively low-level functions. For example, nearly one-third (32.2%) of Couriers and more than one-quarter of Mules (25.4%) were convicted of such offenses.

- While the rate of conviction for an offense carrying a drug mandatory minimum penalty tended to decrease with the culpability level of the offender as reflected by their function, a significant percentage of offenders in every function were nevertheless convicted of such offenses. In fact, a majority of offenders in seven of the ten function categories (including some lower-level functions) were convicted of an offense carrying a drug mandatory minimum penalty.

- Many of the offenders convicted of an offense carrying a drug mandatory minimum penalty had little or no criminal history. Almost half (45.9%) were in Criminal History Category I—37.7 percent of all offenders convicted of an offense carrying a mandatory minimum received no criminal history points under the guidelines, while 8.1 percent received one criminal history point. On the other end of the spectrum, 14.2 percent of all offenders convicted of an offense carrying a mandatory minimum penalty were in Criminal History Category VI.

6.   Statutory relief plays a significant role in the application and impact of drug mandatory minimum penalties and results in significantly reduced sentences when applied.

- More than half (51.6%) of offenders convicted of an offense carrying a drug mandatory minimum penalty received relief at sentencing.

- In fiscal year 2016, 21.8 percent of offenders convicted of a drug mandatory minimum penalty qualified for relief under the safety valve, 21.5 percent received relief for providing substantial assistance, and 8.2 percent received relief for both safety valve and substantial assistance.

- Offenders who received safety valve relief (57 months) or provided substantial assistance (81 months) received significantly lower sentences than those offenders who remained subject to a drug mandatory minimum penalty at sentencing (126 months). Offenders who received both safety valve relief and provided substantial assistance had even lower average sentences (41 months).

Key Findings

7.   Additionally, drug mandatory minimum penalties appear to provide a significant incentive to provide substantial assistance to the government pursuant to 18 U.S.C. § 3553(e) and the related guideline provision at USSG §5K1.1.

- In fiscal year 2016, offenders convicted of an offense carrying a drug mandatory minimum penalty were nearly twice as likely to have provided substantial assistance to the government as those not convicted of such an offense (29.8% compared to 15.2%).

- Nearly a quarter of offenders facing a five-year drug mandatory minimum penalty (22.2%) received a substantial assistance reduction, while 36.0 percent of offenders facing a ten-year mandatory minimum penalty and more than half of offenders facing a mandatory minimum penalty of 20 years or more received a substantial assistance reduction (52.3%).

8.   However, neither the statutory safety valve provision at 18 U.S.C. § 3553(f) nor the substantial assistance provision at 18 U.S.C. § 3553(e) fully ameliorate the impact of drug mandatory minimum penalties on relatively low-level offenders.

- A significant portion of offenders who performed relatively low-level functions did not qualify under the safety valve provision. For example, a significant portion of Couriers (31.9%), Mules (28.8%), and Employees/Workers (33.9%) did not qualify for the safety valve in fiscal year 2016.

- The likelihood of receiving relief for substantial assistance varied depending on the offender's function in the offense. Offenders who performed higher-level functions were generally more likely to receive relief for providing substantial assistance than offenders who performed low-level functions, reflecting the fact that low-level offenders often do not have valuable information to provide due to their more limited role in the offense. For example, offenders with the Broker (50.0%), Street-Level Dealer (38.6%), and Organizer/Leader (36.2%) functions were more likely to receive substantial assistance relief than Couriers (26.6%) and Mules (17.3%).

- Low-level offenders who remained subject to a drug mandatory minimum penalty because they did not qualify for relief received long sentences. For example, Couriers, Mules, and Employees/Workers who remained subject to a drug mandatory minimum penalty received average sentences significantly exceeding five years at 101 months, 82 months, and 100 months, respectively.

Key Findings

9.   There were significant demographic shifts in the data relating to mandatory minimum penalties.

- As they did in fiscal year 2010, Hispanic offenders continued to represent the largest group of offenders (51.9%) convicted of an offense carrying a drug mandatory minimum penalty in fiscal year 2016. However, other demographic data has shifted.

- White offenders and Black offenders shared the highest average sentence among offenders convicted of an offense carrying a drug mandatory minimum penalty (103 months) in fiscal year 2016. White offenders also had the highest average sentence among both offenders relieved of the application of a drug mandatory minimum penalty at sentencing (69 months) and offenders subject to a drug mandatory minimum penalty at sentencing (136 months). This is a change from fiscal year 2010, when Black offenders had the longest average sentences in each of the above categories.

- While Black offenders convicted of an offense carrying a drug mandatory minimum penalty continued to receive relief from the drug mandatory minimum penalty least often, the gap between Black offenders and White offenders has narrowed. In fiscal year 2016, 64.5 percent of Black offenders convicted of an offense carrying a drug mandatory minimum penalty remained subject to that penalty compared to 50.8 percent of White offenders convicted of such an offense (a difference of 13.7 percentage points). By comparison, the difference was 24.2 percentage points in fiscal year 2010 (59.5% of Black offenders convicted of an offense carrying a drug mandatory minimum penalty compared to 35.3% of White offenders).

10.   Although likely due in part to an older age at release, drug trafficking offenders convicted of an offense carrying a drug mandatory minimum penalty had a lower recidivism rate than those drug trafficking offenders not convicted of such an offense.

- Of those offenders convicted of an offense carrying a drug mandatory minimum penalty, nearly half (47.7%) were rearrested during the eight-year study period, compared to 54.7 percent of drug trafficking offenders not convicted of an offense carrying a drug mandatory minimum penalty.

- However, the longer sentences received by offenders convicted of drug mandatory minimum penalties result in older ages at release, which is also an important factor in recidivism. Offenders who were not convicted of an offense carrying a mandatory minimum penalty were approximately four years younger at release than those convicted of an offense carrying a ten-year mandatory minimum penalty (34 compared to 38 years old).

3 Mandatory Minimums

Statutory Mandatory Minimum Provisions Applicable to Federal Drug Offenses

Penalty Provisions

Federal drug trafficking offenders are primarily convicted of offenses under Title 21 of the United States Code. These statutes prohibit the distribution, manufacture, or importation of controlled substances, and possession with intent to distribute controlled substances,[8] in addition to certain specific acts like distributing drugs to persons who are under the age of 21 or who are pregnant, using persons under the age of 18 in drug operations, and distributing drugs in or near schools and colleges.[9] The most commonly prosecuted drug offenses that carry mandatory minimum penalties are 21 U.S.C. §§ 841 and 960. Section 841 prohibits the knowing or intentional manufacture, distribution, dispensation, or possession with intent to manufacture, distribute or dispense a controlled substance. Section 960 prohibits the knowing and intentional importation or exportation of a controlled substance.[10]

Under both provisions, mandatory minimum penalties are tied to the quantity and type of controlled substance involved in the offense. When certain quantity thresholds are met, a five-year mandatory minimum penalty and a maximum term of 40 years applies, while larger amounts increase the mandatory minimum to ten years, with a maximum of life imprisonment.[11] These penalties may be enhanced further based on an offender's record of previous drug offenses.[12] For example, offenders who otherwise qualify for the five-year mandatory minimum penalty face an increased statutory range of ten years to life

if they have a prior conviction for a felony drug offense.[13] Similarly, a qualifying prior conviction increases a ten-year mandatory minimum to a 20-year mandatory minimum (the maximum remains life), while offenders previously convicted of two or more prior drug felonies are subject to a mandatory term of life.[14]

Triggering Thresholds for Common Controlled Substances		
21 U.S.C. § 841	5-year Mandatory Minimum	10-year Mandatory Minimum
Heroin	100 G	1 KG
Powder Cocaine	500 G	5 KG
Cocaine Base (crack)	28 G	280 G
Marijuana	100 KG	1,000 KG
Methamphetamine (pure)	5 G	50 G
Methamphetamine (mixture)	50 G	500 G

The penalties for committing other drug offenses under Title 21 are also tied to the above-referenced penalty structure. For example, attempts or conspiracies to commit any drug offense are subject to the same penalty structure as the substantive offense.[15] Higher penalty ranges apply if death or serious bodily injury results from use of the controlled substance.[16]

As discussed in greater detail in the Commission's previous reports,[17] some legislative history leading up to passage of the Anti-Drug Abuse Act of 1986 discusses the establishment of this two-tiered mandatory penalty structure targeted to "major" traffickers and "serious" traffickers. In particular, floor statements[18] from various members in support of the 1986 Act suggest that the two-tiered penalty structure was designed to target discrete categories of traffickers by linking the five-year mandatory minimum penalties to "serious" traffickers and the ten-year mandatory minimum penalties to "major" traffickers.[19] Drug quantity would serve as a proxy to identify those types of traffickers.

Relatedly, a committee report from the House Judiciary Subcommittee on Crime, issued just over a month before the 1986 Act passed, summarized the committee's consideration of a predecessor bill (House Bill 5394)[20] discussing the establishment of the two-tiered mandatory minimum penalties for serious and major traffickers. According to the report, "the Committee strongly believe[d] that the Federal government's most intense focus ought to be on major traffickers, the manufacturers or the heads of organizations, who are responsible for creating and delivering very large quantities of drugs," and "determined that a second level of focus ought to be on the managers of the retail level traffic, the person who is filling the bags of heroin, packing crack into vials … and doing so in substantial street quantities."[21] The report referred to this second level of trafficker as "serious traffickers because they keep the street markets going."[22]

Congress also referenced these deliberations in later committee reports as indicative of a "general congressional desire to link the Act's minimum penalties and specified drug quantities such that 'kingpin' traffickers would be subject to the ten-year minimum sentence and 'middle-level' traffickers would be subject to the five-year minimum sentence."[23]

Statutory Relief Provisions

Offenders may receive relief from the statutory mandatory minimum penalty, even when otherwise applicable based on drug quantity, in two ways. First, if the prosecution files a motion based on the defendant's "substantial assistance" to authorities in the investigation or prosecution of another person, a sentencing court may impose a sentence below the statutory minimum pursuant to 18 U.S.C. § 3553(e).[24] Second, if the defendant meets the "safety valve" criteria provided in 18 U.S.C. § 3553(f), the statute provides that the court shall impose a sentence pursuant to the sentencing guidelines without regard to the otherwise applicable statutory minimum.[25] For the safety valve to apply, the court must find, on motion of the government, that:

1. the defendant does not have more than one criminal history point;
2. the defendant did not use violence or credible threats of violence or possess a firearm or other dangerous weapon in connection with the offense;
3. the offense did not result in death or serious bodily injury to any person;
4. the defendant was not an organizer, leader, manager or supervisor of others or engaged in a continuing criminal enterprise; and
5. the defendant has, by the time of sentencing, truthfully provided to the Government all relevant information.

Unlike a substantial assistance departure—which applies to all federal offenses carrying a mandatory minimum penalty—the safety valve statute applies only in cases in which a defendant

faces a mandatory minimum penalty after being convicted of a drug trafficking offense listed in the statute.[26] These relief mechanisms are described in greater detail in the 2017 *Overview Publication*.[27]

Guideline Provisions

Defendants convicted of violating these statutes are sentenced under Part D of Chapter Two of the *Guidelines Manual*. The principal drug trafficking guideline is USSG §2D1.1 (Unlawful Manufacturing, Importing, Exporting, or Trafficking), which typically applies to convictions for distributing, manufacturing, importing, or possessing with intent to distribute controlled substances. The primary drivers of the severity of an offender's punishment under this guideline are the type and quantity of drugs for which he or she is accountable, although other factors, discussed in greater detail below, may also affect sentence length.

Section 2D1.1 has five alternate base offense levels (BOL). Four of the five apply if the defendant was convicted under a specific statute listed in the guideline and death or serious bodily injury resulted from the offense.[28] The fifth base offense level, which is the most commonly applied, ties the base offense level to the type and quantity of drugs involved in the offense, ranging from an offense level of 6 up to offense level 38.[29] As a result of the Commission's 2014 "drugs minus two" amendment, offenses that involve drug quantities triggering the five-year mandatory minimum are set at base offense level 24 (51 to 63 months at Criminal History Category I), and offenses involving quantities triggering the ten-year mandatory minimum are set at level 30 (97 to 121 months at Criminal History Category I).[30]

In addition to §2D1.1, drug offenders are also sentenced under other guidelines in Chapter Two, Part D. These guidelines apply when an offender is convicted of violating particular statutes—for example, §2D1.2 applies when an offender is convicted under one of several statutes prohibiting the sale of drugs in certain locations or to specified classes of persons.[31] While these guidelines contain some unique provisions reflecting the specific nature of the offense of conviction, they also incorporate the drug quantity table at §2D1.1, and the drug quantity for which an offender is held responsible is likely to be a major driver of his or her recommended guideline range under any of the Chapter Two, Part D guidelines.

The guidelines incorporate both statutory mechanisms for relief from mandatory minimum penalties. Section 5K1.1 authorizes a departure from the guideline range if the offender provided substantial assistance to law enforcement and the government files a motion to that effect. However, because §5K1.1 cannot authorize courts to impose a sentence below a mandatory minimum penalty, the sentencing court may not do so unless the government files a motion pursuant to 18 U.S.C. § 3553(e). For defendants who qualify for relief from the mandatory minimum penalty pursuant to the statutory safety valve, the guideline at §5C1.2 directs the court to "impose a sentence in accordance with the applicable guidelines without regard to any statutory minimum sentence."[32] The drug trafficking guideline at §2D1.1 also provides for a 2-level decrease if the defendant meets the safety valve subdivision criteria listed at §5C1.2.[33] This decrease applies regardless of whether the defendant was convicted of an offense carrying a mandatory minimum penalty.

4 Data Analysis

The Commission's Updated Study of Drug Mandatory Minimum Penalties

In its 2011 *Mandatory Minimum Report*, the Commission made several recommendations to Congress regarding the use of, and improvement to, mandatory minimum penalties generally and with respect to the four major offense types. The Commission made two specific recommendations regarding the use of mandatory minimum penalties in drug offenses. These were that Congress: (1) consider expanding the safety valve at 18 U.S.C. § 3553(f); and (2) reassess the severity and scope of the recidivist enhancements for drug offenses at 21 U.S.C. §§ 841 and 960.

2011 RECOMMENDATIONS

In its 2011 *Mandatory Minimum Report*, the Commission recommended that Congress marginally expand the safety valve at 18 U.S.C. § 3553(f), and reassess the severity and scope of the recidivist enhancements for drug offenses.

Since the 2011 *Mandatory Minimum Report*, the Commission has continued its study of the scope, use, and impact of mandatory minimum penalties in the federal system, providing regular updates through the issuance of Quick Facts publications, as well as in testimony before Congress. Given the changes highlighted in the 2017 *Overview Publication*, as well as ongoing interest in this subject, the Commission provides this publication to update the information and analyses in its 2011 *Mandatory Minimum Report* and to further inform discussion of the Commission's recommendations regarding the use of mandatory minimum penalties for drug offenses.

For purposes of this publication, focusing on drug offenses[34] carrying mandatory minimum penalties, the Commission analyzed 62,251 cases from the Commission's datafile, identifying relevant offender and offense characteristics, including demographic data, the types of underlying offenses, and basic criminal history information.[35] This publication provides general comparisons between all federal drug offenders, offenders convicted of an offense carrying a drug mandatory minimum penalty, and offenders who remained subject to a drug mandatory minimum penalty at the time of sentencing. The Commission also provides data about sentencing outcomes involving the application of drug mandatory minimum penalties. Where appropriate, this publication highlights key changes between the data set forth in the Commission's 2011 *Mandatory Minimum Report* and the fiscal year 2016 sentencing data, as well as key differences by drug type. Detailed analysis and figures are provided for each drug type in the appendices.

It is the Commission's intent that the data in this publication will further inform the ongoing discussion regarding mandatory minimum penalties by Congress, the Department of Justice, and others.

Recent Trends in Mandatory Minimum Penalties

As discussed in the 2017 *Overview Publication*, the prevalence of convictions for an offense carrying any mandatory minimum among all federal offenders decreased in fiscal year 2016. From fiscal years 1991 to 2014, the percentage of federal offenders convicted of an offense carrying a mandatory minimum penalty remained relatively stable, fluctuating between 26.0 percent and 31.9 percent. Over the past three years, the percentage has decreased to 21.9 percent in fiscal year 2016, a difference of 5.3 percentage points from fiscal year 2010 (27.2%).[36]

While the percentage of offenders convicted of an offense carrying a mandatory minimum penalty steadily decreased, the percentage of offenders subject to a mandatory minimum at sentencing remained relatively stable during the same time period, falling only slightly from 14.5 percent in fiscal year 2010 to 13.4 percent in fiscal year 2016. This is because offenders have been increasingly less likely to receive relief from a mandatory minimum penalty through a substantial assistance motion or application of the statutory safety valve. In fiscal year 2016, 38.7 percent offenders convicted of an offense carrying a mandatory minimum

penalty received relief, down from 46.7 percent in 2010.[37]

Although the use of mandatory minimum penalties decreased overall, different trends appeared with respect to different offenses carrying mandatory minimum penalties. Drug offenses, along with firearms offenses, continued to top the list of the most frequently used mandatory minimum penalty statutes. Drug offenses accounted for slightly more than two-thirds of the offenses (67.3%) carrying a mandatory minimum penalty in fiscal year 2016, significantly higher than the next closest category of offenses.[38] As in fiscal year 2010, the most frequently reported conviction of an offense carrying a mandatory minimum penalty in fiscal year 2016 was 21 U.S.C. § 846 (Attempt and Conspiracy [to Commit a Drug Trafficking Offense]). Violations of section 846 accounted for almost a quarter (24.9%) of the convictions under statutes carrying a mandatory minimum penalty. The primary drug trafficking penalty provisions of 21 U.S.C. § 841—sections 841(b)(1)(A) and

Figure 1. Offenders Convicted of an Offense Carrying a Mandatory Minimum Penalty and Offenders Subject to a Mandatory Minimum Penalty at Sentencing
Fiscal Years 1991 - 2016

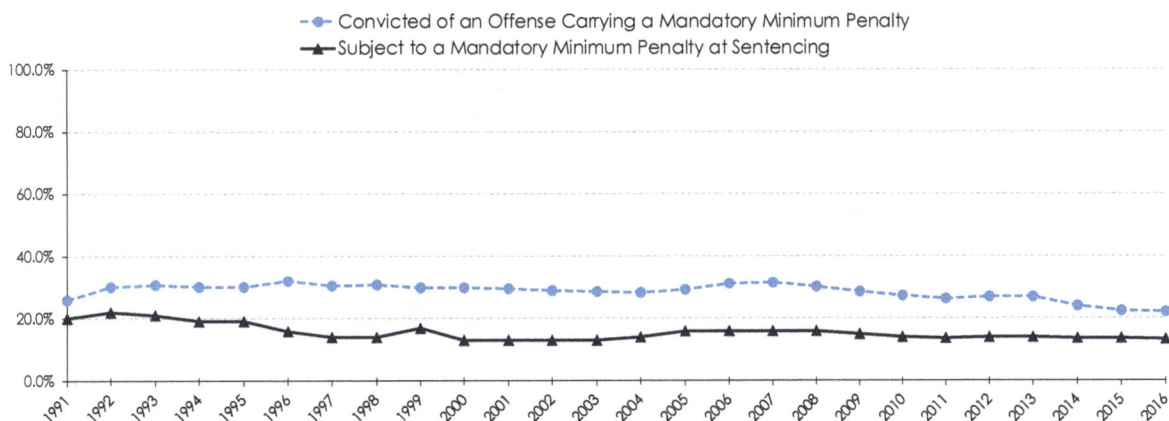

SOURCE: U.S. Sentencing Commission 1991 through 2016 Datafiles, USSCFY1991–USSCFY2016.

Table 1. Number of Convictions for Most Frequently Used Statutes Carrying a Mandatory Minimum Penalty *Fiscal Year 2016*

STATUTE	Total Number of Counts of Convictions	Percentage of Counts of Conviction
21 U.S.C. § 846	5,982	24.9%
21 U.S.C. § 841(b)(1)(B)	2,478	10.3%
21 U.S.C. § 841(b)(1)(A)	2,224	9.3%
18 U.S.C. § 924(c)(1)(A)(i)	1,974	8.2%
18 U.S.C. § 924(c)(1)(A)(ii)	1,019	4.2%

SOURCE: U.S. Sentencing Commission, 2016 Datafile, USSCFY16.

(B)—remain in the top five most frequent statutes of conviction carrying a mandatory minimum penalty.[39]

Though drug offenses remain the most commonly charged offenses carrying mandatory minimum penalties, over time, the percentage of drug offenders convicted of a drug offense carrying a mandatory minimum penalty has decreased significantly while the percentage of offenders convicted of other offenses carrying a mandatory minimum penalty—violent, firearms, sexual abuse,

pornography and "other" offenses—has steadily increased.[40] Figure 2 shows that the percentage of drug trafficking offenders convicted of an offense carrying a mandatory minimum penalty remained relatively stable from 1992 through 2013, fluctuating between 60 and 72 percent. However, after 2013, there was a significant decrease in the percentage of drug trafficking offenders convicted of an offense carrying a mandatory minimum penalty. It decreased to 52.2 percent in fiscal year 2014, 47.9 percent in fiscal year 2015, and reached its lowest rate of 46.8 percent in 2016.[41]

These trends are consistent with recent legislative changes and changes in Department of Justice charging policy. The last significant change to mandatory minimum penalties—the Fair Sentencing Act of 2010 (FSA)—repealed the mandatory minimum penalties established for simple possession of crack cocaine and increased the quantities required to trigger the five- and ten-year mandatory minimum penalties for crack cocaine trafficking offenses from five to 28 grams and 50 to 280 grams, respectively.[42] The FSA also directed the Commission to provide higher

Figure 2. Offenders in Select Offense Types Convicted of an Offense Carrying a Mandatory Minimum Penalty *Fiscal Years 1991 - 2016*

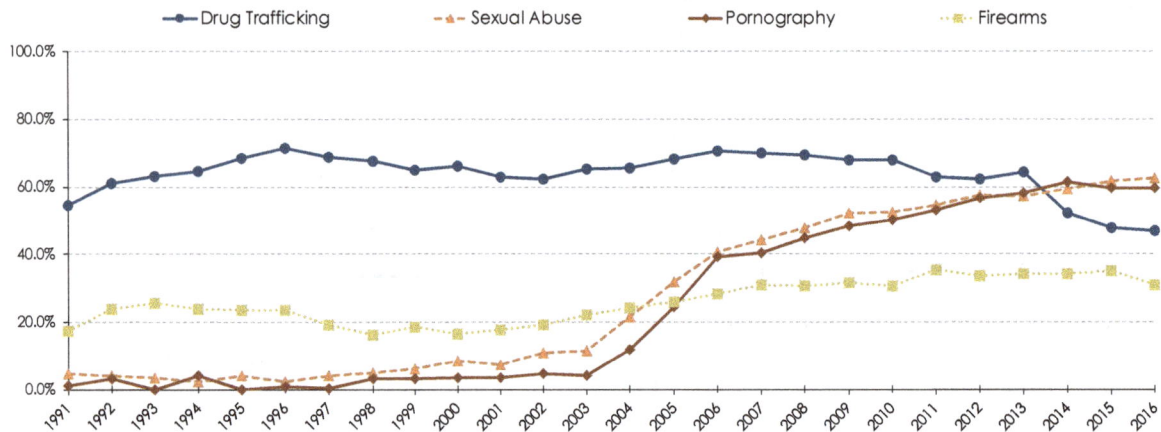

SOURCE: U.S. Sentencing Commission, 1991 through 2016 Datafiles, USSCFY91 – USSCFY16.

guideline sentences for drug offenders based on certain aggravating factors and to provide lower guideline sentences for offenders who received an adjustment for being a minimal participant in the offense.[43] In 2011, the Commission implemented the FSA's new penalties in the guidelines and subsequently made the changes retroactive,[44] and also recommended that Congress make the statutory provisions retroactive.[45] Following implementation, a Commission study indicated that these changes in the FSA reduced the disparity between crack and powder cocaine sentences, reduced the federal prison population, and appear to have resulted in fewer federal prosecutions for crack cocaine.[46]

In addition to these legislative changes, there were also significant changes to the charging of offenses carrying mandatory minimum penalties that impacted the data in this publication. Beginning in 2010, the Department of Justice amended its guidance to federal prosecutors regarding which offenses to charge, including by requiring more targeted charging of offenses carrying a mandatory minimum penalty. Before 2010, Department of Justice policy had directed prosecutors to charge the most serious, readily provable offenses supported by the facts and that would result in the longest sentence.[47] In 2010, then-Attorney General Eric Holder issued a memorandum instructing that while a prosecutor "should ordinarily charge" the most serious offense, the charging decision requires an individual assessment of the facts of the case, considering the purpose of federal criminal laws and the best use of federal resources. The "Holder Memorandum," as it has come to be called, required the same individualized assessment in plea bargaining and sentencing.[48]

Following the Supreme Court's decision in *Alleyne v. United States*,[49] which held that facts that trigger a mandatory minimum penalty are elements that must be submitted to the jury and proven beyond a reasonable doubt,[50] the Department of Justice further modified its charging policies as part of its Smart on Crime Initiative. Noting that "the Supreme Court's decision in *Alleyne* heightens the role a prosecutor plays in determining whether a defendant is subject to a mandatory minimum sentence," the Department of Justice issued a new policy refining its charging policy regarding mandatory minimums for certain non-violent, low-level drug offenders.[51] The Smart on Crime Initiative instructed that "prosecutors should decline to charge the quantity necessary to trigger the mandatory minimum sentence if the defendant meets" the following criteria:

- the defendant's relevant conduct does not involve the use of violence, the credible threat of violence, the possession of a weapon, the trafficking of drugs to or with minors, or the death or serious bodily injury of any person;
- the defendant is not an organizer, leader, manager, or supervisor of others within a criminal organization;
- the defendant does not have significant ties to large-scale drug trafficking organizations, gangs, or cartels; and
- the defendant does not have a significant criminal history (normally evidenced by three or more criminal history points but may involve fewer or greater depending on the nature of any prior convictions)."[52]

The memorandum further provided that prosecutors should decline to pursue the recidivist enhancements in Title 21 (and therefore not file an information pursuant to 21 U.S.C. § 851) "unless the defendant is involved in conduct that makes the case appropriate for severe sanctions."[53]

It is likely that many, if not all of these, changes have in some way impacted the data discussed in this publication, including the current population of the Federal Bureau of Prisons (BOP). Different trends, however, may emerge because of changed policies with respect to mandatory minimums. Attorney General Jefferson Sessions recently issued guidance reverting to the previous policy that "prosecutors should charge and pursue the most serious, readily provable offense" and stating that "the most serious offenses are those that carry the most substantial guideline sentence, including mandatory minimum sentences."[54] Therefore, any recent data trends reported in this publication may not be permanent.

Prevalence of Drug Offenses Carrying Mandatory Minimum Penalties

How Often Are Drug Offenders Charged with an Offense Carrying a Mandatory Minimum Penalty?

Drug Offenders Overall

As noted above, the prevalence of offenders convicted of an offense carrying a drug mandatory minimum penalty decreased in fiscal year 2016, both in number and as a percentage of all offenders sentenced in that year. As reflected in Figure 3, less than half (44.7%, n=8,760) of the 19,584

drug offenders sentenced in fiscal year 2016 were convicted of an offense carrying a drug mandatory minimum penalty,[55] a significant change from fiscal year 2010 when nearly two-thirds (66.1%, n=15,831) of the 23,964 drug offenders were convicted of such an offense. This reflects a 44.7 percent decrease in the number of drug offenders convicted of an offense carrying a drug mandatory minimum penalty, from 15,831 offenders in fiscal year 2010 to 8,760 offenders in fiscal year 2016. Although this decrease is due in part to the reduction in the federal offender population in recent years, the fact that the number of offenders convicted of an offense carrying a drug mandatory minimum penalty declined at a greater rate than the overall population[56] indicates that changes in charging practices are also responsible.

Figure 3. Drug Offenders Convicted of an Offense Carrying a Drug Mandatory Minimum Penalty *Fiscal Year 2016*

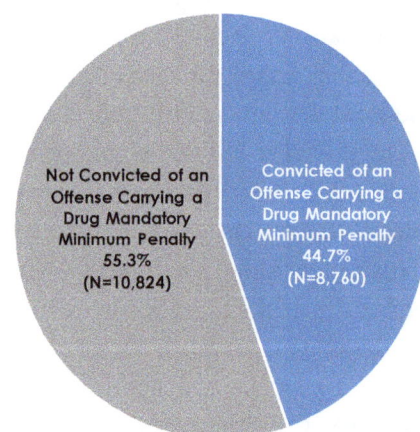

SOURCE: U.S. Sentencing Commission, 2016 Datafile, USSCFY16.

The impact of changes in charging practices is further demonstrated by the recent decrease in the percentage of drug offenders convicted of an offense carrying a drug mandatory minimum, as shown in Figure 4. From fiscal years 1992 to 2013, the percentage of drug offenders convicted of an offense carrying a drug mandatory minimum penalty remained relatively steady, fluctuating between 57.2 percent and 67.0 percent. That trend significantly changed, however, over the past three years, with the percentage of drug offenders convicted of an offense carrying a drug mandatory minimum penalty decreasing from 62.5 percent in fiscal year 2013 to 50.4 percent in fiscal year 2014 and 44.7 percent in this most recent fiscal year.

Despite this considerable decrease, the percentage of drug offenders who remain subject to a drug mandatory minimum remained largely steady over the past seven fiscal years with only a slight downward trend. After reaching 31.6 percent in fiscal year 2005, the rate fell slightly to 28.8 percent in fiscal year 2010 and then to 21.7 percent in fiscal year 2016. While this decrease is notable, it is smaller than the substantial decrease in the drug offenders convicted of any offense carrying a drug mandatory minimum penalty. This is because drug offenders convicted of an offense carrying a drug mandatory minimum were less likely to receive relief from the mandatory minimum through a substantial assistance motion or application of the statutory safety valve. In fiscal year 2016, 51.6 percent of such offenders were relieved from its application at sentencing due to substantial assistance, safety valve, or both.[57] This compares to 54.4 percent who received relief in fiscal year 2010.[58]

These trends are consistent with the stated goals of the Department of Justice's 2010 memorandum and its 2013 Smart on Crime Initiative instructing prosecutors to be more selective in charging offenses with a mandatory minimum penalty, specifically in cases involving certain nonviolent,

Figure 4. Offenders Convicted of an Offense Carrying a Drug Mandatory Minimum Penalty and Offenders Subject to a Drug Mandatory Minimum at Sentencing
Fiscal Years 1991 - 2016

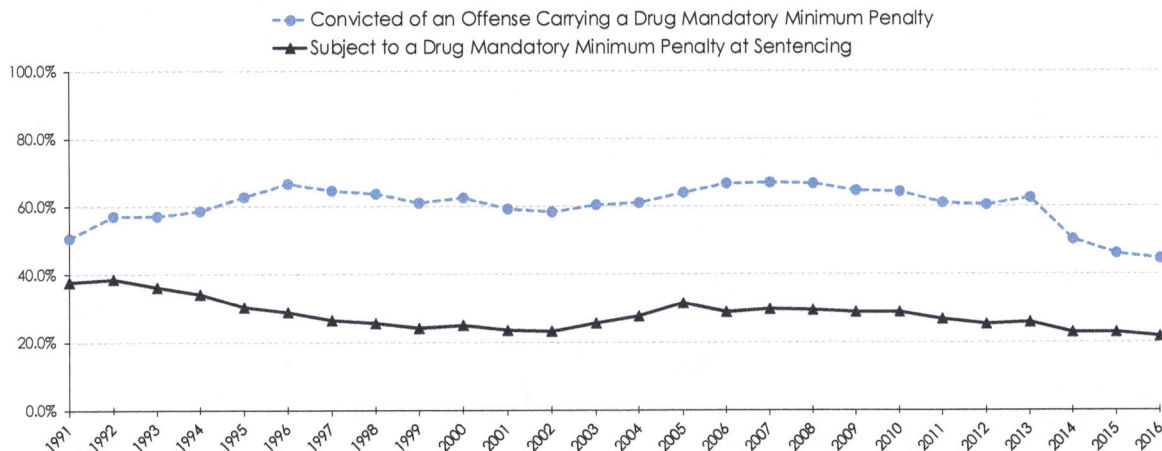

SOURCE: U.S. Sentencing Commission 1991 through 2016 Datafiles, USSCFY1991-USSCFY2016.

low-level drug offenders. As discussed in the 2017 *Overview Publication*, offenders who met certain identified criteria related to the guidance provided in the Smart on Crime Initiative remained subject to a mandatory minimum penalty at a higher rate in 2016 than they did in 2010.[59]

Prevalence by Drug Type

As would be expected given the decline in offenders convicted of an offense carrying a drug mandatory minimum, there was a similar downward trend in the prevalence of offenders convicted of an offense carrying a drug mandatory minimum penalty, both in number and percentage, across each of the primary drug types. In fiscal year 2016, powder cocaine offenders were convicted of an offense carrying a drug mandatory minimum more often than offenders convicted of offenses involving any other drug type (60.2%), followed by methamphetamine offenders (54.6%), crack cocaine offenders (46.6%), and heroin offenders (42.9%).

Marijuana offenders were convicted of an offense carrying a drug mandatory minimum penalty least often (26.1%).

As reflected in Figure 5, however, the extent of the decrease did vary somewhat for each of the drug types. As would be expected following the passage of the FSA, the largest change occurred in the context of crack cocaine offenders. While 80.1 percent of crack cocaine offenders were convicted of an offense carrying a drug mandatory minimum penalty in fiscal year 2010, only 46.6 percent were convicted of such an offense in fiscal year 2016.

Significant shifts also occurred for marijuana offenders, who were convicted of an offense carrying a drug mandatory minimum nearly twice as often in fiscal year 2010 (42.5%) as compared to fiscal year 2016 (26.1%). The rate for methamphetamine offenders fell from 82.0 percent in fiscal year 2010 to 54.6 percent in fiscal year 2016, while the rate for

Figure 5. Percentage of Offenders in Select Drug Types Convicted of an Offense Carrying a Drug Mandatory Minimum Penalty
Fiscal Years 1993 - 2016

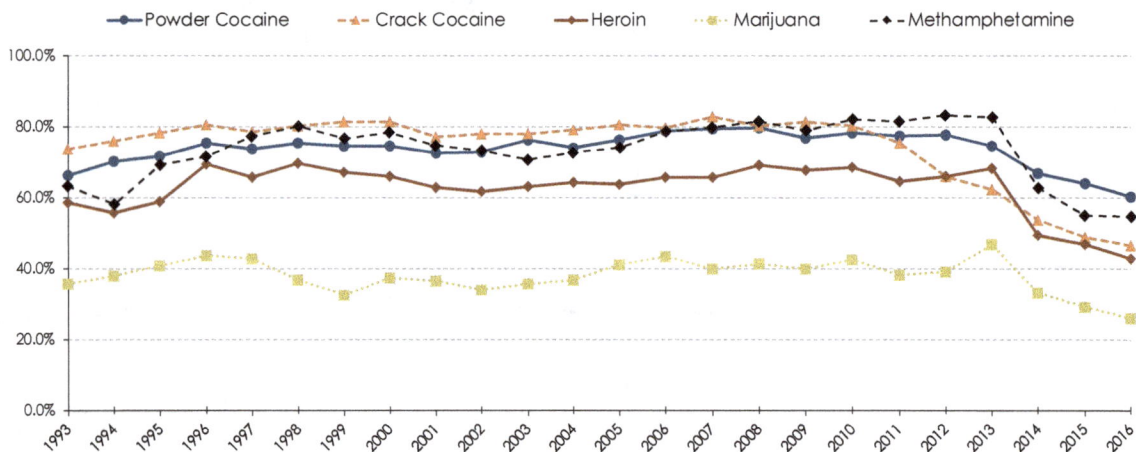

SOURCE: U.S. Sentencing Commission, 1993 through 2016 Datafiles, USSCFY93 – USSCFY16.

heroin offenders fell from 68.5 percent in fiscal year 2010 to 42.9 percent in fiscal year 2016. Powder cocaine offenders experienced a smaller decrease, from 78.4 percent in fiscal year 2010 to 60.2 percent in fiscal year 2016.

Because of these varying rates of decrease, there have also been significant shifts in the prevalence of each drug type among those offenders convicted of an offense carrying a drug mandatory minimum penalty. As reflected in Figure 6, more than one-third (40.6%, n=3,553) of offenses carrying a drug mandatory minimum penalty in fiscal year 2016 involved methamphetamine, followed by powder cocaine (26.2%, n=2,293), heroin (13.6%, n=1,192), marijuana (10.4%, n=914), crack cocaine (8.3%, n=728) and other drugs (0.9%, n=78). This largely reflects the distribution of drug offenses overall, one-third (33.4%, n=6,508) of which involved methamphetamine, followed by powder cocaine (19.5%, n=3,809), marijuana (17.9%, n=3,497), heroin (14.3%, n=2,780), crack cocaine (8.0%, 1,562), and other drugs (7.0%, n=1,356). However, both methamphetamine (40.6%) and powder cocaine (26.2%) are over-represented with

respect to the percentage of offenders convicted of an offense carrying a drug mandatory minimum compared to their portion of the overall drug offender population, which is 33.4 percent and 19.5 percent, respectively. Additionally, in 2016, more offenses carrying a drug mandatory minimum involved heroin (13.6%) than marijuana (10.4%), though marijuana makes up a greater percentage of drug offenses (17.9%, compared to 14.3%).

The proportions represent some significant shifts from those reported in the Commission's 2011 *Mandatory Minimum Report*. Not only were there more drug offenders (n=23,964) and a greater percentage of offenders convicted of an offense carrying a drug mandatory minimum (66.1%) in fiscal year 2010, but the distribution and order of the most common drugs involved has changed significantly. In fiscal year 2010, more than one-quarter (28.1%, n=4,447) of offenses carrying a drug mandatory minimum penalty involved powder cocaine, followed by crack cocaine (24.7%, n=3,905), methamphetamine (21.9%, n=3,466), marijuana (17.2%, n=2,725), heroin (6.9%, n=1,098) and other drugs (1.1%, n=172).

Figure 6. Type of Drug Involved in Drug Offenses
Fiscal Year 2016

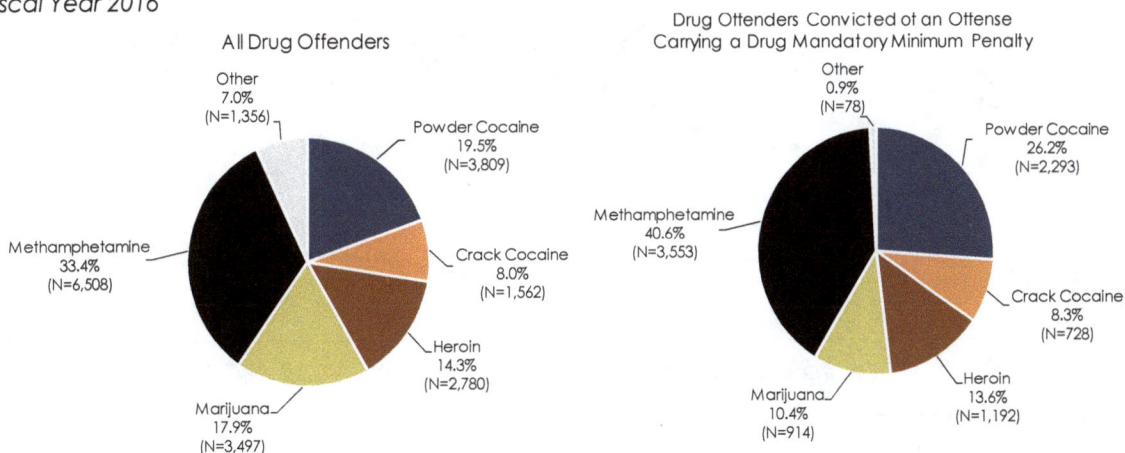

All Drug Offenders

Drug Offenders Convicted of an Offense
Carrying a Drug Mandatory Minimum Penalty

SOURCE: U.S. Sentencing Commission, 2016 Datafile, USSCFY16.

The biggest changes occurred in relation to crack cocaine and methamphetamine offenders. In fiscal year 2010, crack cocaine offenders represented a significantly larger portion of offenders convicted of an offense carrying a drug mandatory minimum penalty in fiscal year 2010 (24.7% compared to 8.3% in fiscal year 2016), while methamphetamine offenders represented a smaller portion of such offenders in fiscal year 2010 (21.9% compared to 40.6% in fiscal year 2016).

This shift is, in large part, due to changes in the number of methamphetamine and crack cocaine offenders since fiscal year 2010. Among all crack cocaine offenders, 728 were convicted of an offense carrying a drug mandatory minimum penalty, down from 3,924 in 2010. While the number of methamphetamine offenders also decreased following the Department of Justice's 2013 Smart on Crime Initiative, Figure 7 shows a marked increase in the number of methamphetamine offenders convicted of an offense carrying a drug mandatory minimum penalty over time when compared to other drug types.

How Severe Were Mandatory Minimum Penalties for Drug Offenders?

As discussed in Section Three, mandatory minimum penalties apply to certain controlled substance offenses and vary in length depending on the type and quantity of drug involved in the offense.

Consistent with fiscal year 2010 data, almost all offenders (96.7%) convicted of an offense carrying a drug mandatory minimum penalty in fiscal year 2016 faced mandatory minimum penalties of ten years or less as shown in Figure 8. At 49.5 percent, such offenders were most frequently convicted of violating a statute carrying a drug mandatory

Figure 7. Number of Offenders in Select Drug Types Convicted of an Offense Carrying a Drug Mandatory Minimum Penalty
Fiscal Years 1993 - 2016

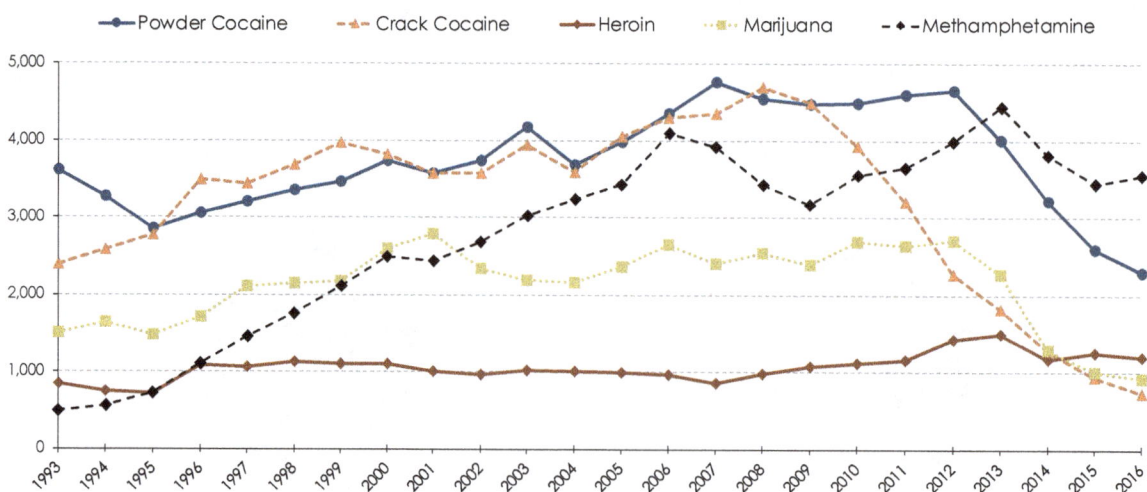

SOURCE: U.S. Sentencing Commission, 1993 through 2016 Datafiles, USSCFY93 – USSCFY16.

minimum penalty of ten years of imprisonment, which is virtually the same as in fiscal year 2010. There was a slight increase in the percentage of offenders convicted of an offense carrying a drug mandatory minimum penalty of five years, from 43.5 percent in fiscal year 2010 to 46.1 percent in fiscal year 2016. In contrast, there was a slight decrease in the percentage of offenders convicted of an offense carrying a drug mandatory minimum penalty of twenty years, from 4.5 percent in fiscal year 2010 to 2.9 percent in fiscal year 2016. The percent of offenders who were sentenced to life

imprisonment remained low—1.0 percent in fiscal year 2010 compared to 0.4 percent in 2016.

There are, however, notable distinctions in the severity of the applicable mandatory minimum penalty depending on drug type. Both powder cocaine and methamphetamine offenders were most frequently convicted under a statute carrying a drug mandatory minimum penalty of ten years of imprisonment—57.0 percent of powder cocaine offenders convicted of an offense carrying a drug mandatory minimum penalty and 59.5 percent of methamphetamine offenders convicted of such an offense faced a ten-year drug mandatory minimum penalty. Conversely, crack cocaine (59.9%), heroin (48.3%), and marijuana offenders (83.3%) convicted of an offense carrying a drug mandatory minimum were most frequently convicted under a statute carrying a five-year drug mandatory minimum penalty.[60]

Figure 8. Length of Mandatory Minimum Penalty for Offenders Convicted of an Offense Carrying a Drug Mandatory Minimum Penalty

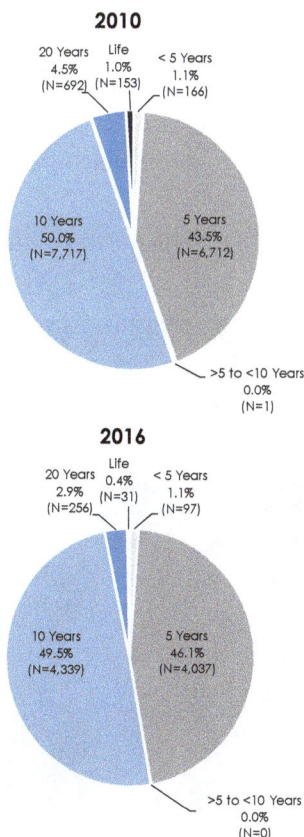

SOURCE: U.S. Sentencing Commission, 2010, and 2016 Datafiles, USSCFY10, and USSCFY16.

Figure 9. Length of Mandatory Minimum Penalty for Offenders Convicted of an Offense Carrying a Mandatory Minimum Penalty

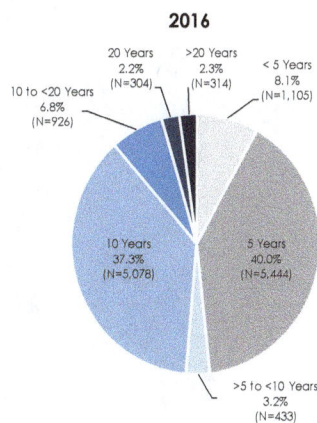

SOURCE: U.S. Sentencing Commission, 2016 Datafile, USSCFY16.

Offenders convicted of an offense carrying a drug mandatory minimum also differed in several ways from the group of offenders convicted of any mandatory minimum offense discussed in the 2017 *Overview Publication*. *See* Figure 9. First, when convicted of an offense carrying a drug mandatory minimum penalty, offenders generally face a higher minimum than offenders convicted of such offenses overall. As reflected in Figure 9, such drug offenders were most frequently convicted for violating a statute carrying a ten-year drug mandatory minimum, whereas the most frequent mandatory minimum penalty was five years imprisonment in 2016 (40.0%) for offenders convicted of an offense carrying any mandatory minimum penalty. Equally notable, however, is the fact that only 3.3 percent of drug offenders convicted of an offense carrying a drug mandatory minimum penalty faced a minimum of more than ten years. Conversely, 11.3 percent of offenders convicted of any mandatory minimum offense faced such penalties.

This distinction is, of course, driven in part by the differing mandatory minimum statutory provisions applicable to the various offense types.[61]

Where Were Offenders Convicted of Offenses Carrying Drug Mandatory Minimums?

There continued to be geographic differences in the rates at which drug mandatory minimum penalties apply.[62] Two-thirds (66.7%) of the 8,760 cases involving a drug mandatory minimum penalty were brought in the district courts within five circuits: 2,145 (24.5%) were in the Fifth Circuit, 1,065 (12.2%) were in the Eleventh, 979 (11.2%) were in the Ninth, 910 (10.4%) were in the Eighth, and 742 (8.5%) were in the Sixth.

In fiscal year 2016, courts in only one district (Southern District of Texas) sentenced more than 750 offenders who were convicted of an offense

Figure 10. Number of Offenders Convicted of an Offense Carrying a Drug Mandatory Minimum Penalty by District
Fiscal Year 2016

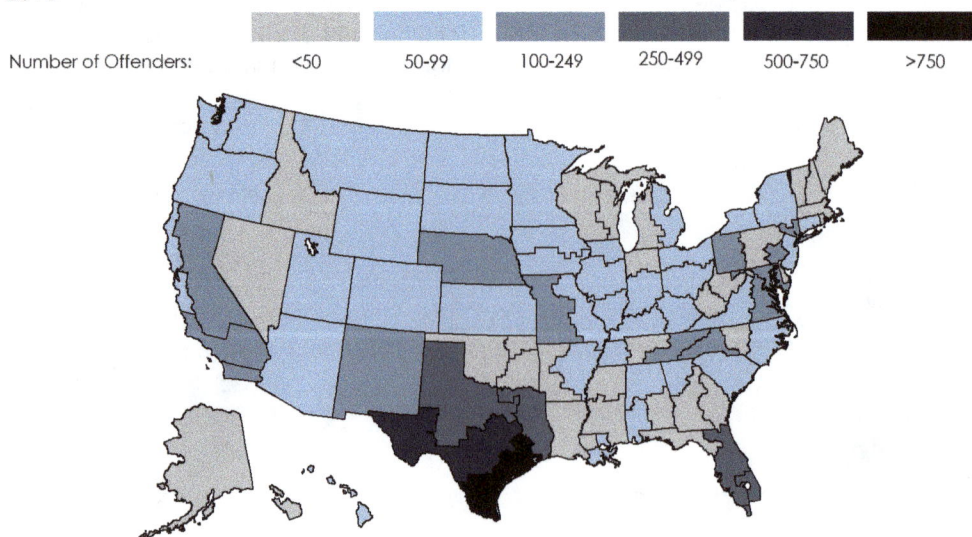

SOURCE: U.S. Sentencing Commission, 2016 Datafile, USSCFY16.

carrying a drug mandatory minimum. That one district accounted for 10.1 percent (n=882) of the 8,760 cases involving a drug mandatory minimum in fiscal year 2016. The four districts reporting the next highest number of cases involving a drug mandatory minimum penalty were: Western Texas (6.7%, n=590), Middle Florida (5.0%, n=439), Southern Florida (4.2%, n=370), and Puerto Rico (4.0%, n=349). Most often, districts had 50 to 99 such convictions (40 of the 94 districts, or 42.6%), while 33 districts (35.1%) had less than 50 such convictions.

Offender Demographics

This section provides an overview of the demographics[63] of drug offenders convicted of an offense carrying a drug mandatory minimum penalty. Demographics of offenders convicted of an offense carrying a drug mandatory minimum penalty vary widely based on the type of drug involved in the offense.

Race, Gender, and Citizenship

In fiscal year 2016, Hispanic offenders continued to represent the largest group of offenders (51.9%) convicted of an offense carrying a drug mandatory minimum penalty, as they did in fiscal year 2010 (44.0%). As set forth in Table 2, the 2016 percentage is nearly equal to their proportion of the total federal drug offender population (50.2%). Black offenders (23.6%), White offenders (21.9%), and Other Race offenders (2.6%) accounted for the remaining offenders convicted of an offense carrying a drug mandatory minimum penalty.

Table 2. Demographic Characteristics of Drug Offenders
Fiscal Year 2016

	All Drug Offenders	Convicted of an Offense Carrying a Drug Mandatory Minimum Penalty	Relieved of Mandatory Minimum Penalty	Subject to Drug Mandatory Minimum Penalty at Sentencing
Total (# of offenders)	**19,584**	**8,760**	**4,519**	**4,241**
RACE				
White	23.4%	21.9%	20.9%	23.0%
Black	23.5%	23.6%	16.3%	31.4%
Hispanic	50.2%	51.9%	60.3%	43.0%
Other	2.9%	2.6%	2.6%	2.6%
CITIZENSHIP				
U.S. Citizen	71.9%	71.4%	61.0%	82.4%
Non-U.S. Citizen	28.1%	28.7%	39.0%	17.6%
GENDER				
Male	84.6%	88.9%	85.2%	92.8%
Female	15.4%	11.1%	14.8%	7.2%

SOURCE: U.S. Sentencing Commission, 2016 Datafile, USSCFY16.

Hispanic offenders were also the largest group to be relieved of a drug mandatory minimum penalty (60.3%), just as they were in fiscal year 2010 (47.7%). This is mainly due to the large number of Hispanic offenders who received relief through the safety valve. In fiscal year 2016, 44.1 percent of Hispanic offenders convicted of an offense carrying a drug mandatory minimum penalty received relief through the safety valve, compared to 16.5 percent of White offenders, 12.4 percent of Black offenders, and 26.9 percent of Other Race offenders.

Of the 4,241 offenders subject to a drug mandatory minimum penalty at sentencing, Hispanic offenders were the largest group (43.0%) followed by Black offenders (31.4%) and White offenders (23.0%). This is a change from fiscal year 2010, when Black offenders were the largest group (40.4%) subject to a drug mandatory minimum penalty at sentencing, followed by Hispanic offenders (39.6%).

As shown in Table 1 in each of the drug specific appendices,[64] the demographics of offenders convicted of drug offenses varied widely by specific drug type in fiscal year 2016. More than three-quarters (82.6%) of all crack cocaine offenders were Black; most powder cocaine offenders were Hispanic (61.8%); most methamphetamine offenders were Hispanic (50.4%) or White (38.8%); most marijuana offenders were Hispanic (76.8%); and most heroin offenders were Hispanic (42.0%) or Black (40.0%). Hispanic offenders represented the largest group of offenders convicted of an offense carrying a mandatory minimum penalty involving powder cocaine (67.9%), as well as the largest group convicted of such an offense involving marijuana (73.9%), methamphetamine

(46.2%), and heroin (46.7%). White offenders also represented a large proportion (42.7%) of offenders convicted of an offense carrying a mandatory minimum penalty involving methamphetamine. Similarly, Black offenders represented a large proportion (41.7%) of offenders convicted of an offense carrying a mandatory minimum penalty involving heroin. Black offenders represented the largest group of offenders convicted of an offense carrying a mandatory minimum penalty involving crack cocaine (85.0%).

As reflected in Table 2, almost three-fourths of offenders convicted of an offense carrying a drug mandatory minimum penalty were U.S. citizens (71.4%).[65] Similarly, most offenders who remained subject to a drug mandatory minimum penalty were U.S. citizens (82.4%). Offenders convicted of an offense carrying a drug mandatory minimum are more commonly U.S. citizens for all drug types except marijuana, for which non-U.S. citizens constituted a greater percentage (55.5%) than U.S. Citizens (44.5%).

Males were most common across all three groups—offenders convicted of an offense carrying a drug mandatory minimum (88.9%), relieved of a drug mandatory minimum (85.2%), and subject to a drug mandatory minimum penalty at sentencing (92.8%). Males were over-represented in the population of offenders who remained subject to a mandatory minimum at sentencing compared to their proportion of overall drug offenders (84.6%). With respect to drug type, methamphetamine and heroin offenders had the highest percentage of female offenders, 20.4 percent and 16.3 percent, respectively, approximately double the next highest drug type, powder cocaine, at 10.8 percent.

Age

Offenders convicted of an offense carrying a drug mandatory minimum penalty are fairly evenly distributed throughout age brackets between 26 through 50, with fewer younger than 26 or older than 50.

The average age of offenders in all categories and for all drug types ranges from 33 to 38. Marijuana offenders are, on average, slightly younger than offenders convicted of offenses involving other drug types, while powder cocaine offenders are the oldest across all categories.[66]

Figure 11. Age of Offenders Convicted of an Offense Carrying a Drug Mandatory Minimum Penalty *Fiscal Year 2016*

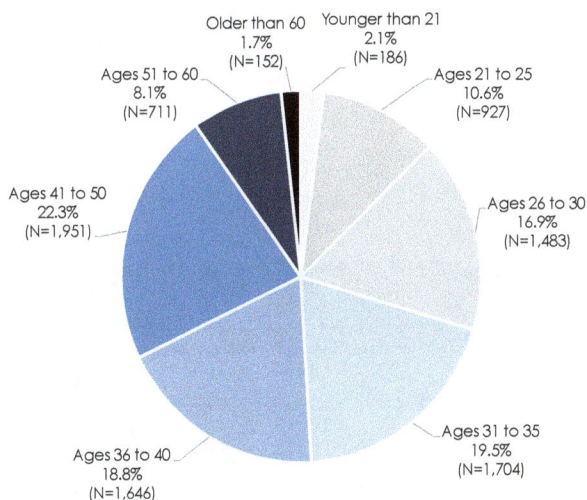

SOURCE: U.S. Sentencing Commission, 2016 Datafile, USSCFY16.

Criminal History and Offense Characteristics

Criminal History

Nearly half of offenders convicted of an offense carrying a drug mandatory minimum penalty (45.9%) were in Criminal History Category I. As reflected in Figure 12, 37.7 percent of offenders convicted of an offense carrying a drug mandatory minimum received no criminal history points under the guidelines, while 8.1 percent received one criminal history point. On the other end of the spectrum, 13.7 percent of all offenders convicted of an offense carrying a drug mandatory minimum penalty received more than ten criminal history points.

A distinct difference appears when looking at offenders relieved of the application of the mandatory minimum penalty and offenders who remain subject to such penalty at sentencing. As set forth in Table 3, offenders in Criminal History Category I were substantially more likely to be relieved of the drug mandatory minimum penalty than offenders in higher criminal history categories, which is unsurprising as only drug offenders who fall within Criminal History Category I are eligible for relief through the statutory safety valve. Thus, even though less than half of offenders convicted of a drug mandatory minimum penalty were in Criminal History Category I (45.9%), offenders in that category accounted for almost two-thirds (66.4%) of those who were relieved of the mandatory minimum penalty. By contrast,

Figure 12. Criminal History Scores of Offenders Convicted of an Offense Carrying a Drug Mandatory Minimum Penalty
Fiscal Year 2016

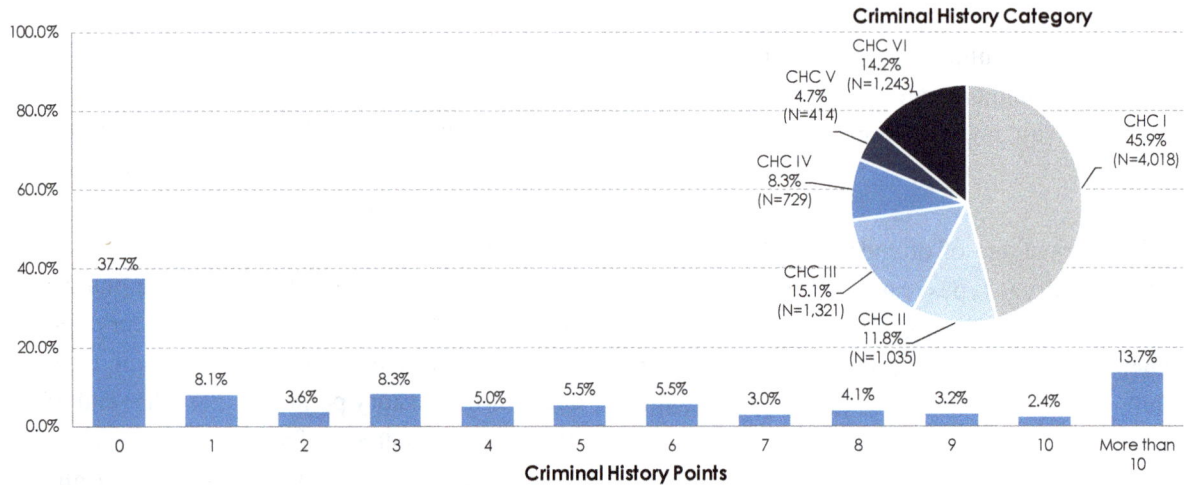

SOURCE: U.S. Sentencing Commission, 2016 Datafile, USSCFY16.

offenders in Criminal History Category VI represented 14.2 percent of offenders convicted of an offense carrying a drug mandatory minimum penalty, but represented 20.3 percent of offenders who were subject to a drug mandatory minimum penalty at sentencing.

Criminal history does vary by drug type. For example, marijuana offenders had the highest percentage of offenders in CHC I (65.9%).[67] Crack cocaine offenders had the lowest percentage in CHC I (18.3%) and the highest percentage in CHC VI (28.7%).[68]

Table 3. Criminal History of Drug Offenders
Fiscal Year 2016

	All Drug Offenders	Convicted of an Offense Carrying a Drug Mandatory Minimum Penalty	Relieved of Mandatory Minimum Penalty	Subject to Drug Mandatory Minimum Penalty at Sentencing
Total (# of offenders)	19,584	8,760	4,519	4,241
CRIMINAL HISTORY CATEGORY				
I	49.6%	45.9%	66.4%	24.0%
II	12.4%	11.8%	7.9%	16.0%
III	14.1%	15.1%	9.7%	20.8%
IV	7.4%	8.3%	4.9%	12.0%
V	4.2%	4.7%	2.7%	6.9%
VI	12.2%	14.2%	8.5%	20.3%

SOURCE: U.S. Sentencing Commission, 2016 Datafile, USSCFY16.

Table 4. Guideline Sentencing Characteristics of Drug Offenders
Fiscal Year 2016

	All Drug Offenders	Convicted of an Offense Carrying a Drug Mandatory Minimum Penalty	Relieved of Mandatory Minimum Penalty	Subject to Drug Mandatory Minimum Penalty at Sentencing
Total (# of offenders)	19,584	8,760	4,519	4,241
SENTENCING CHARACTERISTICS				
Weapon Specific Offense Characteristic	13.4%	17.4%	10.5%	24.8%
Used Violence or Threat of Violence	0.8%	1.2%	0.6%	1.8%
Bodily Injury	4.2%	4.1%	1.9%	6.4%
Firearms Mandatory Minimum Applied	4.4%	5.4%	3.7%	7.1%
Safety Valve Reduction	34.0%	30.1%	58.3%	0.0%

SOURCE: U.S. Sentencing Commission, 2016 Datafile, USSCFY16.

Offense Characteristics

Certain offense characteristics were more prevalent among drug offenders who remained subject to the mandatory minimum penalty at sentencing. As reflected in Table 4, nearly a quarter of offenders subject to a drug mandatory minimum penalty received a guideline enhancement for having a weapon involved in the offense (24.8%), while 7.1 percent were also convicted of an offense carrying a firearm mandatory minimum penalty. In both instances, these rates were higher than the application rate for all drug offenders, 13.4 percent and 4.4 percent, respectively. Similarly, the data demonstrate that offenses in which the offender remained subject to a drug mandatory minimum penalty were more likely to have involved the use or threat of violence (1.8%) compared to 0.8 percent of all drug offenders, and to have resulted in bodily injury (6.4%) compared to 4.2 percent among all drug offenders. In each instance, these rates are also higher than the rate among all offenders convicted of an offense carrying any mandatory minimum penalty.

As reflected in Figure 13, drug offenders who remained subject to a drug mandatory minimum penalty were more than twice as likely to have received an adjustment for aggravating role (16.4%) compared to all drug offenders in fiscal year 2016 (7.5%). Conversely, such offenders were over five times less likely to have received an adjustment for mitigating role (4.4%) compared to all drug offenders (20.5%).

Consistent with the stated goals of the Department of Justice's Smart on Crime Initiative, the prevalence of many of the aggravating factors discussed above has increased over time, indicating that those convicted of an offense carrying a drug mandatory minimum penalty in fiscal year 2016 tended to be more serious offenders. Convictions for offenses carrying a drug mandatory minimum penalty were more likely to involve the use of a weapon as evidenced by the application of a guideline enhancement for having a weapon involved in the offense (17.4% in fiscal

Figure 13. Role in the Offense of Drug Offenders
Fiscal Year 2016

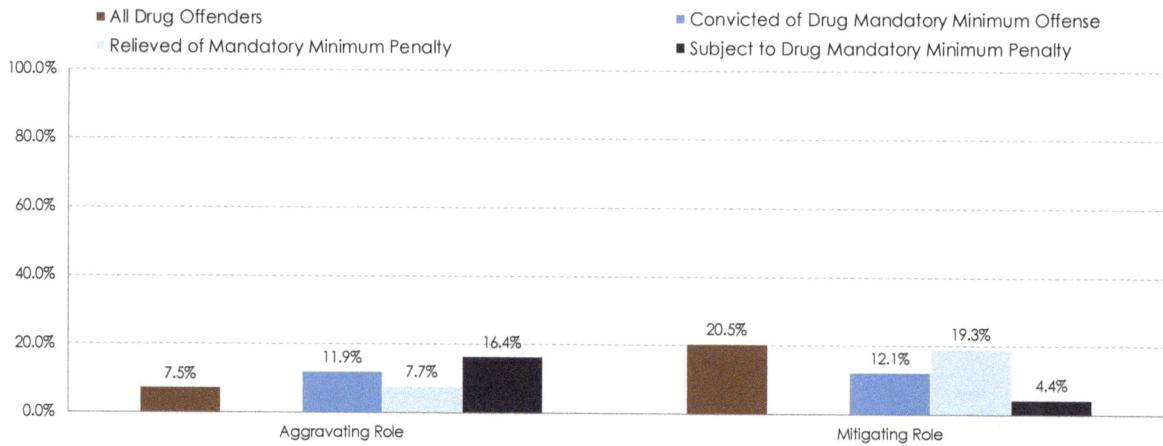

SOURCE: U.S. Sentencing Commission, 2016 Datafile, USSCFY16.

year 2016 compared to 12.5% in fiscal year 2010) or a conviction for a firearms offense carrying a mandatory minimum (5.4% in fiscal year 2016 compared to 5.1% in fiscal year 2010). Similarly, convictions for offenses carrying a drug mandatory minimum penalty were also more likely to have resulted in bodily injury (4.1% in fiscal year 2016 compared to 1.9% in fiscal year 2010).

Offenders convicted of such offenses were also more likely to have played a leadership role, as evidenced by application of a guideline adjustment for aggravating role (11.9% in fiscal year 2016 compared to 7.7% in fiscal year 2010), while the reverse was true for those who received a mitigating role adjustment (12.1% compared to 16.3%).

As reflected in Table 2 in each of the drug specific appendices,[69] crack cocaine offenders have significantly higher instances of firearm or weapon involvement than all drug offenders and offenders in other specific drug types in all categories (all offenders, convicted of an offense

carrying a mandatory minimum, relieved of a mandatory minimum, and subject to a mandatory minimum). Of all crack cocaine offenders, 22.9 percent received a guideline weapon enhancement and 9.7 percent were convicted of a firearms offense carrying a mandatory minimum penalty. In contrast, marijuana offenders had fewer instances of firearm or weapon involvement in all categories (4.7% received a weapon enhancement and 1.9% were subject to a firearm mandatory minimum). Marijuana offenders also had the highest percentage of offenders who received a mitigating role adjustment and remained subject to the mandatory minimum penalty (10.0% compared to 4.4% for drug offenders overall).

Relief from Mandatory Minimum Penalties

Despite a significant decrease in the percentage of offenders who were convicted of an offense carrying a drug mandatory minimum penalty, the percentage of offenders who remain subject to a drug mandatory minimum was steadier over the

Figure 14. Offenders Relieved of a Drug Mandatory Minimum Penalty
Fiscal Year 2016

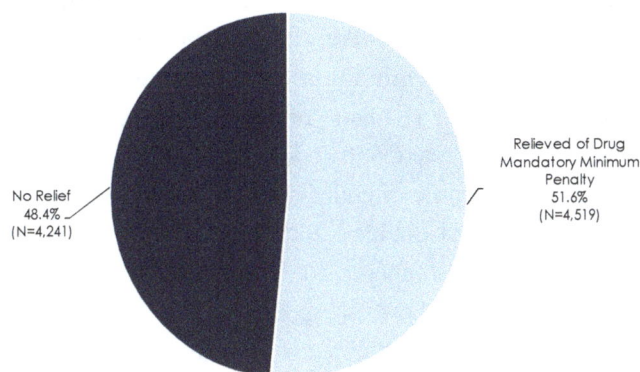

No Relief
48.4%
(N=4,241)

Relieved of Drug
Mandatory Minimum
Penalty
51.6%
(N=4,519)

SOURCE: U.S. Sentencing Commission, 2016 Datafile, USSCFY16.

past seven fiscal years.[70] This is because the rate at which drug offenders convicted of an offense carrying a drug mandatory minimum penalty received relief at sentencing has also decreased in recent years.

As demonstrated in Figure 14, over half (51.6%) of the offenders convicted of an offense carrying a drug mandatory minimum penalty were relieved from its application at sentencing due to substantial assistance, safety valve, or both, while less than half (48.4%) remained subject to the drug mandatory minimum penalty at sentencing. By comparison, 54.4 percent of offenders convicted of a drug mandatory minimum penalty received relief in fiscal year 2010.

The decrease in the rate of relief is the result of a reduction in the percentage of offenders qualifying for the statutory safety valve. Of offenders convicted of an offense carrying a drug mandatory minimum penalty, 30.0 percent received relief pursuant to the safety valve (21.8% for safety valve only, and 8.2% for both safety valve and substantial assistance). By comparison, 35.1 percent of such offenders received safety valve relief in fiscal year

2010 (26.1% for safety valve only, and 9.0% for both safety valve and substantial assistance).

The likelihood of receiving substantial assistance has increased slightly since fiscal year 2010. In fiscal year 2016, 29.7 percent received relief for substantial assistance (21.5% for substantial assistance only, and 8.2% for both substantial assistance and safety valve), compared to 28.3 percent in fiscal year 2010.

While relief for drug offenders decreased, it is notable that offenders receive relief from drug mandatory minimum penalties at a higher rate than offenders convicted of an offense carrying any mandatory minimum penalty. In fiscal year 2016, 48.4 percent of offenders convicted of an offense carrying a drug mandatory minimum received no relief from that penalty and were still subject to a mandatory minimum penalty at sentencing. This compares to 61.3 percent of offenders subject to any mandatory minimum penalty.[71]

Figure 15. Offenders Relieved of a Drug Mandatory Minimum Penalty by Relief Type
Fiscal Year 2016

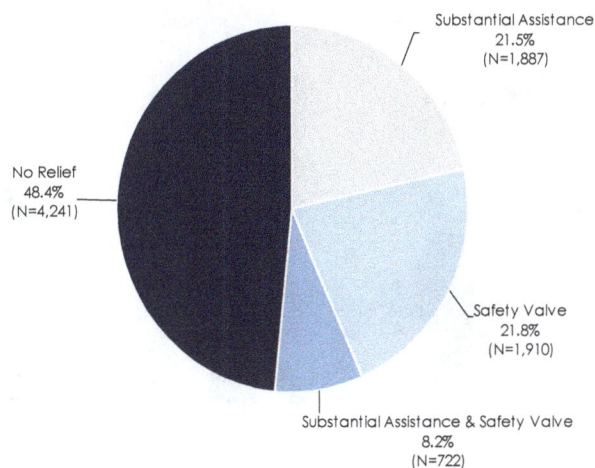

Substantial Assistance
21.5%
(N=1,887)

No Relief
48.4%
(N=4,241)

Safety Valve
21.8%
(N=1,910)

Substantial Assistance & Safety Valve
8.2%
(N=722)

SOURCE: U.S. Sentencing Commission, 2016 Datafile, USSCFY16.

Frequency of relief also varied by drug type: marijuana offenders received relief from a drug mandatory minimum most often (69.4%), with over half receiving safety valve relief (54.5%), while crack cocaine offenders received relief the least often (30.3%), with only 6.9 percent receiving safety valve relief. This is primarily the result of differences in criminal history; marijuana offenders had the highest percentage of offenders in CHC I (65.9%), the only CHC eligible for safety valve relief, while crack cocaine offenders had the lowest (18.3%).

Demographics

As reflected in Figure 16, demographic differences also appeared in the rates of relief for offenders convicted of an offense carrying a drug mandatory minimum penalty. Black offenders continued to receive relief least often. Of Black offenders convicted of an offense carrying a drug mandatory minimum penalty, 64.5 percent remained subject to that penalty. White offenders had the second highest rate (50.8%). Hispanic offenders were least likely to remain subject to a drug mandatory minimum at sentencing (40.1%). This is because Hispanic offenders received relief at the highest rate (59.9%) due, in large part, to the fact that Hispanic offenders qualified for the safety valve at almost double the rate of the next closest group (44.1% compared to 26.9% for Other Race offenders), and at over three times the rate of Black offenders (44.1% compared to 12.4%).

With respect to safety valve relief, the difference between Hispanic offenders and the other demographic groups could be partially attributable to the fact that Black and White offenders who commit drug offenses often do not qualify for the safety valve because of their criminal history. In fiscal year 2016, 78.0 percent of White offenders and 76.7 percent of Black offenders convicted of

Figure 16. Percent of Offenders Convicted of an Offense Carrying a Drug Mandatory Minimum Penalty Who Were Relieved of the Penalty by Race of Offender
Fiscal Year 2016

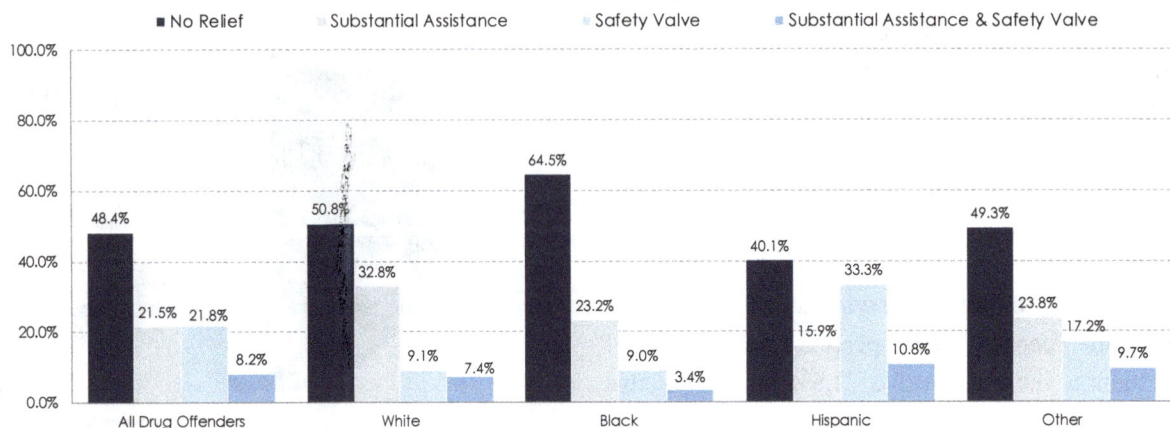

SOURCE: U.S. Sentencing Commission, 2016 Datafile, USSCFY16.

an offense carrying a drug mandatory minimum penalty were in Criminal History Categories II – VI, which disqualified them from consideration for the safety valve. By contrast, only 35.7 percent of Hispanic offenders convicted of a drug mandatory minimum penalty were in Criminal History Categories II – VI.

Weapon involvement is also another factor relating to the likelihood of qualifying for safety valve relief among demographic groups. In fiscal year 2016, 7.6 percent of Black drug offenders convicted of an offense carrying a drug mandatory minimum penalty were convicted of a firearm offense under 18 U.S.C. § 924(c). This compares to 5.4 percent of White drug offenders, 4.4 percent of Hispanic drug offenders, and 5.3 percent of Other Race drug offenders. In addition, 24.1 percent of Black drug offenders convicted of an offense carrying a drug mandatory minimum penalty received an increase under §2D1.1(b)(1) for weapon involvement. This

compares to 23.0 percent of White offenders, 12.0 percent of Hispanic offenders, and 18.6 percent of Other Race drug offenders. However, the difference in safety valve rates only partially explains Black offenders' lower rate of relief as Black drug offenders also receive substantial assistance relief at the lowest rate (26.6%) among all demographic groups.

Since fiscal year 2010, the rate of offenders receiving relief from a drug mandatory minimum penalty decreased across all demographic groups, except for Hispanic offenders, for which it remained constant. Commission data demonstrates, however, that the decreased likelihood of relief has not been uniform. In fiscal year 2016, 50.8 percent of White offenders remained subject to a drug mandatory minimum penalty at sentencing, an increase of 15.5 percentage points since fiscal year 2010 (35.3%). The percentage of Black offenders who remained subject to a drug mandatory minimum penalty also increased, but only by 5.0 percent (from 59.5% in

Figure 17. Demographics of Offenders Who Remained Subject to a Drug Mandatory Minimum Penalty at Sentencing by Race
Fiscal Years 2010 and 2016

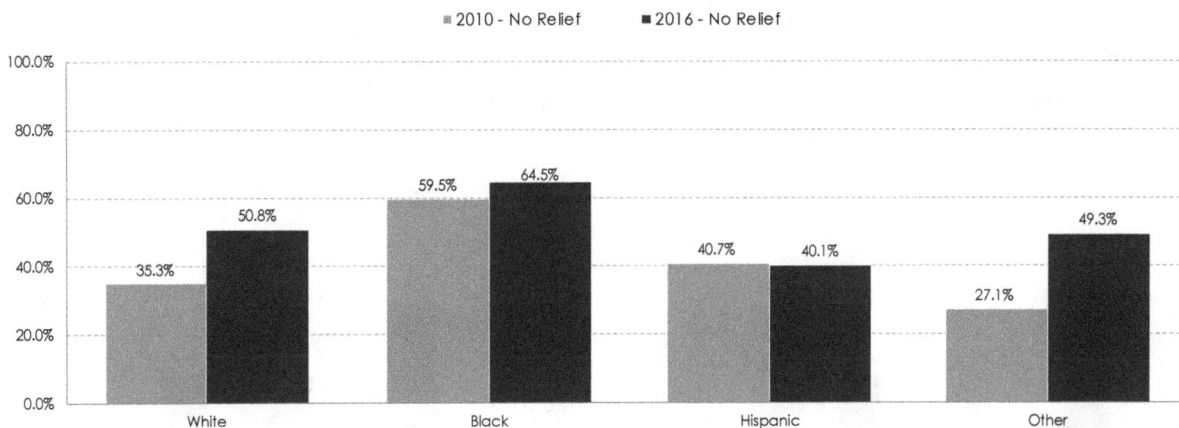

SOURCE: U.S. Sentencing Commission, 2010, and 2016 Datafiles, USSCFY10, and USSCFY16.

fiscal year 2010 to 64.5% in fiscal year 2016). As a result, the gap between White drug offenders and Black drug offenders has decreased since the Commission's 2011 *Mandatory Minimum Report*, from a difference of 24.2 percentage points in 2010 to a difference of 13.7 percentage points in 2016 (59.5% of Black offenders convicted of an offense carrying a mandatory minimum penalty remained subject to that penalty at sentencing compared to 35.3% of White offenders in fiscal year 2010). This gap, however, has not closed as significantly as the gap between White and Black offenders who remain subject to any mandatory minimum penalty, which decreased from 11.6 percent in 2010 to 3.2 percent in 2016.[72]

These changes are most likely the result of differences in the types of offenses charged. For example, the number of crack cocaine offenders, who tend to be predominantly Black,[73] significantly decreased by 67.1 percent in recent years.[74] Conversely, the number of methamphetamine offenders, who tend to be Hispanic or White,[75] increased by 56.1 percent.[76] As reflected in Table E4 in Appendix E, only 30.3 percent of crack cocaine offenders convicted of an offense carrying a drug mandatory minimum received relief, which was least among all drug types. Additionally, Black crack cocaine offenders received relief less often than any other racial group in all drug types (28.2%), followed closely by Black heroin offenders (31.4%).[77]

As reflected in Figure 18, non-U.S. citizens received relief (70.2%) at a significantly higher rate than U.S. citizens (44.1%). This is due, in large part, to the fact that non-U.S. citizens qualified for relief from the drug mandatory minimum penalty under the safety valve (57.0%) more often than U.S. citizen offenders (19.2%) because of their lower criminal history scores.

Female offenders continued to receive relief at a higher rate than male offenders. In fiscal year 2016, more than half of female offenders (68.6%) obtained relief from the drug mandatory minimum penalty at sentencing compared to 49.4 percent of male offenders. Female offenders qualified for each type of relief at a higher rate than male offenders.

Figure 18. Demographics of Offenders Relieved of a Drug Mandatory Minimum Penalty by Citizenship and Gender *Fiscal Year 2016*

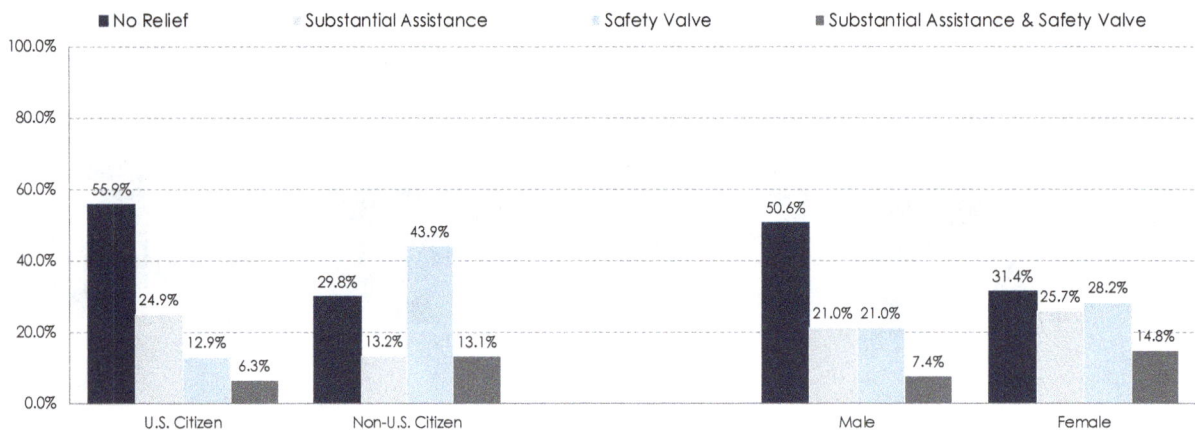

SOURCE: U.S. Sentencing Commission, 2016 Datafile, USSCFY16.

Substantial Assistance

Lastly, the Commission analyzed the extent to which mandatory minimum penalties encourage cooperation with law enforcement. Offenders convicted of an offense carrying a drug mandatory minimum penalty are provided an incentive to plead guilty and cooperate with law enforcement officials. Namely, when the government files a motion indicating that the defendant has substantially cooperated, 18 U.S.C. § 3553(e) grants the court authority to impose a sentence below a mandatory minimum penalty. Because the Commission has also incorporated this incentive into the guidelines at §5K1.1, non-mandatory minimum offenders are also eligible to receive a departure from the applicable guideline range by providing substantial assistance to the government.

Commission data indicates that the longer sentences required by an offense carrying a mandatory minimum penalty provide a significant incentive for offenders to cooperate with law enforcement officials. In fiscal year 2016, offenders convicted of an offense carrying a drug mandatory minimum penalty were nearly twice as likely to have provided substantial assistance to the government.

Figure 19. Percent of Drug Offenders Receiving Substantial Assistance
Fiscal Year 2016

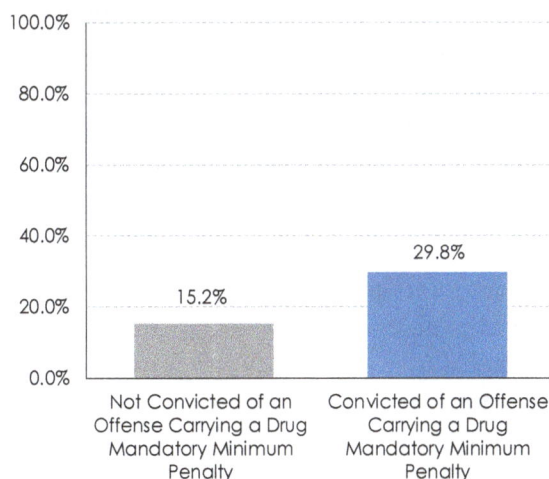

SOURCE: U.S. Sentencing Commission, 2016 Datafile, USSCFY16.

As reflected in Figure 19, 29.8 percent of offenders convicted of an offense carrying a mandatory minimum received a substantial assistance motion. This compares to 15.2 percent of offenders not convicted of an offense carrying a mandatory minimum penalty.

Figure 20. Percentage of Offenders Receiving Substantial Assistance

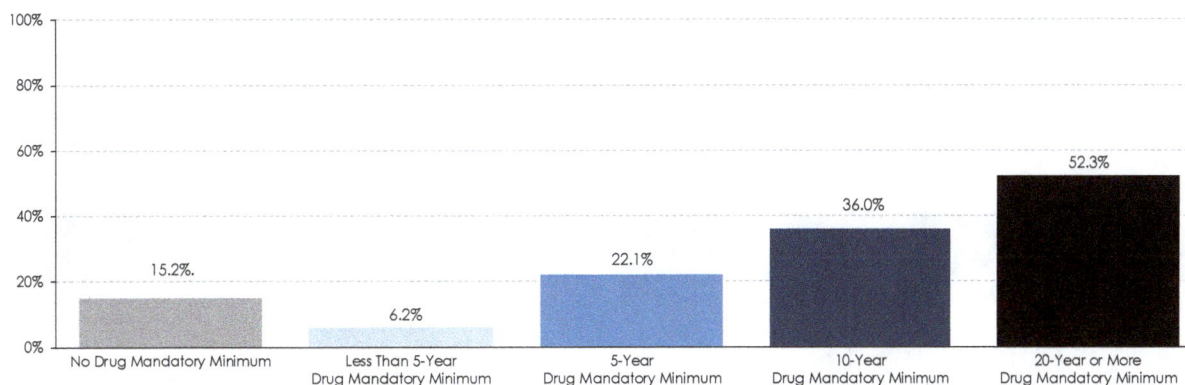

SOURCE: U.S. Sentencing Commission, 2016 Datafile, USSCFY16.

Additionally, as reflected in Figure 20, the percentage of offenders who received substantial assistance generally increased as the drug mandatory minimum penalty increased. Nearly a quarter of offenders facing a five-year drug mandatory minimum penalty (22.1%) received substantial assistance, while 36.0 percent of offenders facing a ten-year mandatory minimum penalty and more than half of offenders facing a mandatory minimum penalty of twenty years or more received substantial assistance (52.3%). Only 6.2 percent of offenders facing a drug mandatory minimum penalty of less than five years received substantial assistance, less than offenders who had no drug mandatory minimum (15.2%).

Of course, the length of mandatory minimum penalties is just one factor that affects whether an offender receives substantial assistance. The availability of substantial assistance relief is also often dependent on the offender's function in the offense. For example, low-level offenders, who may face shorter mandatory minimum penalties are often unable to provide relevant information to

receive credit for substantial assistance. The rate of substantial assistance as related to the offender's function in the offense is explored in greater detail in the Offender Function discussion of this publication.[78]

Sentencing of Offenders Convicted of an Offense Carrying a Drug Mandatory Minimum Penalty

Average Sentence Length

The Commission compared the average sentence imposed for all drug offenders, offenders convicted of an offense carrying a drug mandatory minimum penalty, offenders relieved from application of a drug mandatory minimum penalty, and offenders who remained subject to the drug mandatory minimum penalty at sentencing. In fiscal year 2016, the average sentence for offenders convicted of an offense carrying a drug mandatory minimum penalty was 94 months of imprisonment, more than double the average sentence for drug offenders not convicted of an offense carrying a drug mandatory minimum penalty.

Figure 21. Average Sentence Length for Drug Offender with Base Offense Levels of 24 and 30*
Fiscal Year 2016

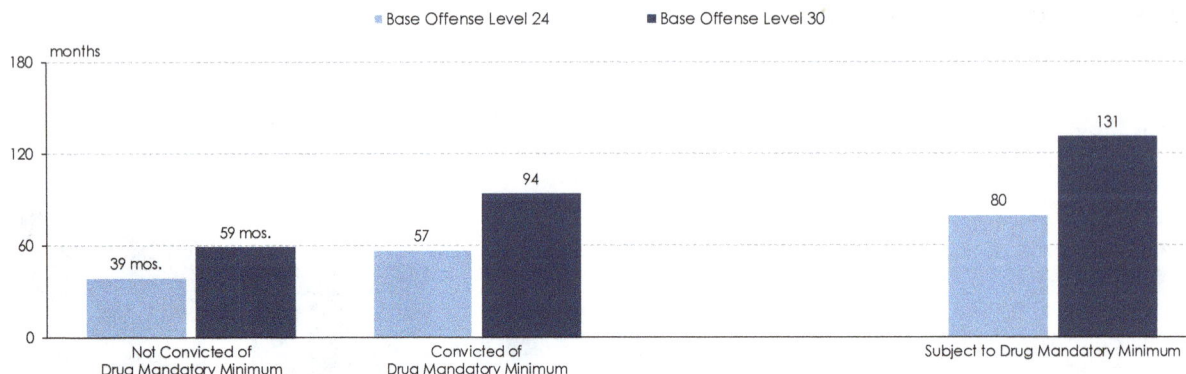

*Included in offenders with a base offense level of 30 are offenders who were subject to the base offense level under §2D1.1(b)(5)(B)(i) (the "Mitigating Role Cap").
SOURCE: U.S. Sentencing Commission, 2016 Datafile, USSCFY16.

Recognizing that this difference in average sentence length could be explained in part by the quantity of drugs involved in the offense, the Commission also analyzed average sentence lengths, controlling for the base offense level (BOL), looking specifically at offenders at BOL 24, which corresponds to a five-year mandatory minimum, and 30, which corresponds to a ten-year mandatory minimum. As demonstrated in Figure 22, while quantity might be one factor contributing to the longer average sentence length, the existence of a drug mandatory minimum penalty still had a significant impact on the average sentence length even when controlling for base offense level. For offenders with a BOL of 24, those who were convicted of an offense carrying a drug mandatory minimum had sentences 18 months longer than those not convicted of an offense carrying a drug mandatory minimum (57 months compared to 39 months), while the sentences for those subject to a drug mandatory minimum were twice the length (80 months). Similarly, for offenders with a BOL of 30, those who were convicted of an offense carrying a drug mandatory minimum had sentences 35

months longer than those not convicted of an offense carrying a drug mandatory minimum (94 months compared to 59 months), while the sentences for those subject to a drug mandatory minimum were more than twice the length (131 months).

As set forth in Figure 21, the average sentence length for offenders who remained subject to a drug mandatory minimum penalty at sentencing was almost twice as high at 126 months compared to offenders who ultimately received relief from such penalty at sentencing (64 months). For those relieved of the drug mandatory minimum penalty, the average sentence imposed also varied depending on the type of statutory relief. Offenders who provided substantial assistance to the government received longer average sentences (81 months) than offenders who qualified for the safety valve provision (57 months). Offenders who qualified for both received the lowest average sentence of 41 months.

Figure 22. Average Sentence Length
Fiscal Year 2016

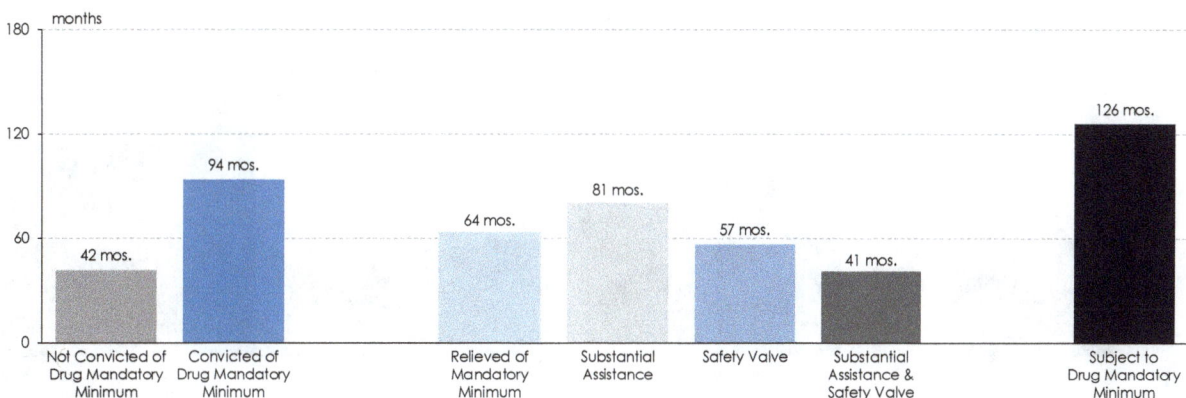

SOURCE: U.S. Sentencing Commission, 2016 Datafile, USSCFY16.

These differences may also be attributable to the fact that offenders who qualify for safety valve relief are generally less culpable than other offenders and, therefore, would be expected to receive lower sentences on average. First, by statute, offenders must fall within Criminal History Category I to qualify for safety valve relief. Additionally, offenders must not have possessed a dangerous weapon in connection with the offense and must not have received an aggravating role adjustment under the guidelines (for being an organizer, leader, manager, or supervisor in any criminal activity).[79] Offenders who received a substantial assistance departure had the highest guideline minimum (164 months on average), followed by offenders with no relief (145 months), those with a substantial assistance departure and safety valve (76 months) and those with just relief through safety valve (65 months).

As reflected in Figure 6 in each of the drug specific appendices,[80] the Commission also compared average sentence length by drug type. For offenders not convicted of an offense carrying a drug mandatory minimum penalty, crack cocaine offenders had the longest average sentence (60 months), while marijuana offenders had the shortest (17 months). While marijuana offenders continued to have the shortest average sentences of offenders convicted of (50 months), relieved of (32 months) and subject to (91 months) a drug mandatory minimum penalty, methamphetamine offenders had the longest average sentences in these categories (110 months, 78 months, and 140 months, respectively). For those convicted of an offense carrying a drug mandatory minimum penalty, crack cocaine offenders were closely behind methamphetamine offenders, with average sentences of 101 months.

The Commission next compared the average length of sentences imposed for offenders by race. When considering all drug offenders, Black drug offenders were sentenced to longer terms than any other racial group (75 months) in fiscal year 2016. White drug offenders (69 months) had the second highest average sentence, followed by Hispanic drug offenders (60 months), and Other Race drug offenders (52 months).

Figure 23. Average Sentence for Drug Offenders by Race
Fiscal Year 2016

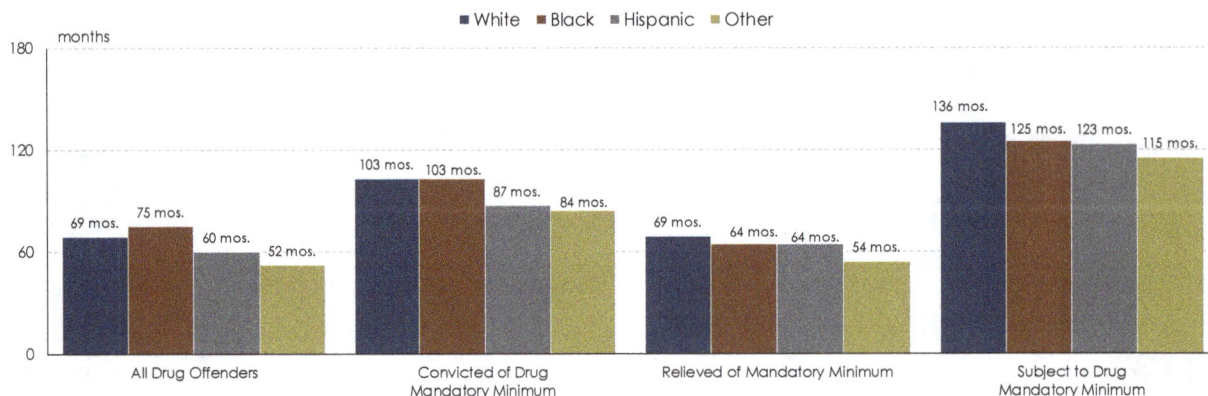

SOURCE: U.S. Sentencing Commission, 2016 Datafile, USSCFY16.

However, among offenders convicted of an offense carrying a drug mandatory minimum penalty, White offenders and Black offenders had the highest average sentence (103 months), followed by Hispanic offenders (87 months) and Other Race offenders (84 months). White offenders also received the longest average sentences among offenders who were relieved of the application of a drug mandatory minimum penalty at sentencing (69 months), and among those offenders who remained subject to a drug mandatory minimum penalty at sentencing (136 months).

There were several notable changes after fiscal year 2010 in the average sentence of drug offenders, particularly White and Black offenders. While Black drug offenders continued to receive the highest average sentence among all drug offenders, the average sentence length in fiscal year 2016 (75 months) represents a 25.7 percent decrease from fiscal year 2010 (101 months). Conversely, White offenders saw an increase in average sentence between 2010 and 2016, going from 61 months in fiscal year 2010 to 69 months in fiscal year 2016, a 13.1 percent increase.

Differences are also seen for offenders convicted of, relieved of, or ultimately subject to a drug mandatory minimum penalty. Most notably, Black offenders no longer had the highest average sentences in each of those categories. As noted, White offenders either had the same (in the cases of those convicted of an offense carrying a drug mandatory minimum) or received the longest average sentences in fiscal year 2016.

This is a significant change from fiscal year 2010 when Black offenders convicted of a statute carrying a drug mandatory minimum penalty had the highest average sentence (120 months), followed by White offenders with 82 months. This change is a result of the fact that White offenders convicted of a statute carrying a drug mandatory minimum penalty had a 25.6 percent increase in their average sentence between fiscal years 2010 and 2016, from 82 months to 103 months.

Figure 24. Comparison of Average Sentence for White and Black Drug Offenders *Fiscal Years 2010 and 2016*

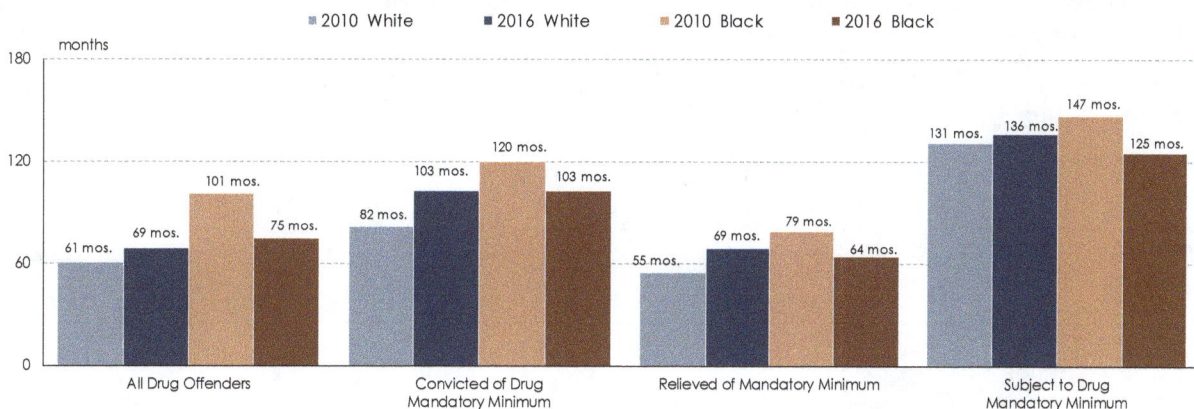

SOURCE: U.S. Sentencing Commission, 2010, and 2016 Datafiles, USSCFY10, and USSCFY16.

For offenders who were relieved of a drug mandatory minimum penalty at sentencing, White offenders saw a 14-month increase (25.5%) in their average sentence from fiscal year 2010 (from 55 months to 69 months). Black offenders, on the other hand, saw a 19.0 percent decrease from fiscal year 2010 (from 79 months to 64 months). White offenders who remained subject to a drug mandatory minimum penalty at sentencing had an average sentence of 136 months in fiscal year 2016, which is 3.8 percent higher than the average in fiscal year 2010 (131 months). Black offenders had an average sentence of 125 months—a 22-month (15.0%) decrease from fiscal year 2010 (147 months).

Finally, the Commission also compared the average sentence length of sentences imposed for offenders by citizenship and gender.

Sentence lengths in all four instances (all drug offenders, offenders convicted of an offense carrying a drug mandatory minimum penalty,

offenders relieved of a drug mandatory minimum penalty, and offenders subject to a drug mandatory minimum penalty at sentencing) between U.S. and non-U.S. citizens remain relatively close to each other. U.S. citizens have longer average sentences for all drug offenders and offenders convicted of an offense carrying a drug mandatory minimum penalty, while non-U.S. citizens have slightly longer average sentences for offenders relieved of a drug mandatory minimum penalty and offenders subject to a drug mandatory minimum penalty. Male offenders also have longer sentences than female offenders in all four categories. The average sentences for each group are provided in Table 5.

Sentences Relative to the Guideline Range

As demonstrated in Figure 25, both the average guideline minimum and the average sentence for offenders convicted of an offense carrying a drug mandatory minimum penalty have remained relatively stable over the past three decades.

Table 5. Average Sentence for Drug Offenders by Citizenship and Gender
Fiscal Year 2016

	All Drug Offenders	Convicted of an Offense Carrying a Drug Mandatory Minimum Penalty	Relieved of Mandatory Minimum Penalty	Subject to Drug Mandatory Minimum Penalty at Sentencing
Total (# of offenders)	19,584	8,760	4,519	4,241
CITIZENSHIP				
U.S. Citizen	69 months	99 months	64 months	126 months
Non-U.S. Citizen	55 months	84 months	65 months	128 months
GENDER				
Male	70 months	98 months	67 months	128 months
Female	41 months	68 months	51 months	104 months

SOURCE: U.S. Sentencing Commission, 2016 Datafile, USSCFY16.

Throughout this time, the average guideline minimum has exceeded the average sentence by approximately two years. The parallel nature of the average guideline minimum and average sentence imposed over time is unsurprising as the Commission has incorporated the applicable mandatory minimums into the Drug Quantity Table at USSG §2D1.1, extrapolating upward and downward to set sentencing guideline ranges for all drug quantities. In order to further explore this relationship and the impact the guidelines have on sentences imposed on offenders convicted of an offense carrying a drug mandatory minimum penalty, the Commission compared the sentence imposed to the applicable guideline range.

Among offenders convicted of a drug mandatory minimum penalty, those who remained subject to such penalty at sentencing were most likely to receive a sentence within the guideline range (58.2%). Offenders who remained subject to a drug mandatory minimum penalty at sentencing were also most likely to receive a non-government sponsored below range sentence. One-quarter (25.0%) of such offenders received a non-government sponsored departure or variance, a higher rate than all drug offenders generally (22.8%) and larger than the subset of offenders convicted of an offense carrying a drug mandatory minimum penalty (19.6%).

For offenders subject to a drug mandatory minimum penalty, marijuana offenders had the highest rate of within range sentences, at 78.2 percent. For offenders subject to a drug mandatory minimum penalty, crack cocaine offenders received a non-government sponsored below range sentence more frequently than any other drug type (28.9%).

As with offenders subject to any mandatory minimum, this high rate of non-government sponsored below range sentences is, in part, because

Figure 25. Average Guideline Minimum and Average Sentence for Offenders Convicted of an Offense Carrying a Drug Mandatory Minimum Penalty
Fiscal Years 1991 - 2016

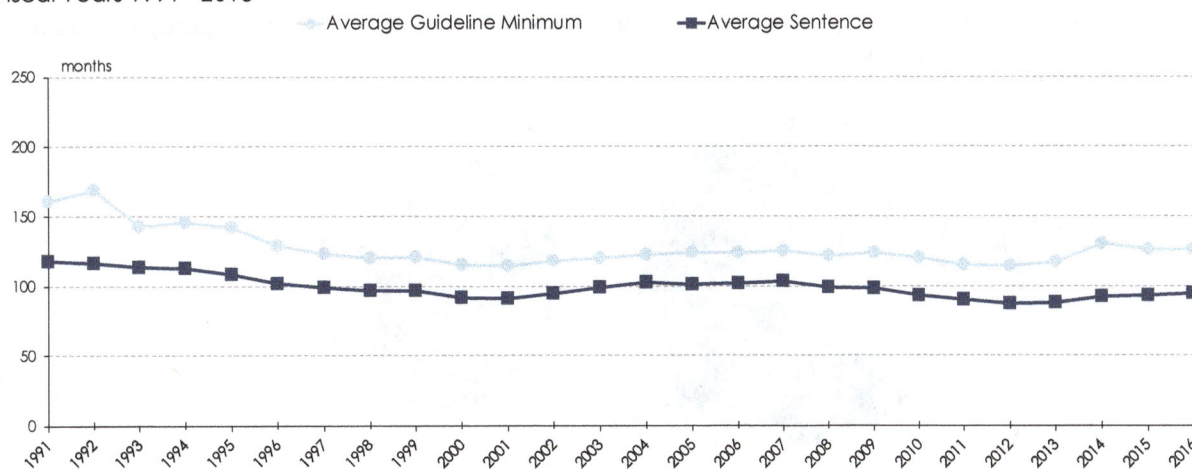

SOURCE: U.S. Sentencing Commission, 1991 through 2016 Datafiles, USSCFY91 – USSCFY16.

Table 6. Sentence Relative to the Guideline Range of Drug Offenders
Fiscal Year 2016

	All Drug Offenders	Convicted of an Offense Carrying a Drug Mandatory Minimum Penalty	Subject to a Drug Mandatory Minimum Penalty at Sentencing
Total (# of offenders)	19,584	8,760	4,241
SENTENCE RELATIVE TO THE GUIDELINE RANGE			
Within Range	37.5%	40.3%	58.2%
Above Range	1.4%	0.9%	1.6%
Substantial Assistance §5K1.1	21.7%	29.8%	0.0%
Other Government Sponsored (no §5K1.1)	16.7%	9.4%	15.2%
Non-Government Sponsored Below Range	22.8%	19.6%	25.0%

SOURCE: U.S. Sentencing Commission, 2016 Datafile, USSCFY16.

courts often sentence such offenders to the statutory mandatory minimum term of imprisonment regardless of the applicable guideline range. As reflected in Figure 26, the majority of offenders who remained subject to a drug mandatory minimum penalty (72.6%) had a guideline minimum that was above the applicable mandatory minimum. In these cases, while courts were bound by the minimum penalty, they were free to sentence below the otherwise applicable guideline range. In such instances, the within guideline range rate fell to 43.9 percent, lower than the overall rate in fiscal year 2016 (46.4%), but still above the within guideline range rate for all drug offenders (37.5%). Conversely, both the non-government sponsored and government sponsored below range increased to 34.4 percent and 20.7 percent, respectively.

Figure 26. Position of Sentence Relative to the Guideline Range for Offenders Subject to a Drug Mandatory Minimum Penalty at Sentencing
Fiscal Year 2016

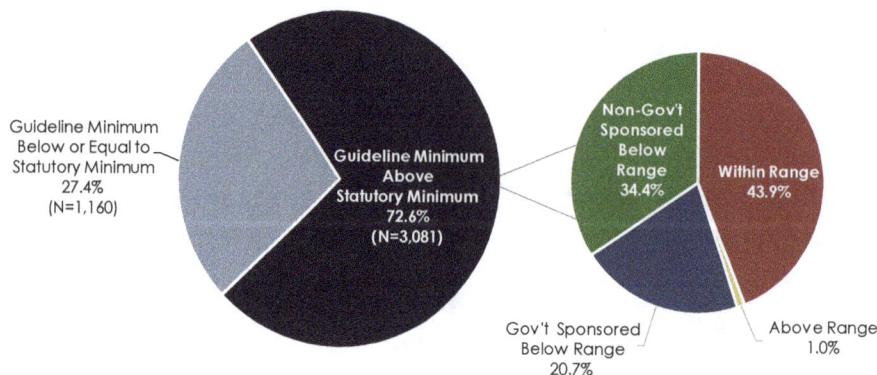

SOURCE: U.S. Sentencing Commission, 2016 Datafile, USSCFY16.

Figure 27. Sentence Imposed on Offenders Subject to a Drug Mandatory Minimum Penalty Compared to Statutory Minimum*
Fiscal Year 2016

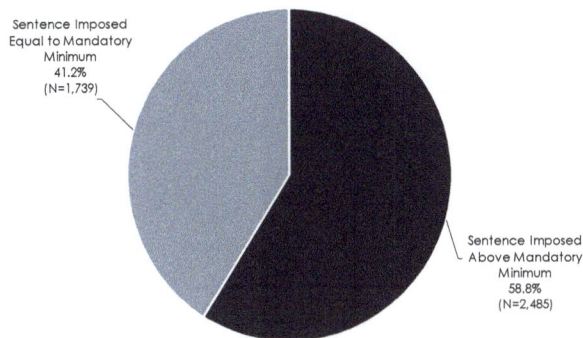

Sentence Imposed Equal to Mandatory Minimum
41.2%
(N=1,739)

Sentence Imposed Above Mandatory Minimum
58.8%
(N=2,485)

*In fiscal year 2016, there were 17 cases that were convicted of an offense carrying drug mandatory minimum penalty, received no form of relief, and were sentenced below the statutory minimum. These cases are not included in the figure above.
SOURCE: U.S. Sentencing Commission, 2016 Datafile, USSCFY16.

In total, 41.2 percent of offenders who remained subject to the mandatory minimum penalty at sentencing received a sentence at the mandatory minimum penalty. While this certainly explains the increased rate of below range sentences, the majority (58.8%) of offenders subject to a mandatory minimum penalty were sentenced above the statutory mandatory minimum.

Offender Function

In order to further explore how mandatory minimums apply across the spectrum of offender functions, the Commission also analyzed the function of those drug offenders convicted of an offense carrying a drug mandatory minimum penalty. Using a 20-percent sample of drug offenders sentenced in fiscal year 2016, the Commission assessed the functions performed by drug offenders as part of the offense. Offender function was defined as the offender's activity coupled with the drug amount he or she was held liable for in one transaction.

Offender function was determined by a review of the offense conduct section of the presentence report. The Commission assessed the most serious function an offender performed during an offense, independent of any application of sentencing enhancements and reductions. In those cases where an offender performed different functions at different times, the Commission determined the most serious function the offender performed. Offender function was assigned based on the most serious function performed by the offender in the drug offense, even if the offender more frequently performed a less serious function. Finally, offenders at higher levels of the drug distribution chain were presumed to be more culpable based on their greater responsibilities and higher levels of authority as compared to other participants in the offense.

The Commission assigned each offender to one of 21 separate function categories based on his or her most serious conduct as described in the presentence report and not rejected by the court on the statement of reasons form.[81] This report only presents data on the ten most common functions in order to facilitate analysis and presentation of the data. Function categories are displayed on the figures in this chapter in decreasing order of culpability from left to right. The categories described below represent a continuum of decreasing culpability:

Importer/High Level Supplier: Imports or otherwise supplies large quantities of drugs (generally sells/possesses or purchases 1 kilogram or more in a single transaction); is near the top of the distribution chain; has ownership interest in drugs; usually supplies drugs to other drug distributors and generally does not deal in retail amounts; may employ no or very few subordinates.

Organizer/Leader: Organizes, leads, directs, or otherwise runs a drug distribution organization; has the largest share of the profits and the most decision-making authority.

Grower/Manufacturer: Grows, cultivates, or manufactures a controlled substance and is the principal owner of the drugs.

Wholesaler: Sells more than retail/user-level quantities in a single transaction; sells at least 1 ounce (28 grams) but less than 1 kilogram at one time; possesses or buys at least 2 ounces (56 grams) at one time, sells any amount to another dealer.

Manager/Supervisor: Serves as a lieutenant to assist one of the above; manages all or a significant portion of a drug manufacturing, importation, or distribution operation; takes instructions from one of the above and conveys to subordinates; supervises directly at least one other co-participant in an organization of at least five co-participants.

Street-Level Dealer: Distributes retail quantities directly to the user; sells less than 1 ounce (28 grams) quantities to any user(s).

Broker: Arranges for two parties to buy/sell drugs, or directs potential buyer to a potential seller.

Courier: Transports or carries drugs with the assistance of a vehicle or other equipment. Includes situations where the offender, who is otherwise considered to be a crew member, is the only participant directing a vessel onto which drugs had been loaded from a "mother-ship."

Mule: Transports or carries drugs internally or on their person, often by airplane, or by walking across a border. Also, includes an offender who only transports or carries drugs in baggage, souvenirs, clothing, otherwise.

Employee/Worker: Performs very limited, low-level function in the offense (whether or not ongoing); includes running errands, answering the telephone, scouts, receiving packages, packaging the drugs, manual labor, acting as a lookout to provide early warnings [during meetings, exchanges, or on/offloading], passengers in vehicles, or acting as a deckhand/crew member on vessel or aircraft used to transport large quantities of drugs.

Distribution of Offender Function

As reflected in Figure 28, Wholesaler (22.4%) was the most common function in the 2016 sample data, followed by Courier (18.6%), Street-Level Dealer (16.2%), High-Level Supplier/Importer (12.5%), and Mule (9.7%). The frequency and order of functions changed from 2009, when the most common function was Courier (23.1%), followed by Wholesaler (21.2%), then Street-Level Dealer (17.2%).

While the prevalence of many of the functions remained largely stable, there were some notable shifts. The frequency of Couriers decreased from 23.1 percent in 2009 to 18.6 percent in 2016. The decrease in the frequency of the Courier function occurred across all drug types, except for methamphetamine offenders, and was most significant in the context of marijuana offenders. In 2009, over half (54.7%) of all marijuana offenders were Couriers, compared to under one-third (32.1%) in 2016.

Significant increases occurred in the frequency of both the Mule (4.8% to 9.7%) and Employee/Worker (5.1% to 9.0%) functions. The increase in Employee/Worker percentage is largely related to the nature of offenders' roles in powder cocaine and marijuana offenses. For offenders convicted of a powder cocaine offense, the percentage performing the "Employee/Worker" function increased significantly, from 6.6 percent in 2009 to 14.4 percent in 2016.[82] These offenders generally served in the role of deckhand or other worker assisting in offloading powder cocaine shipments from ships. For marijuana offenses, the percentage of offenders performing the Employee/Worker function rose

Figure 28. Offender Function*
*Fiscal Years 2009 and 2016 Sample Data***

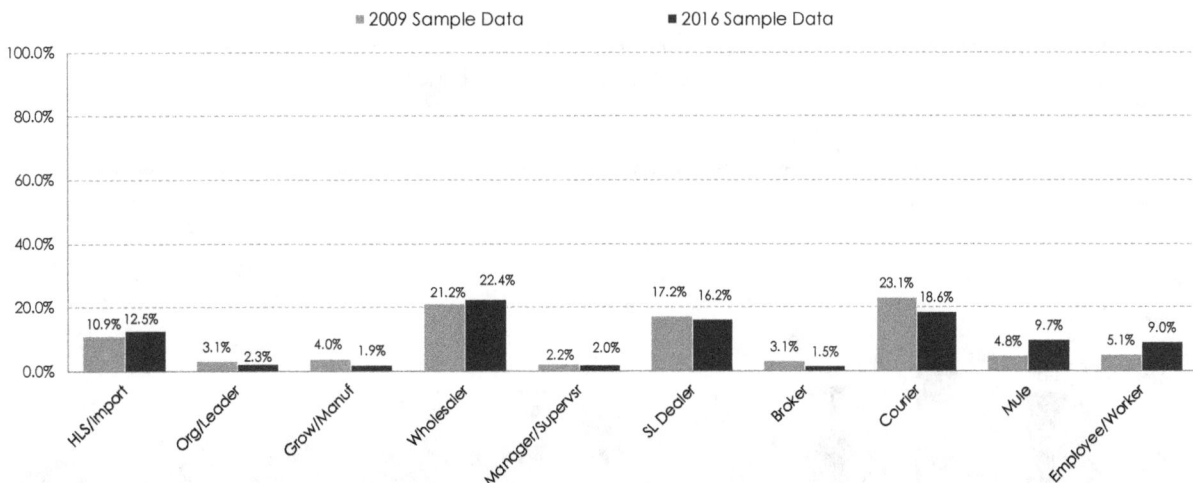

* There were offenders in the samples whose function could not be determined. These offenders are not included in the overall percentages.
** In the fiscal year 2009 sample, 5.3 percent of offenders had "Other" or "Miscellaneous" functions. In the fiscal year 2016 sample, 4.2 percent of offenders had "Other" or "Miscellaneous" functions. These percentages are not represented in the figure above.

SOURCE: U.S. Sentencing Commission, 2009 and 2016 Function Datafiles, FUNCSAMPFY09 and FUNCSAMPFY16.

from 5.0 percent in 2009 to 12.5 percent in 2016.[83] Marijuana had the highest percentage of lower level functions (Couriers, Mules, and Employees/Workers) among all drug types (78.3%).[84]

Prevalence of Offenses Carrying Drug Mandatory Minimum Penalties by Offender Function

When analyzing the function of those drug offenders convicted of an offense carrying a drug mandatory minimum penalty, two trends emerge. First, mandatory minimum penalties are not limited to offenders on the highest end of the culpability scale. As reflected in Figure 29, a significant percentage of offenders in each function were convicted of an offense carrying a drug mandatory minimum penalty in fiscal year 2016. In fact, the majority of offenders in seven of the ten function categories were convicted of an offense carrying a drug mandatory minimum penalty, and no fewer than a quarter of offenders in every category were

convicted of such an offense. Thus, while some legislative history suggests that drug mandatory minimums were aimed at "serious" and "major" traffickers, the data indicate that mandatory minimum penalties apply more broadly.

Nevertheless, the rate at which offenders were convicted of an offense carrying a drug mandatory minimum penalty generally did decrease with the culpability level of the offender as reflected by function. Thus, offenders who functioned as a High-Level Supplier/Importer or Organizer/Leader[85] were convicted of an offense carrying a drug mandatory minimum penalty at high rates,[86] 70.6 percent and 73.4 percent respectively, while Courier and Mule offenders were convicted of such offenses at the lowest rates (32.2% and 25.4%, respectively). There was an exception, however in the "Employee/Worker" category. These offenders were convicted of an offense carrying a drug mandatory minimum penalty 53.3 percent of the time, a significantly higher percentage than more

Figure 29. Percent of Offenders Convicted of an Offense Carrying a Drug Mandatory Minimum Penalty and Subject to a Drug Mandatory Minimum Penalty by Offender Function
Fiscal Year 2016 Sample Data

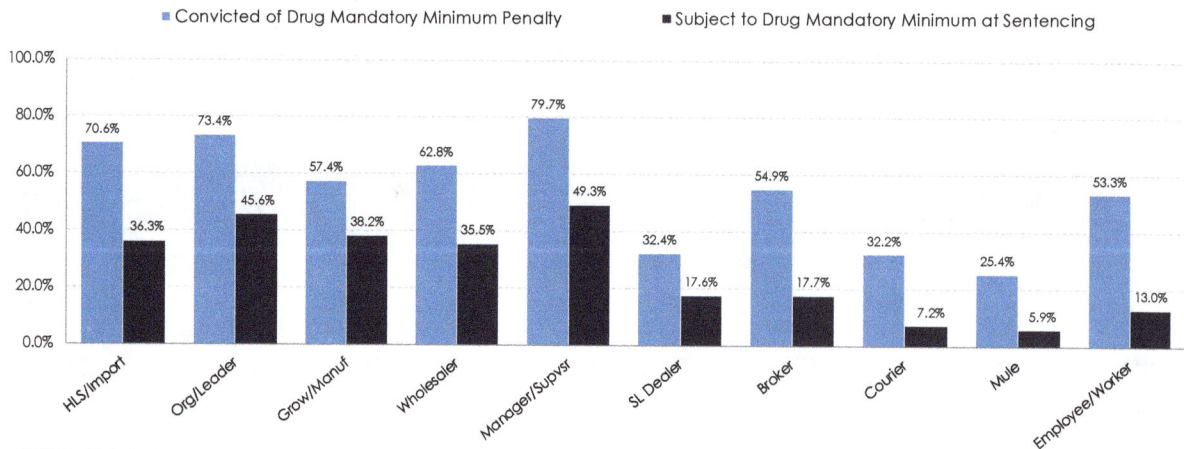

SOURCE: U.S. Sentencing Commission, 2016 Function Datafile, FUNCSAMPFY16.

culpable offenders who performed the functions of Street-Level Dealer (32.4%), Courier (32.2%), and Mule (25.4%). This seems to be the result of the nature of certain powder cocaine offenders and trafficking patterns, as the majority of offenders in this category (53.9%) were low-level powder cocaine offenders, including deckhands who work as powder cocaine off-loaders from small boats, who handled and were held responsible for large quantities of cocaine but who had no actual control or authority over the drugs or the distribution organization.

While the data demonstrates that offenses carrying drug mandatory minimum penalties applied across all functions, the rate at which offenders remained subject to a drug mandatory minimum at sentencing also tended to decrease with the culpability of the offender. Manager/Supervisor offenders were subject to a drug mandatory minimum penalty most often at 49.3 percent, while Mule offenders were subject to these

penalties least often at 5.9 percent. Once again, Employee/Worker offenders were an exception to this rule, remaining subject to a drug mandatory minimum penalty 13.0 percent of the time, higher than the more-culpable Courier (7.2%) and Mule (5.9%) functions.

There is a general downward trend in the percentage of offenders convicted of an offense carrying a drug mandatory minimum penalty across all functions when comparing the 2009 sample to the 2016 sample. As reflected in Figure 30, the largest decrease was for Street-Level Dealer offenders (60.7% in 2009 to 32.4% in 2016), which is largely due to marijuana and crack cocaine drug types. In 2016, no marijuana offenders convicted of an offense carrying a drug mandatory minimum penalty fell into the Street-Level Dealer category,[87] compared to 40.0 percent in 2009 (with 35.0% remaining subject to the mandatory minimum).[88] Similarly, the percentage of crack cocaine offenders convicted of an offense carrying a drug

Figure 30. Comparison of Offenders Convicted of an Offense Carrying a Drug Mandatory Minimum Penalty by Offender Function
Fiscal Years 2009 and 2016 Sample Data

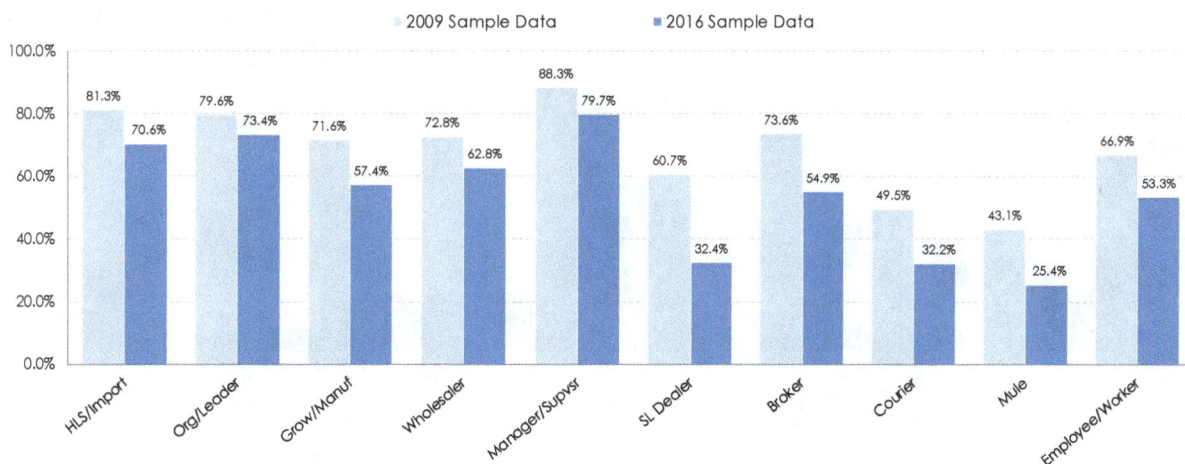

SOURCE: U.S. Sentencing Commission, 2009 and 2016 Function Datafiles, FUNCSAMPFY09 and FUNCSAMPFY16.

mandatory minimum penalty in the Street-Level Dealer category fell from 77.8 percent (with 56.1% remaining subject to a drug mandatory minimum) in 2009,[89] to 37.0 percent (with 22.5% remaining subject to a drug mandatory minimum) in 2016.[90]

While there was a downward trend in the percentage of offenders convicted of an offense carrying a drug mandatory minimum penalty, the percentage who remained subject to a drug mandatory minimum penalty was largely stable for the majority of drug functions. The exception to this rule is the Street-Level Dealer function, which saw a large decrease in the percentage of offenders who remained subject to a drug mandatory minimum (40.4% in 2009 to 17.6% in 2016). As discussed in the 2017 *Overview Publication*, this is likely attributable to changes in the charging and sentencing of drug offenders, including changes made as a result of the Fair Sentencing Act and the Department of Justice's Smart on Crime Initiate.[91]

Relief from Mandatory Minimum Penalties by Offender Function

The Commission also examined the rates and types of relief that offenders received from drug mandatory minimum penalties. In general, offenders who performed low-level functions obtained relief from drug mandatory minimums at a higher rate than offenders who performed high-level functions. For the functions higher in culpability than Street-Level Dealer, the highest percentage of relief from a drug mandatory minimum was 48.5 percent (for the High-Level Suppler/Importer offenders). Conversely, every function lower in culpability than Street-Level Dealer received relief in at least 67.9 percent of the cases, which was the percentage for the Broker function. Courier and Mule offenders obtained relief at the highest rates, at 77.6 percent and 77.0 percent, respectively.

Figure 31. Comparison of Offenders Subject to a Drug Mandatory Minimum Penalty by Offender Function *Fiscal Years 2009 and 2016 Sample Data*

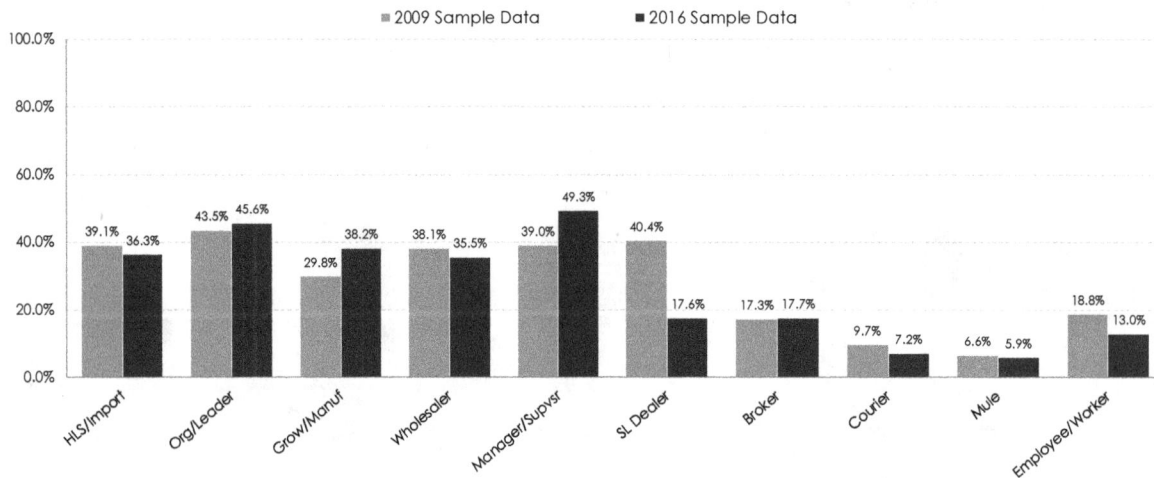

SOURCE: U.S. Sentencing Commission, 2009 and 2016 Function Datafiles, FUNCSAMPFY09 and FUNCSAMPFY16.

The correlation between function in the offense and relief from mandatory minimum penalties varied depending on the type of relief. Offenders who performed higher-level functions were generally more likely to receive relief for providing substantial assistance to law enforcement, while low-level functions were more likely to obtain relief pursuant to the statutory safety valve. Thus, offenders with the Broker (50.0%), Street-Level Dealer (38.6%), and Organizer/Leader (36.2%) functions were substantially more likely to receive substantial assistance relief than those in the Mule (17.3%) category. Conversely, every function lower than Street-Level Dealer obtained safety valve relief in at least 39.3 percent of the cases, with Courier and Mule offenders receiving safety valve relief at the highest rates (68.1% and 71.3%, respectively). By comparison, offenders in the Organizer/Leader, Grower/Manufacturer, and Street-Level Dealer categories received safety valve at the lowest rates (1.7%, 10.3%, and 10.9%, respectively).

This correlation between function in the offense and correlation likely reflects the fact that low-level offenders tend to have less significant criminal histories, but generally do not have valuable information to provide to law enforcement due to their more limited role in the offense. High-level offenders, on the other hand, are generally more involved in the offense and therefore are often able to provide more and better information to law enforcement.

Figure 32. Percent of Offenders Convicted of an Offense Carrying a Drug Mandatory Minimum Penalty Who Were Relieved of the Drug Penalty by Offender Function
Fiscal Year 2016 Sample Data

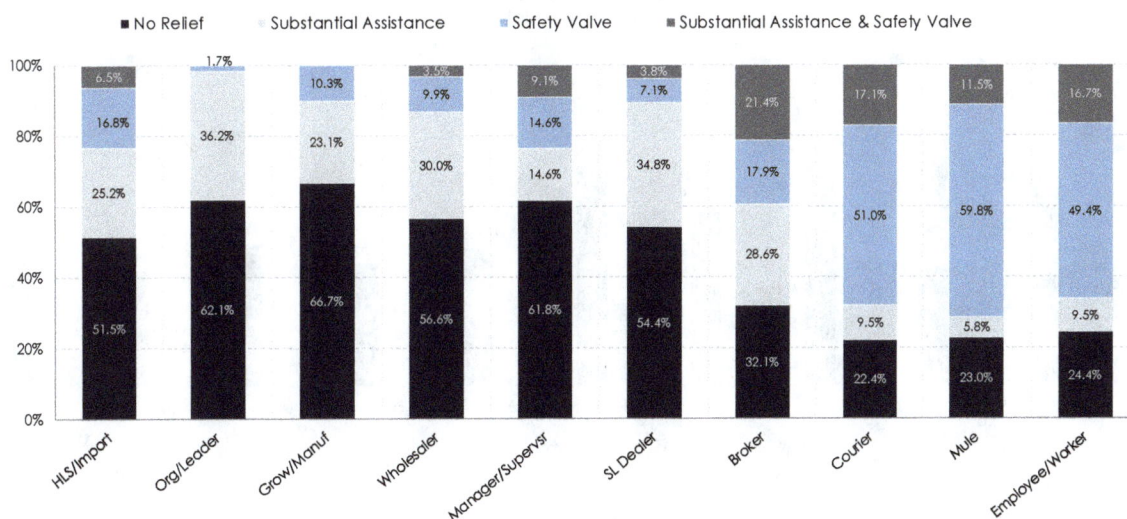

SOURCE: U.S. Sentencing Commission, 2016 Function Datafile, FUNCSAMPFY16.

Average Sentence Length by Offender Function

Lastly, the Commission analyzed the average sentence length imposed on offenders convicted of an offense carrying a drug mandatory minimum penalty by offender function. Both the average sentence for those relieved of such penalty and those who remained subject to such penalty at sentencing are compared. Again, several trends emerge.

First, this analysis demonstrates the significant impact of relief from a drug mandatory minimum sentence. Sentences for those who remain subject to a drug mandatory minimum were significantly longer than those who received relief across all functions. This was particularly true for many low-level functions, such as Mules and Couriers. As reflected in Figure 33, the average sentence length of 82 months for Mules who remained subject to a

mandatory minimum penalty was over three times longer than for Mules who received relief from such penalty at sentencing (26 months). Similarly, the average sentence for Couriers who remained subject to a drug mandatory minimum penalty at sentencing was 101 months compared to 52 months for those who received relief.

These differences may be attributable to the fact that offenders who qualify for safety valve relief are generally less culpable than other offenders and, therefore, would normally receive lower sentences on average. By statute, offenders must fall within Criminal History Category I to qualify for safety valve relief. Additionally, offenders must not have possessed a dangerous weapon in connection with the offense and must not have received an aggravating role adjustment under the guidelines (for being an organizer, leader, manager, or supervisor in any criminal activity).[92]

Figure 33. Average Sentence by Offender Function
Fiscal Year 2016 Sample Data

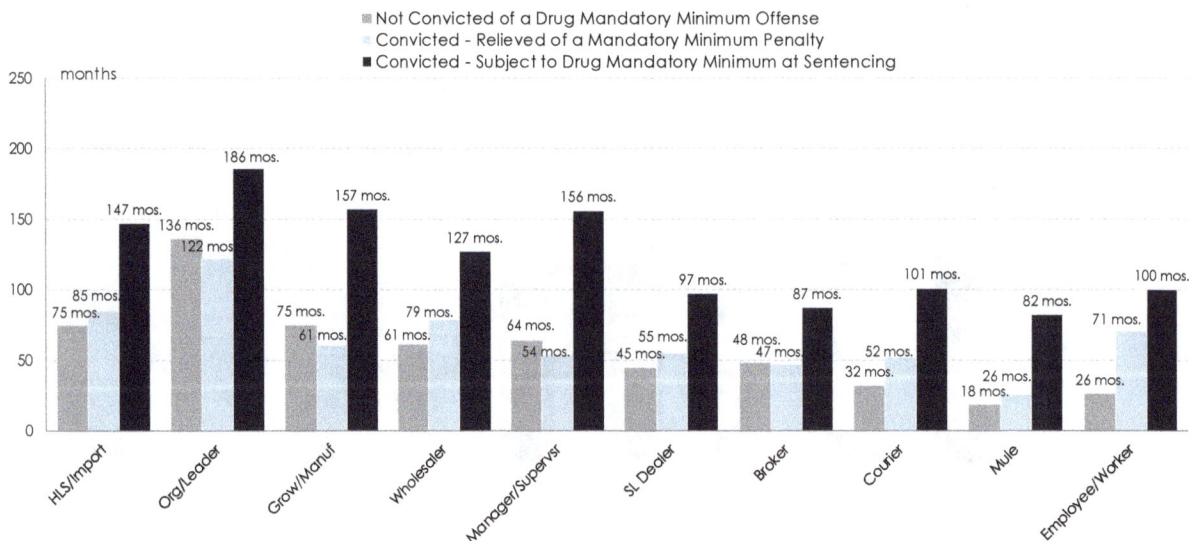

SOURCE: U.S. Sentencing Commission, 2016 Function Datafile, FUNCSAMPFY16.

When comparing offender functions to each other, the data continue to show that higher culpability offenders generally receive higher sentences than lower culpability offenders. For example, of offenders who remained subject to a drug mandatory minimum penalty, Organizers/ Leaders had the highest average sentence (186 months), followed by Growers/Manufacturers (157 months) and Manager/Supervisors (156 months). Mules (82 months), Brokers (87 months), and Street-Level Dealers (97 months) had the lowest average sentences for offenders subject to a drug mandatory minimum penalty. However, sentences for lower culpability offenders who remained subject to drug mandatory minimum sentences (*e.g.*, Couriers (101 months), Mules (82 months) and Employees/Workers (100 months)), were roughly equal to, or higher than, average sentences for more culpable offenders who received relief (*e.g.*, High-Level Suppliers/Importers (85 months), Growers/ Manufacturers (61 months), and Wholesalers (79 months)). This indicates that individuals who received relief from a drug mandatory minimum were more likely to receive less severe sentences regardless of what function they performed in the offense.

The average sentence length is also a function of the varying severities of the mandatory minimum penalties faced by offenders based on offender function. Offenders in the higher culpability categories generally faced longer mandatory minimum penalties. However, Managers/ Supervisors (43.5%) and Employees/Workers (34.9%) were subject to ten-year mandatory minimum penalties more often than functions with greater culpability. By comparison, 23.5 percent of Growers/Manufacturers, 28.9 percent

of Wholesalers, and 18.6 percent of Couriers were convicted of an offense carrying a ten-year mandatory minimum penalty. A more detailed analysis of the length of the mandatory minimum penalties by offender function is provided in Appendix C.

Impact of Drug Mandatory Minimum Penalties on the Federal Prison Population

This section further explores the continuing impact of drug mandatory minimum penalties on the overall prison population, including an update of the Commission's analysis of the current portion of the federal prison population that was convicted of a drug mandatory minimum penalty. This section also provides new analysis regarding the size and composition of the federal prison population convicted of an offense carrying a drug mandatory minimum penalty by race, gender, and citizenship. For this analysis, the Commission obtained prisoner data from the Bureau of Prisons to compare to Commission data. By merging the two datasets, the Commission created snapshots of the federal prison population at different points in time, including what percentage of prisoners were convicted of violating a statute containing a mandatory minimum penalty, and what percentage of prisoners were subject to a mandatory minimum penalty at sentencing.

As discussed in the 2017 *Overview Publication*, many of the changes in the prison population were likely the result of changes in charging practices discussed above.[93] Nevertheless, the full impact of these policies will not be seen for many years, as offenders sentenced between 2010 and 2016 serve out their sentences. Many of these offenders

51

Figure 34. Number of Offenders in Prison on September 30
1995 - 2016

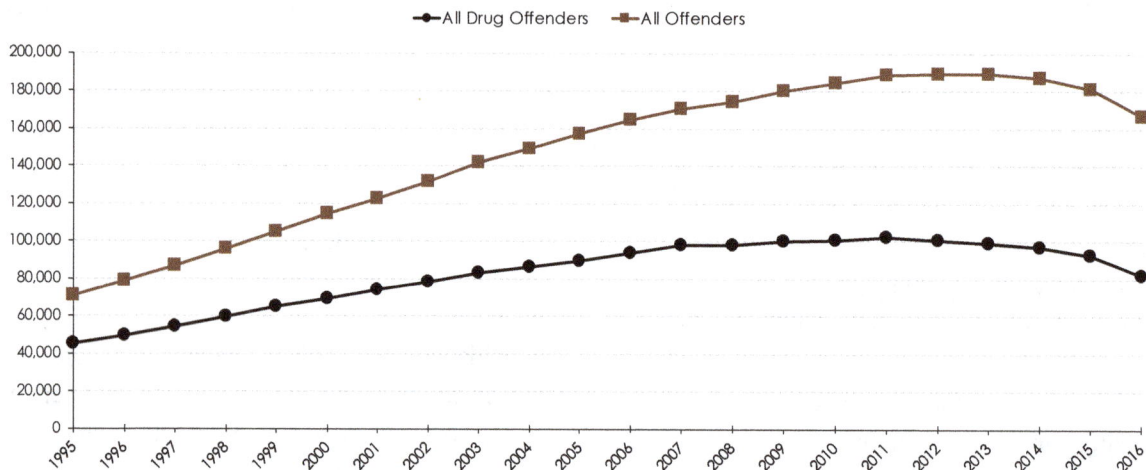

SOURCE: U.S. Sentencing Commission, and Bureau of Prisons Combined 2016 Datafiles, USSCBOP.

received shorter sentences than they would have under different policies, and therefore their release could continue to impact the makeup of the prison population in future years. It is also unclear the extent to which the Department of Justice's recent decision to refocus its efforts on prosecuting the most serious, readily provable offense will reverse the trends seen in the data below.

Federal Drug Offender Population Overall

There have been significant changes to the federal prison population over the past 25 years. The total number of offenders in the federal prison population rose steadily from 1995 to a high of 217,815 in December 2012.[94] The steady increase through 2012 was the result of several factors, including the scope and use of mandatory minimum penalties.[95] However, in recent years, this trend has reversed. Since the high point at the end of 2012, the number of federal inmates fell to 196,455 on December 31, 2015.

To further explore the scope and impact of drug mandatory minimum penalties in the federal system, the Commission merged the BOP dataset with the Commission dataset, identifying those offenders for whom the Commission received complete sentencing information. The Commission used this combined data to determine the number of drug offenders in the federal prison population, which has also declined in recent years. As shown in Figure 34, the drug offender population steadily increased from 45,064 on September 30, 1995 to a high of 102,091 on of September 30, 2011. Since then, the number of federal drug inmates fell to 81,825 inmates (a 19.9% decrease) on September 30, 2016. Changes related to the charging and sentencing of drug offenders likely explain this trend.[96]

As reflected in Figure 35, the number of drug offenders has varied widely over the years based on the type of drug involved in the offense. The number of crack cocaine offenders steadily increased from 1995 to a peak of 32,084 offenders

Figure 35. Number of Offenders in Prison on September 30 by Type of Drug
1995 - 2016

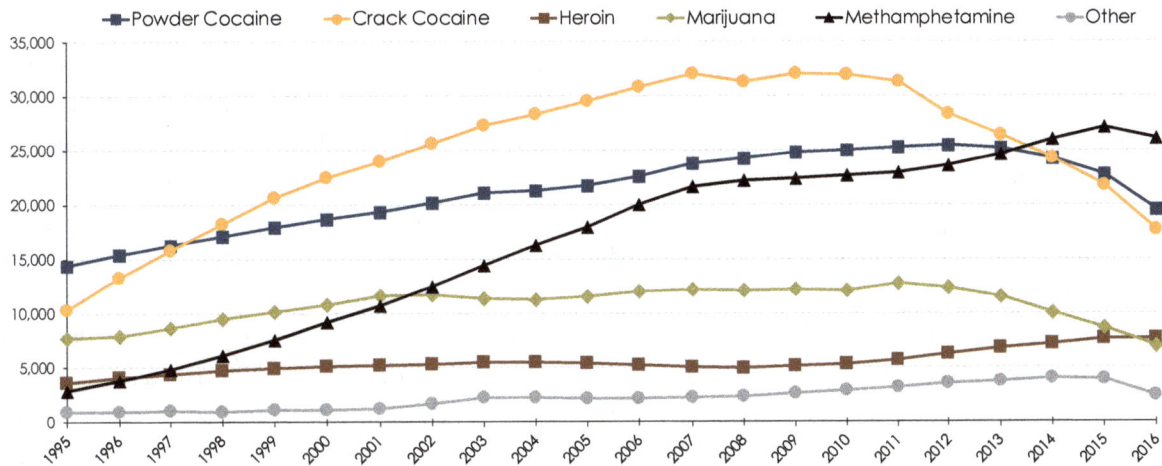

SOURCE: U.S. Sentencing Commission, and Bureau of Prisons Combined 2016 Datafiles, USSCBOP.

in 2007, and has since significantly decreased since 2011. Conversely, methamphetamine offenders have now become the largest drug-type population with 26,089 offenders. The only other drug type for which the number of offenders continued to trend upward was heroin. The population of heroin offenders remained largely stable until a gradual increase began in 2011. The other drug categories, including powder cocaine and marijuana, followed the general trend, with decreasing numbers in recent years.

Drug Mandatory Minimum Offenders in the Federal Prison Population

While the number of drug offenders has decreased over time, drug offenders continued to contribute significantly to the federal prison population. As of September 30, 2016, there were 166,771 offenders in the total BOP population. Of these, 81,825 (49.1%) were drug offenders.

Figure 36. Drug Offenders in the BOP Population
At the End of Fiscal Year 2016

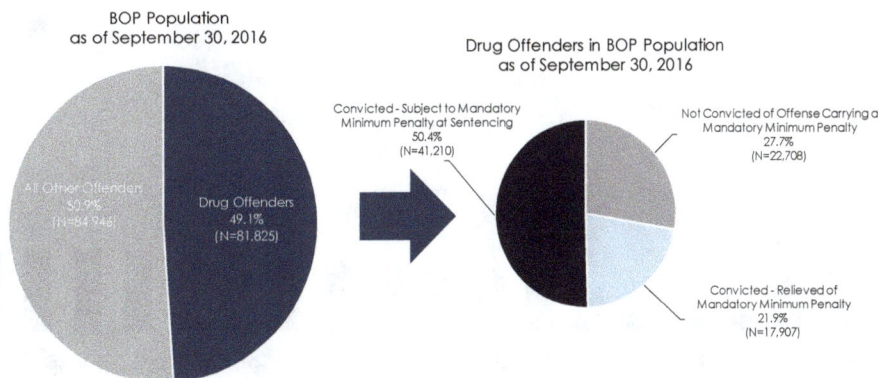

SOURCE: U.S. Sentencing Commission, and Bureau of Prisons Combined 2016 Datafile, USSCBOP.

Within the subset of drug offenders, 72.3 percent were convicted of an offense carrying a mandatory minimum penalty. This is significantly higher than the percentage of the offenders in the total BOP population convicted of an offense carrying a mandatory minimum penalty, which stands at 55.7 percent (n=92,870).[97] As shown in Figure 36, 50.4 percent (n=41,210) of drug offenders were convicted of, and remained subject to, a drug mandatory minimum penalty at sentencing, while 21.9 percent (n=17,907) were convicted of and relieved from an offense carrying a mandatory minimum penalty. The remaining 27.7 percent (n=22,708) of drug offenders were not convicted of an offense carrying a drug mandatory minimum penalty.

As depicted in Figure 37, the number of offenders convicted of an offense carrying a drug mandatory minimum penalty has decreased in recent years, which is consistent with the downward trend in the total federal prison population. As of September 30, 2010, combined Commission

and BOP data identified 81,084 offenders in BOP custody who were convicted of an offense carrying a drug mandatory minimum penalty. By September 30, 2016, there were 59,117 such inmates in BOP custody, a 27.1 percent decrease.

As part of this decline, both the population of offenders who were relieved of a mandatory minimum penalty and those who remained subject to such a penalty at sentencing decreased in number since 2010. Nevertheless, they have done so at significantly different rates. While the number of offenders in BOP custody who remained subject to a mandatory minimum penalty at sentencing decreased 19.3 percent between September 30, 2010 (n=51,038) and September 30, 2016 (n=41,210), the number of offenders who were convicted of but relieved from such a penalty decreased 40.4 percent during the same period (30,046 as of September 30, 2010 to 17,907 as of September 30, 2016). At the same time, there was an increase in the population of offenders convicted

Figure 37. Number of Offenders in Prison Not Convicted of an Offense Carrying a Drug Mandatory Minimum Penalty, Relieved of an Offense Carrying a Drug Mandatory Minimum Penalty, and Subject to a Drug Mandatory Minimum Penalty at Sentencing
At the End of Fiscal Years 1995 - 2016

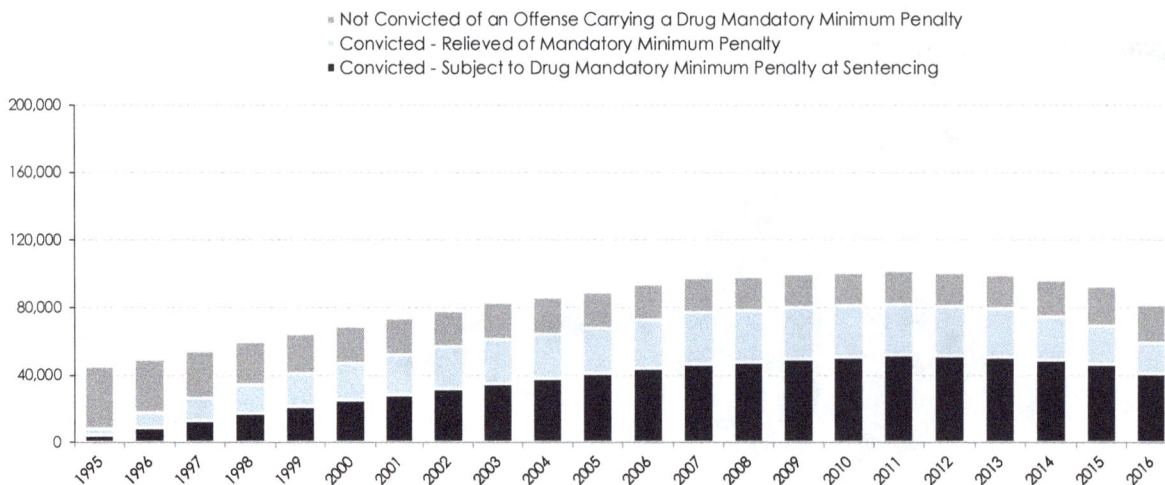

- Not Convicted of an Offense Carrying a Drug Mandatory Minimum Penalty
- Convicted - Relieved of Mandatory Minimum Penalty
- Convicted - Subject to Drug Mandatory Minimum Penalty at Sentencing

SOURCE: U.S. Sentencing Commission, and Bureau of Prisons Combined 2016 Datafiles, USSCBOP.

of violating a statute with no drug mandatory minimum penalty from 19,719 as of September 30, 2010 to 22,708 as of September 30, 2016.

These trends are consistent with the changes in charging and sentencing practices discussed above. As fewer offenders were convicted of offenses carrying drug mandatory minimum penalties, that population declined, while the number of non-mandatory minimum offenders increased slightly. Similarly, the differing rates of decrease between the number of offenders who were relieved of a mandatory minimum and those who remained subject to such penalties also reflected the stated goals of the Department of Justice's 2013 Smart on Crime initiative to more narrowly target mandatory minimum penalties to more serious drug offenders.

Combined Commission and BOP data also reflect changes in the distribution of offenders in the federal prison population who were convicted of violating drug statutes with and without mandatory minimum penalties. Following the general trend of the total BOP population,[98] the percentage of the prison drug population convicted of statutes carrying drug mandatory minimum penalties decreased slightly from a peak of 80.4 percent as of September 30, 2010 to 72.3 percent as of September 30, 2016. Among this group, the percentage of offenders subject to a mandatory minimum penalty remained remarkably stable at between 50.4 percent and 51.0 percent during fiscal years 2010 through 2016. Conversely, the percentage of offenders who were convicted of a statute carrying a drug mandatory minimum penalty but relieved from the penalty at sentencing has steadily decreased from 29.8 percent to 21.9 percent during the same period, which is the lowest percentage since fiscal year 1996.

Figure 38. Percent of Offenders in Prison Not Convicted of an Offense Carrying a Drug Mandatory Minimum Penalty, Relieved of an Offense Carrying a Mandatory Minimum Penalty, and Subject to a Drug Mandatory Minimum Penalty at Sentencing
At the End of Fiscal Years 1995 - 2016

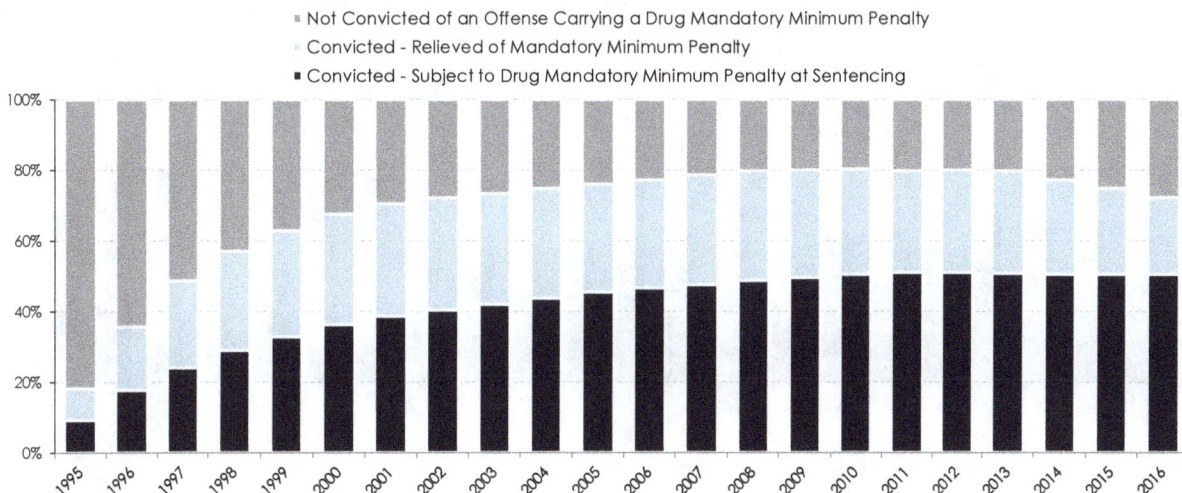

▪ Not Convicted of an Offense Carrying a Drug Mandatory Minimum Penalty
▪ Convicted - Relieved of Mandatory Minimum Penalty
▪ Convicted - Subject to Drug Mandatory Minimum Penalty at Sentencing

SOURCE: U.S. Sentencing Commission, and Bureau of Prisons Combined 2016 Datafiles, USSCBOP.

As demonstrated in Figure 39, the percentages of drug offenders who received relief through substantial assistance, safety valve, or both have hit all-time lows at 18.1 percent, 9.8 percent, and 2.4 percent, respectively. Since the Commission's 2011 *Mandatory Minimum Report*, the portion of federal drug offenders who received substantial assistance relief decreased slightly from 22.2 percent in fiscal year 2010 (18.8% receiving substantial assistance, and 3.4% receiving both substantial assistance and safety valve relief) to 20.5 percent in fiscal year 2016 (18.1% receiving substantial assistance, and 2.4% receiving both substantial assistance and safety valve relief). The frequency of safety valve relief has decreased even more significantly from 18.3 percent in fiscal year 2010 (14.9% receiving substantial assistance, and 3.4% receiving both substantial assistance and safety valve relief) to 12.2 percent in fiscal year 2016 (9.8% receiving substantial assistance, and 2.4% receiving both

substantial assistance and safety valve relief). As a result, over two-thirds (69.7%) of drug offenders convicted of an offense carrying a drug mandatory minimum in 2016 did not receive any form of relief. This compares to 62.9 percent in fiscal year 2010, and is up significantly from the mid-1990s when only half of offenders convicted of an offense carrying a drug mandatory minimum did not receive relief.

These trends again appear consistent with the intent of the Department of Justice's 2013 Smart on Crime Initiative. That is, while fewer offenders were convicted of an offense carrying a mandatory minimum penalty in recent years, those who were tended to be more serious offenders who are less likely to be eligible for relief.

Figure 39. Percent of Offenders in Federal Prison Convicted of an Offense Carrying a Drug Mandatory Minimum Penalty by Type of Relief
At the End of Fiscal Years 1995 - 2016

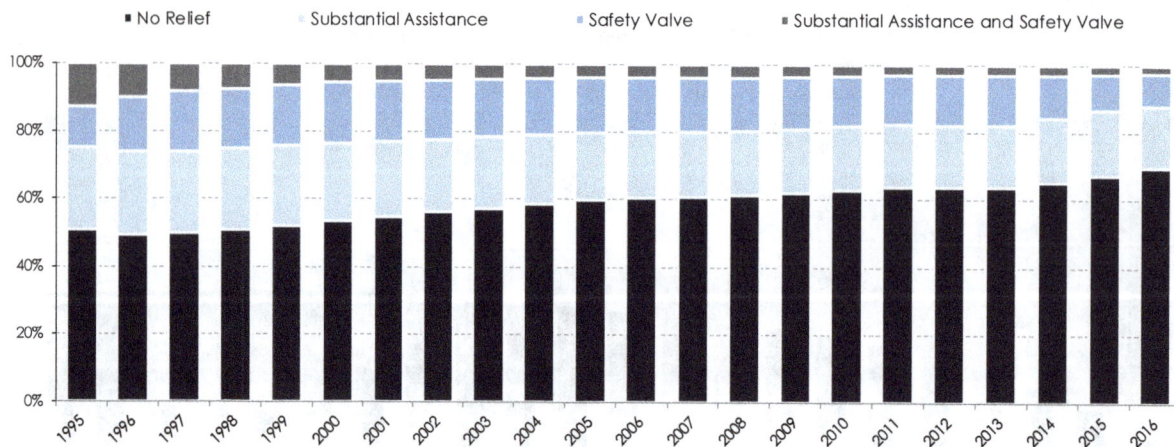

SOURCE: U.S. Sentencing Commission, and Bureau of Prisons Combined 2016 Datafiles, USSCBOP.

Drug Mandatory Minimum Offenders in the Federal Prison Population – By Race

All racial groups experienced a steady decrease in the population of drug offenders since 2013, following more than a decade of increases. At the end of fiscal year 2013, Hispanic offenders (n=38,125) became the most common racial group in the federal prison drug population for the first time, overtaking Black offenders (n=37,067). This trend continued in the years since, with Hispanic offenders (n=33,429) making up the largest portion of drug offenders in BOP custody at the end of fiscal year 2016. Black offenders (n=29,131) comprised the second largest group, followed by White offenders (n=17,295) and Other Race offenders (n=1,852).

In addition to comprising the largest population of drug offenders in BOP custody, Hispanic drug offenders in prison were also more likely than any other race to have been convicted of an offense carrying a drug mandatory minimum penalty in recent years. As shown in Figure 41, 75.3 percent of Hispanic drug offenders in prison were convicted of an offense carrying a drug mandatory minimum penalty at the end of fiscal year 2016. This percentage, however, has declined since fiscal year 2010 (84.1% of all Hispanic drug offenders in prison). Similarly, 73.0 percent of Black drug offenders in prison were convicted of an offense carrying a drug mandatory minimum penalty at the end of fiscal year 2016, a steady decline since fiscal year 2010 (81.6% of all Black drug offenders in prison). The percentage of White drug offenders and Other Race drug offenders convicted of an offense carrying a mandatory minimum penalty also decreased during this time to 66.0 percent and 65.3 percent, respectively, at the end of fiscal year 2016.

In contrast, the percentage of offenders in prison subject to a drug mandatory minimum increased for all demographic groups, except Black drug offenders (which decreased since the end of fiscal year 2010 (from 58.9% to 56.9%)). Despite the decrease, Black drug offenders in prison were the demographic group most likely to have remained subject to a drug mandatory minimum penalty. At the end of fiscal year 2016, 56.9 percent of Black drug offenders in prison were subject to a drug mandatory minimum penalty at sentencing, followed by Hispanic drug offenders (48.6%), White drug offenders (43.7%), and Other Race drug offenders (41.9%).

Drug Mandatory Minimum Offenders in the Federal Prison Population – By Gender

As reflected in Figure 43, the number of male offenders in the federal prison drug population decreased from a high of 94,772 at the end of fiscal year 2011 to 75,299 at the end of fiscal year 2016 (a 20.5% decrease). The population of female drug offenders also decreased slightly in the last three fiscal years, but was more steady over the study period.

The percentage of males in prison who were convicted of an offense carrying a drug mandatory minimum penalty also decreased, from 80.7 percent at the end of fiscal year 2010 to 73.3 percent in 2016. The percentage of female drug offenders in prison convicted of an offense carrying a drug mandatory minimum penalty demonstrated a similar decrease during this period, falling from 76.5 percent at the end of fiscal year 2010 to a low of 60.2 percent at the end of fiscal year 2016.

Figure 40. Number of Drug Offenders in Federal Prison by Race
At the End of Fiscal Years 1995 - 2016

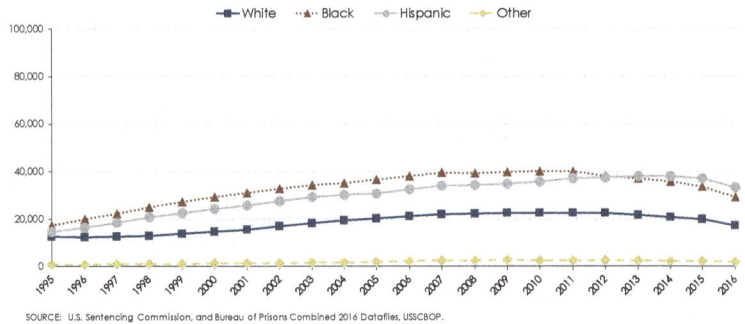

SOURCE: U.S. Sentencing Commission, and Bureau of Prisons Combined 2016 Datafiles, USSCBOP.

Figure 41. Percentage of Offenders in Federal Prison Convicted of an Offense Carrying a Drug Mandatory Minimum Penalty by Race
At the End of Fiscal Years 1995 - 2016

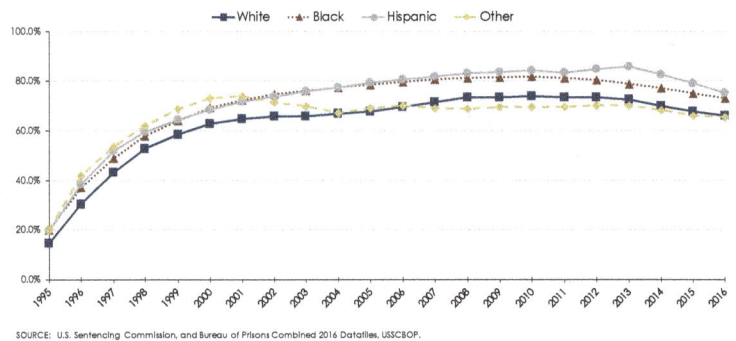

SOURCE: U.S. Sentencing Commission, and Bureau of Prisons Combined 2016 Datafiles, USSCBOP.

Figure 42. Percentage of Offenders in Federal Prison Subject to a Drug Mandatory Minimum Penalty at Sentencing by Race
At the End of Fiscal Years 1995 - 2016

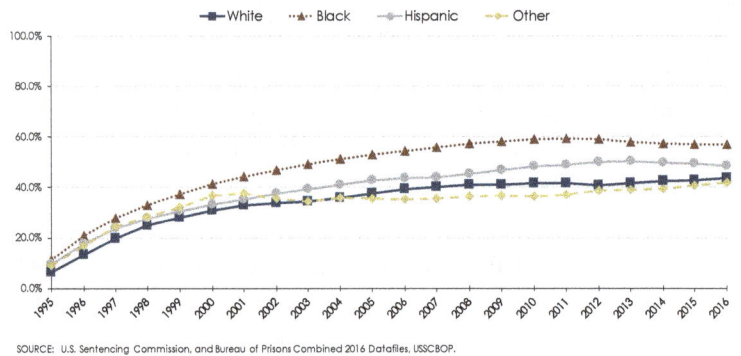

SOURCE: U.S. Sentencing Commission, and Bureau of Prisons Combined 2016 Datafiles, USSCBOP.

The percentage of male offenders in prison who were subject to a drug mandatory minimum steadily increased until 2010 and has remained relatively stable since. At the end of fiscal year 1995, 9.5 percent of male offenders in prison were subject to a drug mandatory minimum penalty at sentencing. This increased to a high of 52.4 percent at the end of fiscal years 2012 and 2013, but has remained stable since, leveling off at 52.1 percent at the end of fiscal year 2016. The percentage of female offenders in prison subject to a drug mandatory minimum penalty, though always lower than the percentage of male offenders, followed a similar pattern but has decreased since 2010. As of the end of fiscal year 2016, 30.9 percent of female offenders in prison were subject to a drug mandatory minimum penalty at sentencing.

Drug Mandatory Minimum Offenders in the Federal Prison Population – By Citizenship

Following a steady increase from the end of fiscal year 1995 (n=33,069) through the end of fiscal year 2011 (n=78,420), the population of U.S. citizens in the federal prison population for drug offenses decreased to 64,223 at the end of fiscal year 2016. The population of non-U.S. citizen drug offenders followed a similar pattern, increasing from the end of fiscal year 1995 (n=11,748) through the end of fiscal year 2011 (n=23,537) before steadily decreasing to 17,519 at the end of fiscal year 2016.

While the percentage has declined in recent years, the majority of both U.S. citizen drug offenders (71.0%) and non-U.S. citizen drug offenders (76.8%) in prison at the end of fiscal year 2016 were convicted of an offense carrying a drug mandatory minimum penalty. As reflected in Figure 47, the percentage of both U.S. citizen drug offenders and non-U.S. citizen drug offenders in prison who were convicted of an offense carrying a drug mandatory minimum penalty significantly increased over the course of the study period (from 18.0% at the end of fiscal year 1995 to 71.0% at the end of fiscal year 2016, and from 19.3% at the end of fiscal year 1995 to 76.8% at the end of fiscal year 2016, respectively), though both have declined in recent years.

A similar trend is seen in Figure 48 when analyzing offenders who remained subject to a mandatory minimum penalty at sentencing. The percentages of U.S. citizen and non-U.S. citizen drug offenders who were in prison and were subject to a drug mandatory minimum penalty at sentencing both increased over the study period (from 9.4% at the end of fiscal year 1995 to 51.8% at the end of fiscal year 2016, and from 9.1% at the end of fiscal year 1995 to 45.1% at the end of fiscal year 2016, respectively).

Figure 43. Number of Drug Offenders in Federal Prison by Gender
At the End of Fiscal Years 1995 - 2016

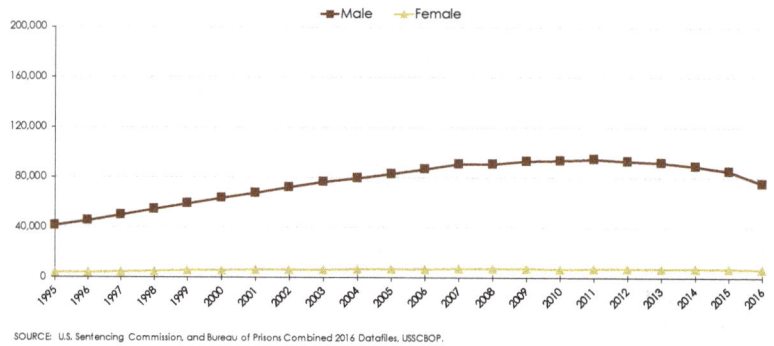

SOURCE: U.S. Sentencing Commission, and Bureau of Prisons Combined 2016 Datafiles, USSCBOP.

Figure 44. Percentage of Offenders in Federal Prison Convicted of an Offense Carrying a Drug Mandatory Minimum Penalty by Gender
At the End of Fiscal Years 1995 - 2016

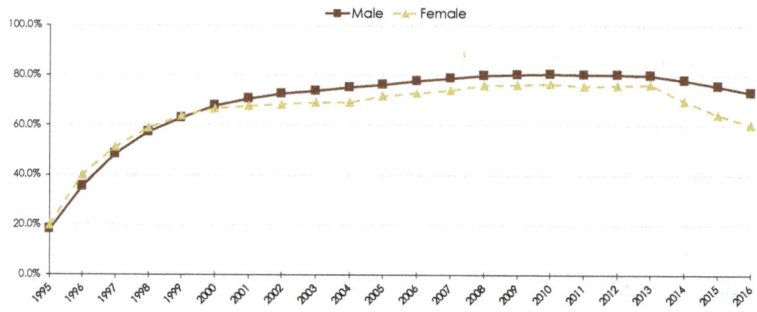

SOURCE: U.S. Sentencing Commission, and Bureau of Prisons Combined 2016 Datafiles, USSCBOP.

Figure 45. Percentage of Offenders in Federal Prison Subject to a Drug Mandatory Minimum Penalty at Sentencing by Gender
At the End of Fiscal Years 1995 - 2016

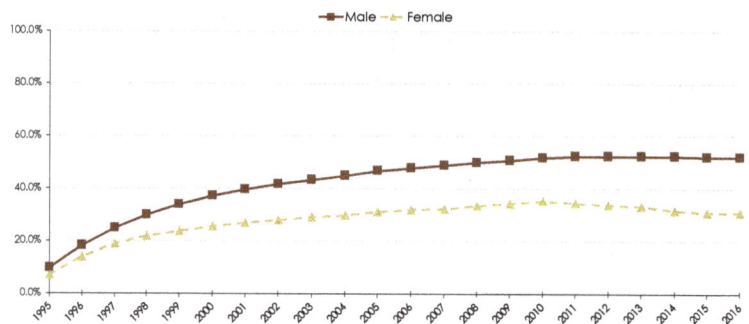

SOURCE: U.S. Sentencing Commission, and Bureau of Prisons Combined 2016 Datafiles, USSCBOP.

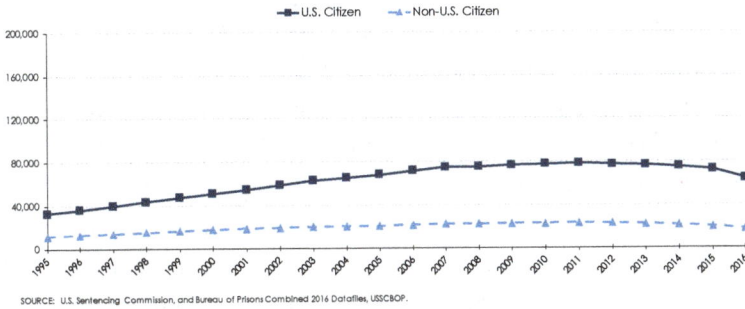

Figure 46. Number of Drug Offenders in Federal Prison by Citizenship
At the End of Fiscal Years 1995 - 2016

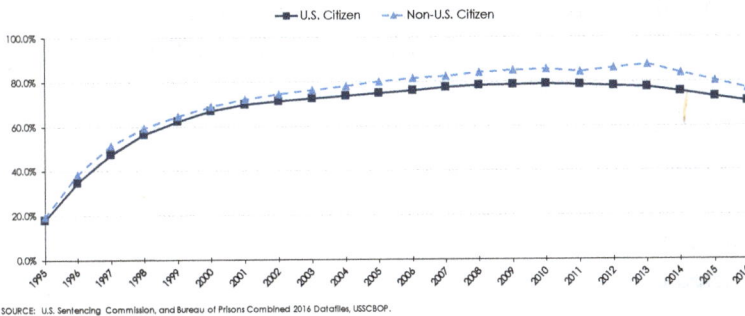

SOURCE: U.S. Sentencing Commission, and Bureau of Prisons Combined 2016 Datafiles, USSCBOP.

Figure 47. Percentage of Offenders in Federal Prison Convicted of an Offense Carrying a Drug Mandatory Minimum Penalty by Citizenship
At the End of Fiscal Years 1995 - 2016

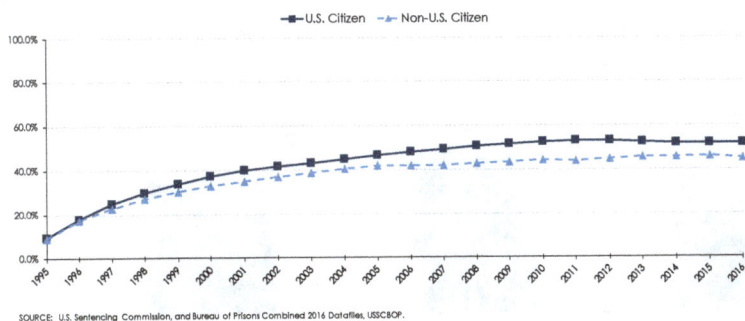

SOURCE: U.S. Sentencing Commission, and Bureau of Prisons Combined 2016 Datafiles, USSCBOP.

Figure 48. Percentage of Offenders in Federal Prison Subject to a Drug Mandatory Minimum Penalty at Sentencing by Citizenship
At the End of Fiscal Years 1995 - 2016

SOURCE: U.S. Sentencing Commission, and Bureau of Prisons Combined 2016 Datafiles, USSCBOP.

Recidivism

Any policy discussion regarding the impact and appropriate use of mandatory minimum penalties would not be complete without consideration of their relationship to recidivism rates. The Commission thus considered the percentage of offenders who recidivated (as measured by rearrest rates) by the length of the drug mandatory minimum term faced, as well as the number of recidivism events, time to recidivism event, and most serious event.

As reflected in Figure 49, the Commission's recidivism data demonstrated that there was an inverse relationship between the length of any drug trafficking mandatory minimum penalty and recidivism rate. Recidivism, as measured by rearrest rates, among drug trafficking offenders not convicted of an offense carrying a drug mandatory minimum penalty was 54.7 percent, while those convicted of an offense carrying a five-year mandatory minimum penalty had a lower recidivism rate of 50.6 percent, those convicted of

an offense carrying a ten-year mandatory minimum penalty had an even lower recidivism rate of 44.7 percent, and those convicted of an offense carrying a mandatory minimum penalty of twenty years had the lowest recidivism rate, 37.0 percent. The longer sentences received by offenders convicted of drug mandatory minimum penalties result in older ages at release. Offenders who were not convicted of an offense carrying a mandatory minimum penalty were approximately four years younger at release than those convicted of an offense carrying a ten-year mandatory minimum penalty (34 compared to 38 years old). This difference in age at release is likely one factor in explaining the link between lower mandatory minimum penalties and higher recidivism.[99]

Figure 49. Rearrest Rates for Offenders by Length of Drug Mandatory Minimum Penalties
Fiscal Year 2016

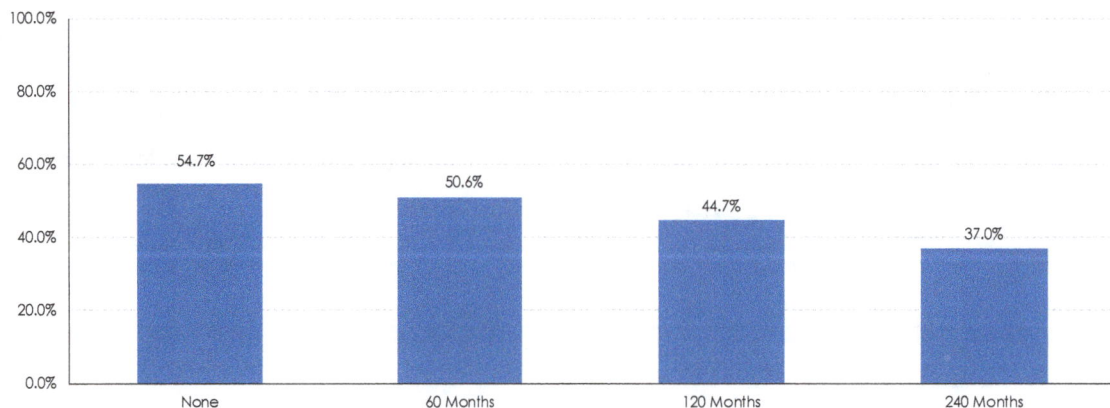

SOURCE: U.S. Sentencing Commission's 2005 Recidivism Release Cohort Datafile, RECID05_OFFUPDT.

Of those offenders convicted of an offense carrying a drug mandatory minimum penalty, nearly half (47.7%) were rearrested during the eight-year study period, while fewer were reconvicted (28.6%) or reincarcerated (21.8%). While the most serious post-release event was most frequently drug trafficking for those reconvicted or reincarcerated (18.7% and 21.9%, respectively), it was assault for those rearrested (24.7%).

The Commission has provided more detailed analysis of recidivism among drug offenders in its recent publication, *Recidivism Among Federal Drug Trafficking Offenders*,[100] which examined the recidivist behavior of a group of 10,888 federal drug trafficking offenders who were released in calendar year 2005.

Table 7. Recidivism Rates for Offenders Convicted of an Offense Carrying a Drug Mandatory Minimum Penalty
Fiscal Year 2016

Recidivism Measure	Rearrest	Reconviction	Reincarceration
Percent	47.7%	28.6%	21.8%
Median Time to Recidivism	28 Months	38 Months	37 Months
Median Number of Recidivism Events	2	1	1
Most Serious Post-Release Event	Assault (24.7%, n=787)	Drug Trafficking (18.7%, n=359)	Drug Trafficking (21.9%, n=321)
Median Age at Release	33	32	32

SOURCE: U.S. Sentencing Commission's 2005 Recidivism Release Cohort Datafile, RECID05_OFFUPDT. The Commission excluded cases from this analysis that were missing information necessary to perform the analysis. Median age at release is shown for recidivist offenders only.

5 Conclusion

Conclusion

Since the Commission's 2011 *Mandatory Minimum Report*, there have been significant legislative and prosecutorial changes, as well as judicial opinions, affecting the use of mandatory minimum penalties. These changes were chiefly directed at low-level, non-violent drug offenders. In particular, the Fair Sentencing Act of 2010 repealed the mandatory minimum penalty for simple possession of crack cocaine and increased the quantities of crack cocaine necessary to trigger a mandatory minimum penalty. In 2013, the Department of Justice's Smart on Crime Initiative instructed prosecutors not to charge the drug quantities necessary to trigger mandatory minimum penalties for certain non-violent, less culpable drug offenders. These changes are reflected in the data trends reported in this publication, including a significant decrease in the number of offenders convicted of an offense carrying a drug mandatory minimum penalty since fiscal year 2010.

At the same time, drug mandatory minimum penalties continue to have a significant impact on the sentencing of drug offenders and on the federal prison population. The data demonstrates that offenders convicted of an offense carrying a drug mandatory minimum penalty continue to receive longer sentences than offenders not convicted of an offense carrying a drug mandatory minimum. These longer sentences, coupled with the fact that drug offenses are the most common offenses carrying mandatory minimum penalties, considerably affect the prison population. At the end of the last fiscal year, nearly half of all federal inmates were drug offenders and nearly three-quarters of those drug offenders in prison were convicted of an offense carrying a drug mandatory minimum penalty. The data also demonstrates that the effects of mandatory minimum penalties on sentencing occur for drug offenders across the culpability spectrum and regardless of an offender's role in the offense.

Endnotes

1   U.S. SENTENCING COMM'N, OVERVIEW OF MANDATORY MINIMUM PENALTIES IN THE FEDERAL CRIMINAL JUSTICE SYSTEM [hereinafter 2017 OVERVIEW PUBLICATION], *available at* https://www.ussc.gov/sites/default/files/pdf/research-and-publications/research-publications/2017/20170711_Mand-Min.pdf.

2   The term "mandatory minimum penalty" refers to a federal criminal statute requiring, upon conviction of a federal criminal offense and the satisfaction of criteria set forth in that statute, the imposition of a specified minimum term of imprisonment. This publication uses the terms "drug mandatory minimum penalty," "drug mandatory minimum sentencing provision," "statute carrying a drug mandatory minimum penalty," "convicted of an offense carrying a drug mandatory minimum penalty," and related terms interchangeably in discussing statutory provisions carrying a minimum term of imprisonment. A provision that requires a mandatory minimum fine, mandatory minimum term of probation, mandatory minimum term of supervised release, or any other mandatory component of a sentence other than imprisonment is not considered a mandatory minimum penalty for purposes of this publication.

3   U.S. SENTENCING COMM'N, 2011 REPORT TO CONGRESS: MANDATORY MINIMUM PENALTIES IN THE FEDERAL CRIMINAL JUSTICE SYSTEM [hereinafter 2011 MANDATORY MINIMUM REPORT], *available at* https://www.ussc.gov/research/congressional-reports/2011-report-congress-mandatory-minimum-penalties-federal-criminal-justice-system.

4   The Commission submitted the 2011 *Mandatory Minimum Report* pursuant to the statutory directive contained in section 4713 of the Matthew Shepard and James Byrd, Jr. Hate Crimes Prevention Act of 2009. *See* Division E of the National Defense Authorization Act for Fiscal Year 2010, Pub. L. No. 111-84, 123 Stat. 2190, 2843 (enacted October 28, 2009). The Commission also submitted its 2011 *Mandatory Minimum Report* pursuant to its general authority under 28 U.S.C. §§ 994–995, and its specific authority under 28 U.S.C. § 995(a)(20) which provides that the Commission shall have authority to "make recommendations to Congress concerning modification or enactment of statutes relating to sentencing, penal, and correctional matters that the Commission finds to be necessary and advisable to carry out an effective, humane, and rational sentencing policy."

5   A detailed historical discussion of statutory mandatory minimum penalties for drug offenses is presented in the Commission's 2011 MANDATORY MINIMUM REPORT, *supra* note 2, at 23–25.

6   *See* 2017 OVERVIEW PUBLICATION, *supra* note 1, at 34 & Figure 7.

7   For definitions of the various offender functions and a description of how the offender function was determined for each case, see *infra* at 43–44. The special coding project for this publication was similar to the coding project the Commission undertook for its analysis in the 2011 *Mandatory Minimum Report*. *See* 2011 MANDATORY MINIMUM REPORT, *supra* note 2, at nn.636–40 & accompanying text.

8   21 U.S.C. §§ 841, 960.

9   *See* 21 U.S.C. §§ 859, 860, and 861. A person who commits one of those offenses is subject to a mandatory minimum penalty of at least one year of imprisonment, unless a greater mandatory minimum penalty otherwise applies.

10   Controlled substance is defined as "a drug or other substance, or immediate precursor, included in Schedule I, II, III, IV, or V of part B of this subchapter," and includes powder cocaine, crack cocaine, marijuana, methamphetamine, and heroin, among others. 21 U.S.C. § 802(6).

11   These mandatory minimum penalties became effective on November 1, 1987, for all drug types, except methamphetamine. *See* Pub. L. No. 99-570, § 1002, 100 Stat. 3207, 3207-2 (1986) (amending 21 U.S.C. § 841(b) (1)). The mandatory minimum penalties for methamphetamine became effective on November 18, 1988. *See* Pub. L. No. 100-690, § 6470(g)(3), 102 Stat. 4181, 4378 (1988) (amending 21 U.S.C. § 841(b)(1)). Congress also added a mandatory minimum penalty for simple possession of crack cocaine in 1988. *See* Pub. L. No. 100-690, § 6371, 102 Stat. 4181, 4370 (1988) (amending 21 U.S.C. § 844(a)). The Fair Sentencing Act of 2010 (FSA) altered the mandatory minimum penalties established by the 1986 and 1988 Acts by repealing the mandatory minimum penalty for simple possession of crack cocaine and by increasing the quantities required to trigger the five- and ten-year mandatory minimum penalties for crack cocaine trafficking offenses from five to 28 grams and 50 to 280 grams, respectively. *See* Pub. L. No. 111-220, § 2, 124 Stat. 2372 (amending 21 U.S.C. §§ 841, 844).

12   These increased mandatory minimum penalties are applicable only if the government provides notice pursuant to 21 U.S.C. § 851, which provides that "[n]o person who stands convicted of an offense under this part shall be sentenced to increased punishment by reason of one or more prior convictions, unless before trial, or before entry of a plea of guilty, the United States attorney files an information with the court (and serves a copy of such information on the person or counsel for the person) stating in writing the previous convictions to be relied upon."

13   *See* 21 U.S.C. §§ 841(b)(1)(B), 960(b)(2)(A)–(C), (G), and (H).

14   *See* 21 U.S.C. §§ 841(b)(1)(A), 960(b)(1)(A)–(C), (G), and (H).

15   *See* 21 U.S.C. §§ 846, 963.

16   *See* 21 U.S.C. §§ 841(b) and 960(b).

17   A more detailed history of drug mandatory minimums can be found in Chapter Two of 2011 *Mandatory Minimum Report*. *See* 2011 MANDATORY MINIMUM REPORT, *supra* note 2, at 23–25. *See also* U.S. SENTENCING COMM'N, REPORT TO THE CONGRESS: COCAINE AND FEDERAL SENTENCING POLICY, at 8, note 26 (May 2007), *available at* https://www.ussc.gov/sites/default/files/pdf/news/congressional-testimony-and-reports/drug-topics/200705_RtC_Cocaine_Sentencing_Policy.pdf; U.S. SENTENCING COMM'N, REPORT TO THE CONGRESS: COCAINE AND FEDERAL SENTENCING POLICY, at 6–7 (May 2002), *available at* https://www.ussc.gov/sites/default/files/pdf/news/congressional-testimony-and-reports/drug-topics/200205-rtc-cocaine-sentencing-policy/200205_Cocaine_and_Federal_Sentencing_Policy.pdf; U.S. SENTENCING COMM'N, SPECIAL REPORT TO THE CONGRESS: COCAINE AND FEDERAL SENTENCING POLICY, at 117–19, (Feb. 1995), *available at* https://www.ussc.gov/sites/default/files/pdf/news/congressional-testimony-and-reports/drug-topics/199502-rtc-cocaine-sentencing-policy/CHAP5-8.pdf; U.S. SENTENCING COMM'N, SPECIAL REPORT TO CONGRESS: MANDATORY MINIMUM PENALTIES IN THE FEDERAL CRIMINAL JUSTICE SYSTEM (AS DIRECTED BY SECTION 1703 OF PUBLIC LAW 101–647), at 28–29 (Aug. 1991), *available at* https://www.ussc.gov/sites/default/files/pdf/news/congressional-testimony-and-reports/mandatory-minimum-penalties/1991_Mand_Min_Report.pdf.

18   Because of the heightened concern and national sense of urgency surrounding drugs generally and crack cocaine specifically, Congress bypassed much of its usual deliberative legislative process in passing the Act. As a result, there were no committee hearings and no Senate or House Reports accompanying the bill that ultimately passed, limiting the legislative history for the bill that was enacted into law to statements made by senators and representatives during floor debates.

19   *See* 132 CONG. REC. 27,193–94 (daily ed. Sept. 30, 1986) (statement of Sen. Robert Byrd) ("For the kingpins—the masterminds who are really running these operations—and they can be identified by the amount of drugs with which they are involved—we require a jail term upon conviction. If it is their first conviction, the minimum term is 10 years. . . . Our proposal would also provide mandatory minimum penalties for the middle-level dealers as well. Those criminals would also have to serve time in jail. The minimum sentences would be slightly less than those for the kingpins, but they nevertheless would have to go to jail—a minimum of 5 years for the first offense."). *See also* 132 CONG. REC. 22,993 (daily ed. Sept. 11, 1986) (statement of Rep. John LaFalce) ("[S]eparate penalties are established for the biggest traffickers, with another set of penalties for other serious drug pushers."); 132 CONG. REC. 13779 (daily ed. Sept. 26, 1986) ("the most serious drug traffickers, so-called 'drug kingpins', would face a mandatory minimum of 10 years and up to life imprisonment") (Senate section-by-section analysis).

20   The House version provided tougher penalties for "cocaine freebase," H.R. 5394, 99th CONG., 2d Sess. § 101 (1986), while the Senate version provided penalties for "cocaine base," S. 2878, 99th CONG., 2d Sess. § 1002, 132 CONG. REC. S13649 (daily ed. Sept. 25, 1986). Congress ultimately enacted the Senate version by incorporating it into H.R. 5484, which became the Anti–Drug Abuse Act of 1986. *See* 132 CONG. REC. H11219–20 (daily ed. Oct. 17, 1986).

21   H.R. Rep. No. 99-845, pt. 1, at 11–12 (1986).

22   *See id.*

23   *See* H.R. Rep. No. 103-460 (1994) (accompanying H.R. 3979 (Mandatory Minimum Sentencing Reform Act of 1994, which ultimately added the statutory safety valve), citing to H.R. Rep. No. 99-845, *supra* note 21, and floor statement of Sen. Byrd, *supra* note 19.

24   *See* 18 U.S.C. § 3553(e) ("Upon motion of the Government, the court shall have the authority to impose a sentence below a level established by statute as a minimum sentence so as to reflect a defendant's substantial assistance in the investigation or prosecution of another person who has committed an offense.").

25   18 U.S.C. § 3553(f).

26   The safety valve provisions apply to offenses under section 401, 404, or 406 of the Controlled Substances Act (21 U.S.C. §§ 841, 844, 846) and section 1010 or 1013 of the Controlled Substances Import and Export Act (21 U.S.C. §§ 960, 963).

27   *See* 2017 OVERVIEW PUBLICATION, *supra* note 1, at 18–19 (explaining the statutory and guideline "substantial assistance" and "safety valve" provisions).

28   USSG §2D1.1(a)(1)–(4).

29   USSG §2D1.1(a)(5).

30   *See* USSG §2D1.1. In 2014, the Commission amended the Drug Quantity Table to reduce by two levels the offense levels assigned to the quantities that trigger mandatory minimum penalties, resulting in corresponding ranges that include the mandatory minimum penalties. *See* USSG App. C, amend. 782 (effect. Nov. 1, 2014). Prior to the amendment, the base offense levels assigned corresponded to guideline ranges that were slightly above the statutory mandatory minimum penalties. Offenses involving drug quantities that trigger a five-year statutory minimum were assigned a base offense level 26 (63 to 78 months for a defendant in Criminal History Category I) and offenses involving drug quantities that trigger a ten-year statutory minimum were assigned a base offense level of 32 (121 months to 151 months for a defendant in Criminal History Category I).

31   The majority of drug offenders (96.3%, n=18,862) were sentenced under USSG §2D1.1. Additional relevant guidelines include USSG §§ 2D1.2 (Drug Offenses Occurring Near Protected Locations or Involving Underage or Pregnant Individuals; Attempt or Conspiracy) (1.6%, n=318); 2D2.1 (Unlawful Possession: Attempt or Conspiracy) (1.1%, n=218); 2D1.11 (Unlawfully Distributing, Importing, Exporting or Possessing a Listed Chemical; Attempt or Conspiracy) (0.4%, n=75); 2D2.2 (Acquiring a Controlled Substance by Forgery, Fraud, Deception, or Subterfuge; Attempt or Conspiracy) (0.3%, n=53); 2D1.8 (Renting or Managing a Drug Establishment: Attempt or Conspiracy) (0.1%, n=18); 2D1.10 (Endangering Human Life While Illegally Manufacturing a Controlled Substance; Attempt or Conspiracy) (0.1%, n=12); 2D1.5 (Continuing Criminal Enterprise: Attempt or Conspiracy) (0.1%, n=12); 2D1.12 (Unlawful Possession, Manufacture, Distribution, Transportation, Exportation, or Importation of Prohibited Flask, Equipment, Chemical, Product, or Material; Attempt or Conspiracy) (0.0%, n=6); 2D1.7 (Unlawful Sale or Transportation of Drug Paraphernalia) (0.0%, n=6); 2D1.13 (Structuring Chemical Transactions or Creating a Chemical Mixture to Evade Reporting or Recordkeeping Requirements; Presenting False or Fraudulent Identification to Obtain a Listed Chemical; Attempt or Conspiracy) (0.0%, n=2); and 2D3.1 (Regulatory Offenses Involving Registration Numbers) (0.0%, n=2).

32   *See* USSG §5C1.2(a). As required by Congressional directive, the new offense level cannot be lower than 17 for offenders whose mandatory minimums were at least five years in length. *See* USSG §5C1.2(b).

33   *See* USSG §2D1.1(b)(17).

34   For purposes of this publication, the phrase "offense carrying a drug mandatory minimum penalty" refers to drug offenses involving mandatory minimum penalties specifically relating to the unlawful distribution, manufacture, or importation of controlled substance, as well as the possession of such substances with the intent to distribute. As such, unless otherwise expressly noted, all analysis in this section is limited to offenders whose primary Chapter Two guideline is found in Chapter Two, Part D (Offenses involving Drugs and Narco-Terrorism) of the *Guidelines Manual.* A "drug offender" may also have a conviction for violating 18 U.S.C. § 924(c), for

possession or use of a firearm during the commission of the drug offense. Those offenders will also be included in the Commission's future publication on firearms mandatory minimum penalties.

35   In fiscal year 2016, the Commission's datafile included 67,742 cases and of those cases, the Commission received complete guideline application information and sufficient documentation for analysis in the 62,251 cases considered for this publication. *See* 2017 OVERVIEW PUBLICATION, *supra* note 1, at 28. The methodology used in this publication, with respect to records collection and data analysis, is described in detail in the 2017 OVERVIEW PUBLICATION *supra* note 1, at 28.

36   *Id.* at 29–30.

37   *Id.*

38   *Id.* at 34 & Figure 7. Drug offenses have accounted for the majority of offenses carrying a mandatory minimum penalty since the 1990s, following passage of the Anti-Drug Abuse Act of 1986, Pub. L. No. 99-570, 100 Stat. 3207, which established mandatory minimum penalties for drug offenses.

39   *Id.* at 35.

40   *Id.* at 35–36 & Figure 8.

41   *Id.*

42   Pub. L. No. 111-220, 124 Stat. 2372, at § 2 (Aug. 2, 2010). *See* 2017 OVERVIEW PUBLICATION, *supra* note 1, at 22–23 (discussing the FSA and Commission response).

43   *See* Pub. L. No. 111-220, 124 Stat. 2372, at §§ 6–7.

44   *See* USSG App. C, amend. 750 (effective Nov. 1, 2011) (implementing as permanent the temporary, emergency amendment (USSG App. C, amend. 748 (effective Nov. 1, 2010)) that implemented the FSA); USSG App. C, amend. 759 (effective Nov. 1, 2011). The statutory changes made by the FSA apply only to offenders sentenced on or after August 3, 2010, the Act's effective date. Thus, the revised penalties apply to offenders who committed a crime after the Act became effective, as well as those who committed a crime before the Act went into effect but were sentenced after the Act's effective date. The revised FSA provisions do not, however, apply retroactively to any offender sentenced before the Act's effective date. *See* Dorsey v. United States, 132 S. Ct. 2321 (2013).

45   *See* Statement of Judge Patti B. Saris, Chair, United States Sentencing Commission, For the Hearing on "S. 2123, Sentencing Reform and Corrections Act of 2015" Before the Committee on the Judiciary, United States Senate (Oct. 19, 2015), *available at* https://www.ussc.gov/sites/default/files/pdf/news/congressional-testimony-and-reports/testimony/20151021_Saris_Testimony.pdf; Statement of Judge Patti B. Saris, Chair, United States Sentencing Commission, For the Hearing on "H.R. 3717, Sentencing Reform Act of 2015" Before the U.S. House of Representatives Judiciary Committee (Nov. 18, 2015), *available at* https://www.ussc.gov/sites/default/files/pdf/news/

congressional-testimony-and-reports/submissions/20151117_HR3713.pdf.

46   *See* U.S. SENTENCING COMM'N, REPORT TO THE CONGRESS: IMPACT OF THE FAIR SENTENCING ACT OF 2010, at 3 (Aug. 2015), *available at* https://www.ussc.gov/sites/default/files/pdf/news/congressional-testimony-and-reports/drug-topics/201507_RtC_Fair-Sentencing-Act.pdf. The Commission completed this study pursuant to the Congressional directive in the FSA to analyze and report on the Act's impact.

47   *See* U.S. Dep't of Justice, Attorney General John Ashcroft, Memorandum: Department Policy Concerning Charging Criminal Offenses, Disposition of Charges, and Sentencing (September 22, 2003).

48   *See* U.S. Dep't of Justice, Attorney General Eric Holder, Memorandum: Department Policy on Charging and Sentencing (May 19, 2010), *available at* https://www.justice.gov/sites/default/files/oip/legacy/2014/07/23/holder-memo-charging-sentencing.pdf.

49   133 S. Ct. 2151 (2013).

50   *Id.* at 2160.

51   *See* U.S. Dep't of Justice, Attorney General Eric Holder, Memorandum: Department Policy on Charging Mandatory Minimum Sentences and Recidivist Enhancements in Certain Drug Cases (August 12, 2013), *available at* https://www.justice.gov/ sites/default/files/ag/legacy/2014/04/11/ag-memo-drug-guidance.pdf ("We must ensure that our most severe mandatory minimum penalties are reserved for serious, high-level, or violent drug traffickers. In some cases, mandatory minimum and recidivist enhancement statutes have resulted in unduly harsh sentences and perceived or actual disparities that do not reflect our Principles of Federal Prosecution.").

52   *Id.*

53   *Id.* The memorandum provided "[w]hen determining whether an enhancement is appropriate, prosecutors should consider the following factors: (1) Whether the defendant was an organizer, leader, manager or supervisor of others within a criminal organization; (2) Whether the defendant was involved in the use or threat of violence in connection with the offense; (3) The nature of the defendant's criminal history, including any prior history of violent conduct or recent prior convictions for serious offenses; (4) Whether the defendant has significant ties to large-scale drug trafficking organizations, gangs, or cartels; (5) Whether the filing would create a gross sentencing disparity with equally or more culpable co-defendants; and (6) Other case-specific aggravating or mitigating factors." *Id.*; *see also* 2017 OVERVIEW PUBLICATION, *supra* note 1, at 23–24 (discussing Department of Justice guidance and relevant Supreme Court case law).

54   *See* U.S. Dep't of Justice, Attorney General Jefferson Sessions, Memorandum: Department Charging and Sentencing Policy (May 10, 2017), *available at* https://www.justice.gov/opa/press-release/file/965896/download.

55   This percentage is significantly higher than the portion of offenders convicted of any mandatory minimum penalty (21.9%). This, however, is unsurprising, given the role of mandatory minimums in drug offenses, as

reflected by the fact that drug trafficking offenses have accounted for approximately two-thirds of offenses carrying a mandatory minimum in recent years, which is significantly higher than the next largest class of offenses. *See* 2017 OVERVIEW PUBLICATION, *supra* note 1, at 34 & Figure 7.

56   There was approximately a 15% decrease in the size of the overall federal offender population. The Commission analyzed 62,251 cases for this publication and 73,239 fiscal year 2010 cases for the 2011 MANDATORY MINIMUM REPORT.

57   *See infra* at 31 & Figure 14.

58   2011 MANDATORY MINIMUM REPORT, *supra* note 2, at 158.

59   *See* 2017 OVERVIEW PUBLICATION, *supra* note 1, at 30–31 (describing the Commission's methodology for tracking factors identified by the Department of Justice in the Smart on Crime Initiative).

60   *See* Figure 2 in Appendices D through H.

61   *See* 2017 OVERVIEW PUBLICATION, *supra* note 1, at 10 (noting that mandatory minimum penalties apply to several different types of federal offenses and are of varying lengths depending on the offense type and specific criteria).

62   A complete distribution of offenders convicted of an offense carrying a drug mandatory minimum penalty, as well as those who remained subject to such a penalty at sentencing is provided for each circuit and district in Appendix A.

63   The Commission obtains data on the race and ethnicity of the offender from the Presentence Report. The "Other Race" category includes offenders of Native American, Alaskan Native, and Asian or Pacific Islander origin. Of the offenders analyzed for this study, there were 2,484 offenders identified as "Other" race offenders: 1,085 (43.7%) were of Asian/Pacific Islander origin, 1,186 (47.8%) were Native-American/Alaskan Native, and 213 (8.5%) were of other origin. For drug offenders in fiscal year 2016, the "Other" race category consists of 52.3% Asian/Pacific Islander (n=295), 39.7% Native-American/Alaskan Native (n=224), and 8.0% were of other origin (n=45).

64   *See* Appendices D through H.

65   This is, in large part, because non-U.S. citizens are often convicted of immigration offenses, which do not carry mandatory minimum penalties.

66   *See* Appendix B.

67   *See* Appendix F, Table F2.

68   *See* Appendix E, Table E2.

69   *See* Appendices D through H.

70   *See supra* at Figure 4.

71   2017 OVERVIEW PUBLICATION, *supra* note 1, at Figure 9.

72   *Id.* at 41.

73   In fiscal year 2016, more than three-quarters of crack cocaine offenders were Black (82.6%), followed by Hispanic (11.3%), White (5.6%), and Other Race (0.5%).

74   There were 1,562 crack cocaine offenders in fiscal year 2016, a 67.1% decrease from fiscal year 2010 (n=4,751).

75   In fiscal year 2016, more than half of methamphetamine offenders were Hispanic (50.4%), followed by White (38.8%), Black (6.0%), and Other Race (4.8%).

76   There were 6,508 methamphetamine trafficking offenders in fiscal year 2016, a 56.1% increase from fiscal year 2010 (n=4,169).

77   Other Race crack cocaine offenders received relief less than Black crack cocaine offenders (0.0%). However, there were only eight offenders in this category. Other Race marijuana offenders had the highest rate of relief (72.7%), followed by White marijuana offenders (71.9%).

78   *See infra* at 48–49.

79   *See* USSG §§5C1.2, 3B1.1.

80   *See* Appendices D through H.

81   Originally developed in the 1990s with consultation from the Drug Enforcement Agency, the Commission has historically used these categories as the basis of its offender function analysis. *See, e.g.,* 2011 MANDATORY MINIMUM REPORT, *supra* note 2, at 165–73; U.S. SENTENCING COMM'N REPORT TO THE CONGRESS: COCAINE AND FEDERAL SENTENCING POLICY A-2 (2007), *available at* https://www.ussc.gov/sites/default/files/pdf/news/congressional-testimony-and-reports/drug-topics/200705_RtC_Cocaine_Sentencing_Policy.pdf. Function categories used in this analysis do not necessarily correlate with guideline definitions of similar terms. For example, the definition of Manager/Supervisor used in the coding project to describe offender function does not match the guideline definition of manager or supervisor in USSG §3B1.1 (Aggravating Role) and the determination of offender function was made without regard to whether §3B1.1 or §3B1.2 applied.

82   *See* Appendix D, Figure D8.

83   *See* Appendix F, Figure F8.

84   *Id.*

85   Powder cocaine Organizers/Leaders had the highest percentage of offenders subject to a drug mandatory minimum penalty at sentencing (63.6%). *See* Appendix D, Figure D9.

86   Offenders who functioned as Managers/Supervisors were convicted of an offense carrying a drug mandatory minimum penalty at the highest rate (79.7%), but as reflected in Figure 28 only accounted for 2.0% of all drug offenders in the 2016 sample.

87   *See* Appendix F, Figure F9.

88   *See* 2011 MANDATORY MINIMUM REPORT, *supra* note 2, at 219 & Figure 8–35.

89   *See id.* at 204 & Figure 8–29.

90   *See* Appendix E, Figure E9.

91   *See supra* nn.32–43 & accompanying text. For a detailed discussion of the changes in the application of mandatory minimum sentences, see Section 4 of the Commission's 2017 *Overview Publication. See* 2017 OVERVIEW PUBLICATION, *supra* note 1, at 22–25.

92   *See* USSG §§5C1.2, 3B1.1.

93   2017 OVERVIEW PUBLICATION, *supra* note 1, at 48–49.

94   These population figures were obtained from the Bureau of Prisons data and reflect complete population figures. The remaining federal prison population analysis in this section is based on matching the BOP data with Commission data and therefore may reflect fewer offenders.

95   *See* 2011 MANDATORY MINIMUM REPORT, at Ch.4. In the 2011 *Mandatory Minimum Report*, the Commission noted that these factors have included changes to mandatory minimum penalties themselves, both in terms of number and scope, as well as other systemic changes to the federal criminal justice system, such as the expanded federalization of criminal law, increased size and changes in the composition of the federal criminal docket, and higher rates of imposition of sentences of imprisonment. *See id.*

96   2017 OVERVIEW PUBLICATION, *supra* note 1, at 49.

97   *Id.*

98   *Id.* at 51 & Figure 21.

99   U.S. Sentencing Comm'n, Recidivism Among Federal Drug Trafficking Offenders 16–17 [hereinafter Drug Recidivism Report], *available at* https://www.ussc.gov/sites/default/files/pdf/research-and-publications/research-publications/2017/20170221_Recidivism-Drugs.pdf.

100   *Id.*

Appendix A

DRUG MANDATORY MINIMUM STATUS FOR ALL OFFENDERS
IN EACH CIRCUIT AND DISTRICT[1]
Fiscal Year 2016

CIRCUIT District	Total		All Drug Offenders		Drug Mandatory Mandatory	
	Number	Percent	Number	Percent	Number	Percent
TOTAL	62,251	100.0	19,584	31.5	8,760	14.1
D.C. CIRCUIT	250	0.4	122	48.8	69	27.6
District of Columbia	250	0.4	122	48.8	69	27.6
FIRST CIRCUIT	1,943	3.1	822	42.3	440	22.6
Maine	198	0.3	105	53.0	20	10.1
Massachusetts	460	0.7	156	33.9	45	9.8
New Hampshire	174	0.3	43	24.7	13	7.5
Puerto Rico	1,021	1.6	486	47.6	349	34.2
Rhode Island	90	0.1	32	35.6	13	14.4
SECOND CIRCUIT	3,257	5.2	1,301	39.9	523	16.1
Connecticut	302	0.5	149	49.3	62	20.5
New York						
Eastern	756	1.2	265	35.1	113	14.9
Northern	277	0.4	110	39.7	54	19.5
Southern	1,292	2.1	475	36.8	219	17.0
Western	449	0.7	173	38.5	66	14.7
Vermont	181	0.3	129	71.3	9	5.0
THIRD CIRCUIT	2,021	3.3	706	34.9	340	16.8
Delaware	69	0.1	25	36.2	13	18.8
New Jersey	657	1.1	196	29.8	85	12.9
Pennsylvania						
Eastern	574	0.9	152	26.5	103	17.9
Middle	299	0.5	126	42.1	33	11.0
Western	365	0.6	189	51.8	103	28.2
Virgin Islands	57	0.1	18	31.6	3	5.3
FOURTH CIRCUIT	4,506	7.0	1,703	37.8	688	15.3
Maryland	660	1.1	229	34.7	120	18.2
North Carolina						
Eastern	543	0.9	196	36.1	90	16.6
Middle	420	0.7	137	32.6	20	4.8
Western	650	1.0	224	34.5	124	19.1
South Carolina	617	1.0	172	27.9	97	15.7
Virginia						
Eastern	814	1.3	255	31.3	147	18.1
Western	305	0.5	181	59.3	53	17.4
West Virginia						
Northern	296	0.5	178	60.1	28	9.5
Southern	201	0.3	131	65.2	9	4.5

| CIRCUIT | | | | | Drug Mandatory | |
| | Total | | All Drug Offenders | | Mandatory | |
District	Number	Percent	Number	Percent	Number	Percent
FIFTH CIRCUIT	**15,297**	**24.6**	**4,157**	**27.2**	**2145**	**14.0**
Louisiana						
Eastern	328	0.5	112	34.1	70	21.3
Middle	160	0.3	51	31.9	23	14.4
Western	207	0.3	74	35.7	33	15.9
Mississippi						
Northern	157	0.3	27	17.2	5	3.2
Southern	226	0.4	78	34.5	29	12.8
Texas						
Eastern	811	1.3	381	47.0	261	32.2
Northern	1,329	2.1	578	43.5	252	19.0
Southern	6,233	10.0	1,155	18.5	882	14.2
Western	5,846	9.4	1,701	29.1	590	10.1
SIXTH CIRCUIT	**4,334**	**7.0**	**1,584**	**36.5**	**742**	**17.1**
Kentucky						
Eastern	432	0.7	230	53.2	75	17.4
Western	285	0.5	119	41.8	86	30.2
Michigan						
Eastern	867	1.4	206	23.8	95	11.0
Western	316	0.5	76	24.1	25	7.9
Ohio						
Northern	560	0.9	167	29.8	62	11.1
Southern	472	0.8	179	37.9	63	13.3
Tennessee						
Eastern	740	1.2	364	49.2	232	31.4
Middle	204	0.3	55	27.0	30	14.7
Western	458	0.7	188	41.0	74	16.2
SEVENTH CIRCUIT	**2,231**	**3.6**	**761**	**34.1**	**376**	**16.9**
Illinois						
Central	258	0.4	102	39.5	63	24.4
Northern	627	1.0	179	28.5	79	12.6
Southern	312	0.5	155	49.7	69	22.1
Indiana						
Northern	285	0.5	62	21.8	29	10.2
Southern	329	0.5	118	35.9	96	29.2
Wisconsin						
Eastern	296	0.5	104	35.1	31	10.5
Western	124	0.2	41	33.1	9	7.3
EIGHTH CIRCUIT	**4,637**	**7.4**	**1,721**	**37.1**	**910**	**19.6**
Arkansas						
Eastern	354	0.6	198	55.9	85	24.0
Western	252	0.4	106	42.1	17	6.7
Iowa						
Northern	347	0.6	130	37.5	99	28.5
Southern	347	0.6	138	39.8	53	15.3
Minnesota	481	0.8	154	32.0	87	18.1
Missouri						
Eastern	740	1.2	216	29.2	92	12.4
Western	804	1.3	306	38.1	184	22.9
Nebraska	532	0.9	243	45.7	144	27.1
North Dakota	356	0.6	145	40.7	97	27.2
South Dakota	424	0.7	85	20.0	52	12.3

CIRCUIT	Total		All Drug Offenders		Drug Mandatory Mandatory	
District	Number	Percent	Number	Percent	Number	Percent
NINTH CIRCUIT	**10,791**	**17.3**	**3,623**	**33.6**	**979**	**9.1**
Alaska	166	0.3	58	34.9	37	22.3
Arizona	4,090	6.6	1,100	26.9	51	1.3
California						
Central	865	1.4	265	30.6	182	21.0
Eastern	655	1.1	244	37.3	107	16.3
Northern	433	0.7	105	24.2	53	12.2
Southern	2,317	3.7	1,067	46.1	128	5.5
Guam	65	0.1	18	27.7	0	0.0
Hawaii	138	0.2	72	52.2	61	44.2
Idaho	254	0.4	100	39.4	37	14.6
Montana	310	0.5	123	39.7	80	25.8
Nevada	391	0.6	95	24.3	43	11.0
Northern Mariana Islands	20	0.0	5	25.0	4	20.0
Oregon	358	0.6	114	31.8	77	21.5
Washington						
Eastern	298	0.5	102	34.2	61	20.5
Western	431	0.7	155	36.0	58	13.5
TENTH CIRCUIT	**7,319**	**11.8**	**1,321**	**18.0**	**483**	**6.6**
Colorado	464	3.0	112	24.1	52	11.2
Kansas	459	0.7	175	38.1	97	21.1
New Mexico	4,954	8.0	632	12.8	130	2.6
Oklahoma						
Eastern	100	0.2	37	37.0	21	21.0
Northern	210	0.3	78	37.1	28	13.3
Western	295	0.5	96	32.5	32	10.9
Utah	623	1.0	102	16.4	64	10.3
Wyoming	214	0.3	89	41.6	59	27.6
ELEVENTH CIRCUIT	**5,665**	**9.1**	**1,763**	**31.1**	**1,065**	**18.8**
Alabama						
Middle	151	0.2	30	19.9	21	13.9
Northern	333	0.5	91	27.3	54	16.2
Southern	313	0.5	93	29.7	52	16.6
Florida						
Middle	1,393	2.2	550	39.5	439	31.5
Northern	241	0.4	62	25.7	41	17.0
Southern	2,130	3.4	581	27.3	370	17.4
Georgia						
Middle	303	0.5	117	38.6	33	10.9
Northern	523	0.8	120	22.9	50	9.6
Southern	278	0.5	119	42.8	5	1.8

[1] Of the 67,742 cases sentenced in fiscal year 2016, the Commission received complete guideline information in 61,958. The Commission did not receive complete guideline information for another 287 cases in which the only statute of conviction was 18 U.S.C. § 924(c) and 111 cases in which an offender was sentenced under 18 U.S.C. § 1028A and the guidelines were not applied, but these cases are included in the analysis. Of the remaining 63,357 cases, 105 were excluded due to missing statutory information.

SOURCE: U.S. Sentencing Commission, 2016 Datafile, USSCFY16.

A

Appendix B

Table B1. Average Age of Drug Offenders at Sentencing
Fiscal Year 2016

	All Drug Offenders	Convicted of an Offense Carrying a Drug Mandatory Minimum Penalty	Relieved of Mandatory Minimum Penalty	Subject to Drug Mandatory Minimum Penalty at Sentencing
Total (# of offenders)	19,584	8,760	4,519	4,241
AGE (YEARS)				
All Drugs	36	37	36	37
Powder Cocaine	37	38	38	38
Crack Cocaine	35	35	36	34
Heroin	36	37	37	37
Marijuana	33	35	34	37
Methamphetamine	36	37	36	37

SOURCE: U.S. Sentencing Commission, 2016 Datafile, USSCFY16.

Appendix C

Figure C1. Length of Drug Mandatory Minimum Penalty for Offenders Convicted of an Offense Carrying a Mandatory Minimum by Function
Fiscal Year 2016 Sample Data

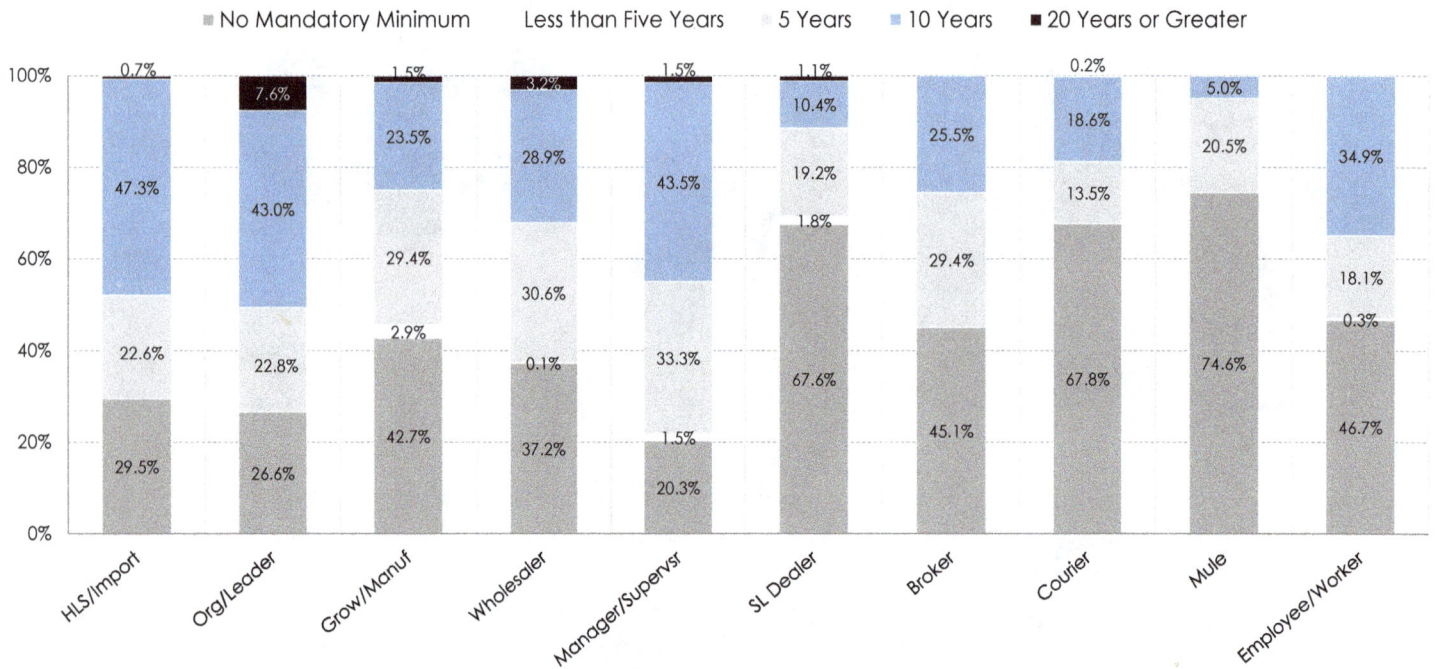

Legend: No Mandatory Minimum | Less than Five Years | 5 Years | 10 Years | 20 Years or Greater

SOURCE: U.S. Sentencing Commission, 2016 Function Datafile, FUNCSAMPFY16.

A

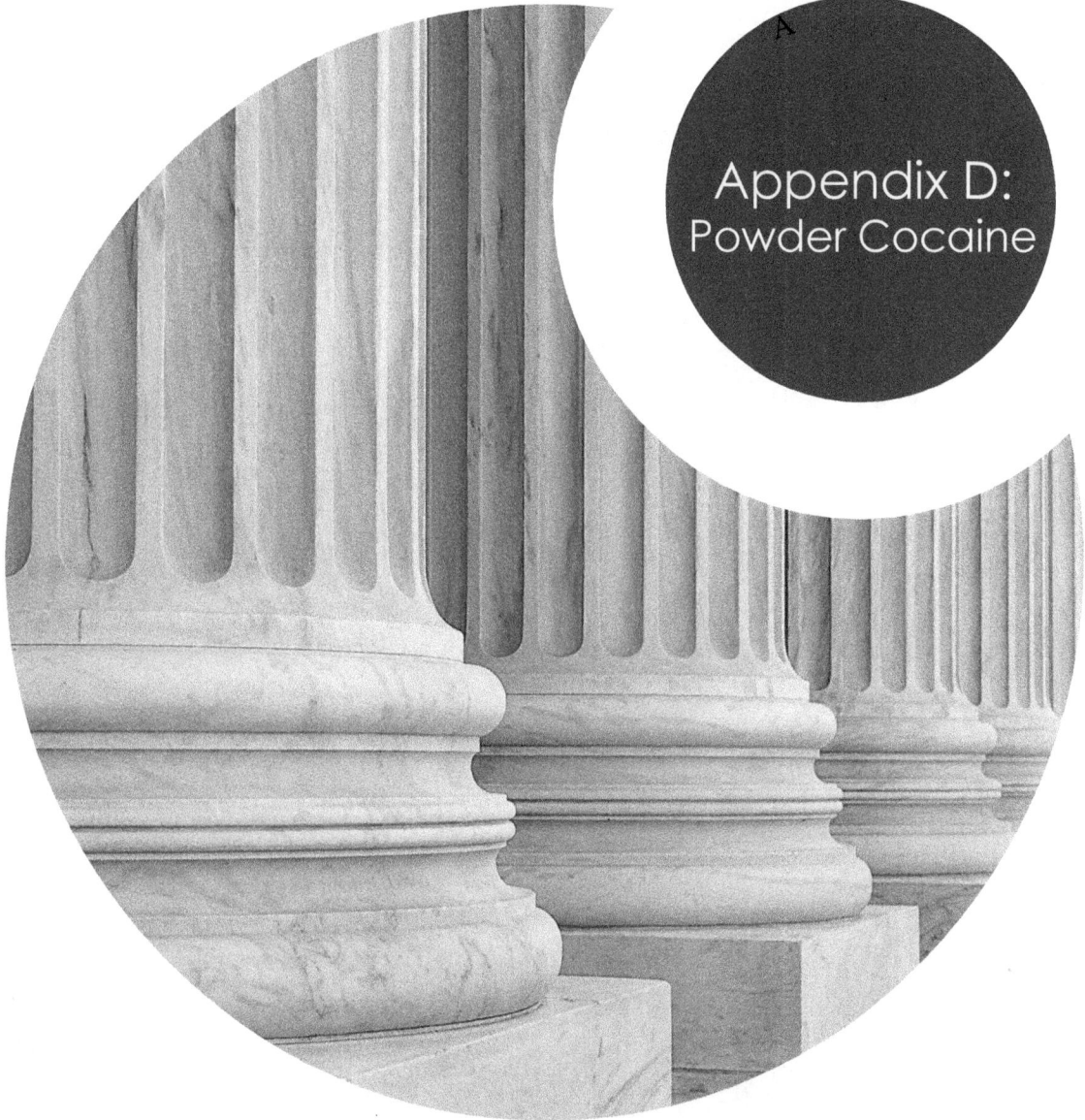

Appendix D:
Powder Cocaine

Figure D1. Powder Cocaine Offenders Convicted of an Offense
Carrying a Drug Mandatory Minimum Penalty
Fiscal Year 2016

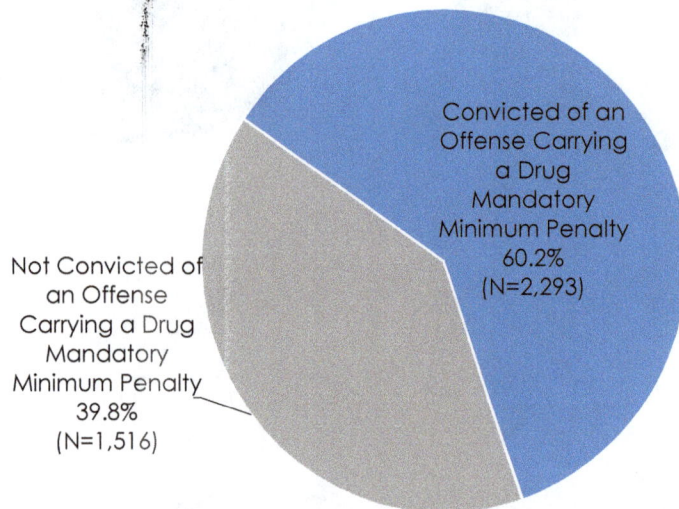

Convicted of an
Offense Carrying
a Drug
Mandatory
Minimum Penalty
60.2%
(N=2,293)

Not Convicted of
an Offense
Carrying a Drug
Mandatory
Minimum Penalty
39.8%
(N=1,516)

SOURCE: U.S. Sentencing Commission, 2016 Datafile, USSCFY16.

Figure D2. Length of Mandatory Minimum Penalty for Powder Cocaine Offenders Convicted of an Offense Carrying a Drug Mandatory Minimum Penalty *Fiscal Year 2016*

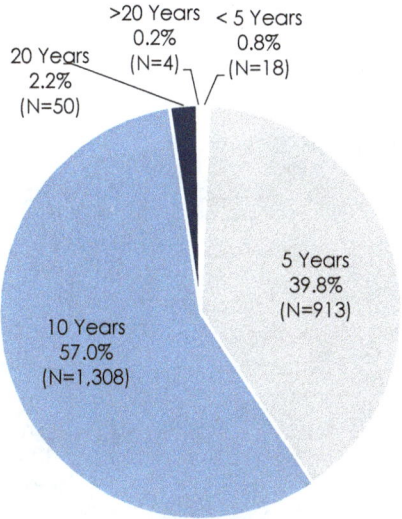

>20 Years
0.2%
(N=4)

< 5 Years
0.8%
(N=18)

20 Years
2.2%
(N=50)

5 Years
39.8%
(N=913)

10 Years
57.0%
(N=1,308)

SOURCE: U.S. Sentencing Commission, 2016 Datafiles, USSCFY16.

Figure D3. Number of Powder Cocaine Offenders Convicted of an Offense Carrying a Drug Mandatory Minimum Penalty by District
Fiscal Year 2016

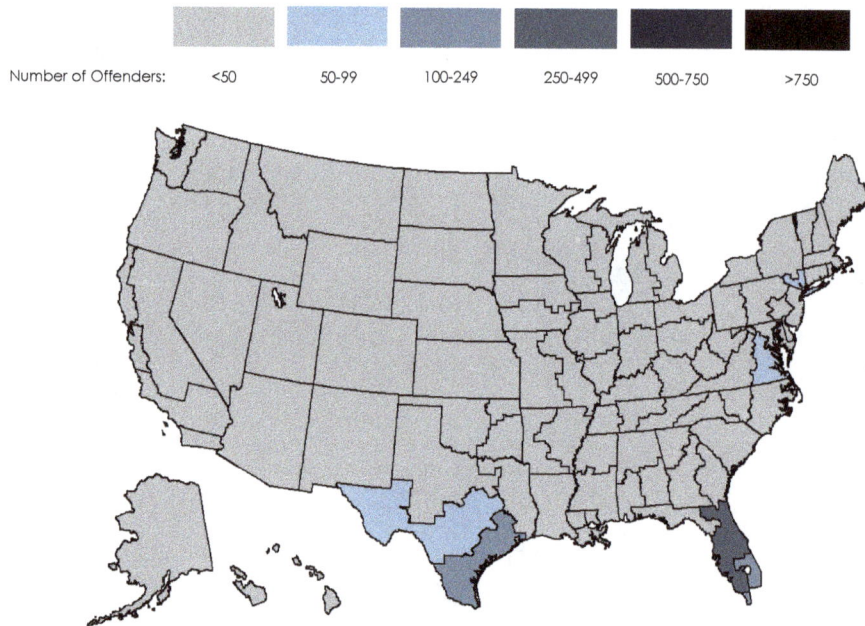

SOURCE: U.S. Sentencing Commission, 2016 Datafile, USSCFY16.

Table D1. Demographic Characteristics of Powder Cocaine Offenders
Fiscal Year 2016

	All Powder Cocaine Offenders	Convicted of an Offense Carrying a Drug Mandatory Minimum Penalty	Relieved of Mandatory Minimum Penalty	Subject to Drug Mandatory Minimum Penalty at Sentencing
Total (# of offenders)	3,809	2,293	1,364	929
RACE				
White	6.9%	5.2%	5.4%	4.7%
Black	30.2%	25.9%	19.6%	35.2%
Hispanic	61.8%	67.9%	74.0%	59.1%
Other	1.1%	1.0%	1.0%	1.0%
CITIZENSHIP				
U.S. Citizen	64.9%	59.9%	47.7%	77.9%
Non-U.S. Citizen	35.1%	40.1%	52.3%	22.1%
GENDER				
Male	89.2%	91.8%	89.3%	95.5%
Female	10.8%	8.2%	10.7%	4.5%

SOURCE: U.S. Sentencing Commission, 2016 Datafile, USSCFY16.

Table D2. Guideline Sentencing Characteristics, Role in the Offense and Criminal History of Powder Cocaine Offenders
Fiscal Year 2016

	All Powder Cocaine Offenders	Convicted of an Offense Carrying a Drug Mandatory Minimum Penalty	Relieved of Mandatory Minimum Penalty	Subject to Drug Mandatory Minimum Penalty at Sentencing
Total (# of offenders)	3,809	2,293	1,364	929
CHARACTERISTICS				
Weapon Specific Offense Characteristic	11.4%	12.1%	7.0%	19.5%
Firearms Mandatory Minimum Applied	6.0%	6.0%	3.2%	10.1%
Safety Valve Reduction	41.0%	42.9%	72.2%	0.0%
ROLE IN THE OFFENSE				
Aggravating Role	10.0%	13.8%	7.8%	22.5%
Mitigating Role	18.0%	12.4%	19.2%	2.5%
CRIMINAL HISTORY CATEGORY				
I	62.3%	65.0%	80.8%	41.8%
II	11.1%	11.3%	6.1%	18.8%
III	11.3%	10.6%	5.9%	17.6%
IV	4.7%	4.1%	2.1%	7.1%
V	2.3%	1.9%	1.2%	2.9%
VI	8.3%	7.2%	4.0%	11.8%

SOURCE: U.S. Sentencing Commission, 2016 Datafile, USSCFY16.

Figure D4. Demographics of Powder Cocaine Offenders Relieved of a
Drug Mandatory Minimum Penalty by Race of Offender
Fiscal Year 2016

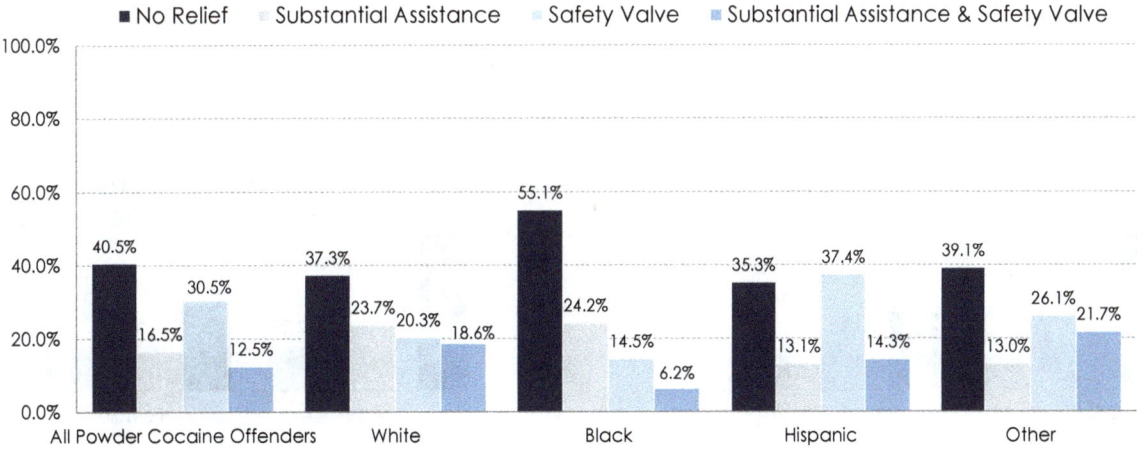

Legend: No Relief | Substantial Assistance | Safety Valve | Substantial Assistance & Safety Valve

All Powder Cocaine Offenders: 40.5%, 16.5%, 30.5%, 12.5%
White: 37.3%, 23.7%, 20.3%, 18.6%
Black: 55.1%, 24.2%, 14.5%, 6.2%
Hispanic: 35.3%, 13.1%, 37.4%, 14.3%
Other: 39.1%, 13.0%, 26.1%, 21.7%

SOURCE: U.S. Sentencing Commission, 2016 Datafile, USSCFY16.

Figure D5. Demographics of Powder Cocaine Offenders Relieved of a
Drug Mandatory Minimum Penalty by Citizenship and Gender
Fiscal Year 2016

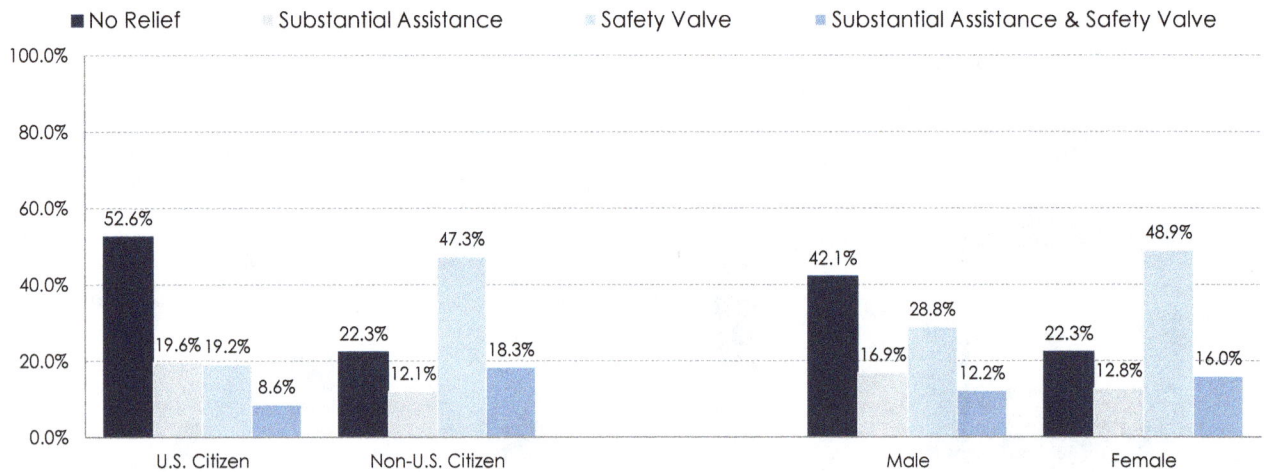

SOURCE: U.S. Sentencing Commission, 2016 Datafile, USSCFY16.

Figure D6. Average Sentence Length of Powder Cocaine Offenders
Fiscal Year 2016

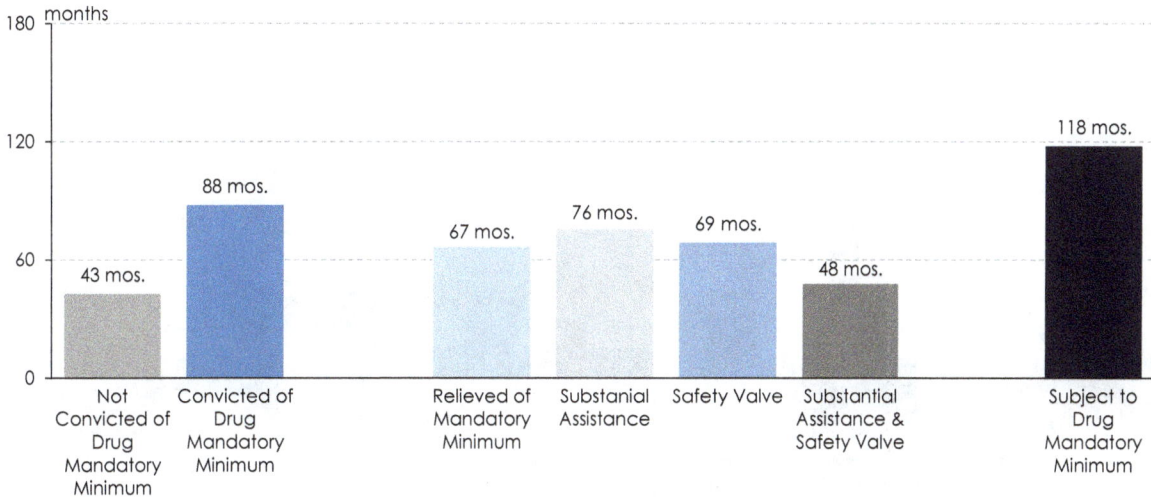

months

180	
120	118 mos.
88 mos.	
76 mos.	
67 mos.	69 mos.
60	
43 mos.	48 mos.
0	

Not Convicted of Drug Mandatory Minimum — 43 mos.
Convicted of Drug Mandatory Minimum — 88 mos.
Relieved of Mandatory Minimum — 67 mos.
Substanial Assistance — 76 mos.
Safety Valve — 69 mos.
Substantial Assistance & Safety Valve — 48 mos.
Subject to Drug Mandatory Minimum — 118 mos.

SOURCE: U.S. Sentencing Commission, 2016 Datafile, USSCFY16.

Figure D7. Average Sentence for Powder Cocaine Offenders by Demographic Characteristics
By Race
Fiscal Year 2016

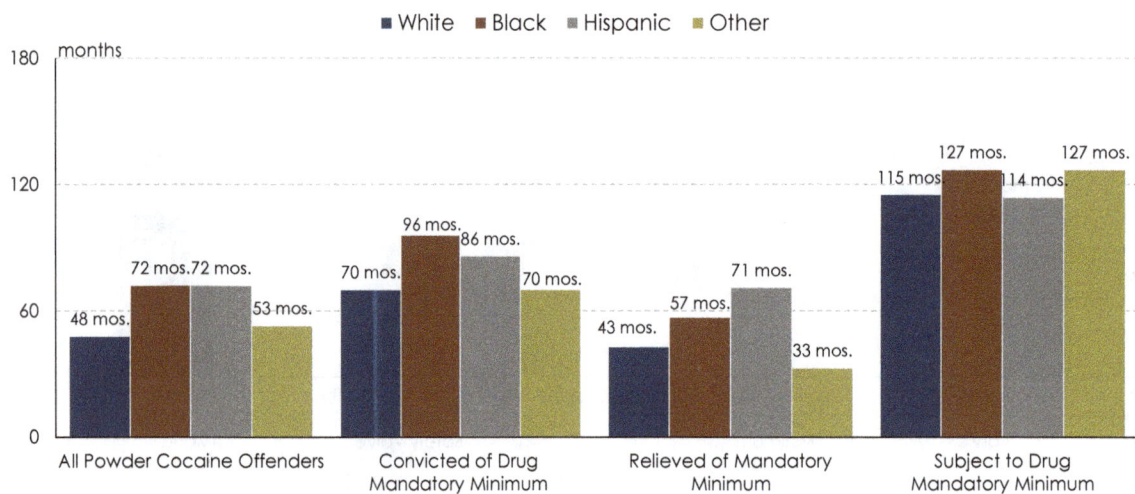

■ White ■ Black ■ Hispanic ■ Other

SOURCE: U.S. Sentencing Commission, 2016 Datafile, USSCFY16.

Table D3. Average Sentence for Powder Cocaine Offenders by Citizenship and Gender
Fiscal Year 2016

	All Powder Cocaine Offenders	Convicted of an Offense Carrying a Drug Mandatory Minimum Penalty	Relieved of Mandatory Minimum Penalty	Subject to Drug Mandatory Minimum Penalty at Sentencing
Total (# of offenders)	3,809	2,293	1,364	929
CITIZENSHIP				
U.S. Citizen	67 months	84 months	51 months	114 months
Non-U.S. Citizen	75 months	93 months	81 months	133 months
GENDER				
Male	74 months	91 months	70 months	120 months
Female	32 months	46 months	35 months	85 months

SOURCE: U.S. Sentencing Commission, 2016 Datafile, USSCFY16.

Table D4. Sentence Relative to the Guideline Range of Powder Cocaine Offenders
Fiscal Year 2016

	All Powder Cocaine Offenders	Convicted of an Offense Carrying a Drug Mandatory Minimum Penalty	Relieved of Mandatory Minimum Penalty	Subject to Drug Mandatory Minimum Penalty at Sentencing
Total (# of offenders)	3,809	2,293	1,364	929
SENTENCE RELATIVE TO THE GUIDELINE RANGE				
Within Range	40.7%	43.4%	29.3%	63.9%
Above Range	1.4%	0.8%	0.2%	1.6%
Substantial Assistance §5K1.1	23.0%	29.0%	48.8%	0.0%
Other Government Sponsored (no §5K1.1)	11.7%	6.8%	3.3%	12.0%
Non-Government Sponsored Below Range	23.2%	20.0%	18.3%	22.5%

SOURCE: U.S. Sentencing Commission, 2016 Datafile, USSCFY16.

Figure D8. Offender Function[1]
Powder Cocaine Offenders[2]
Fiscal Year 2009 and 2016 Sample Data

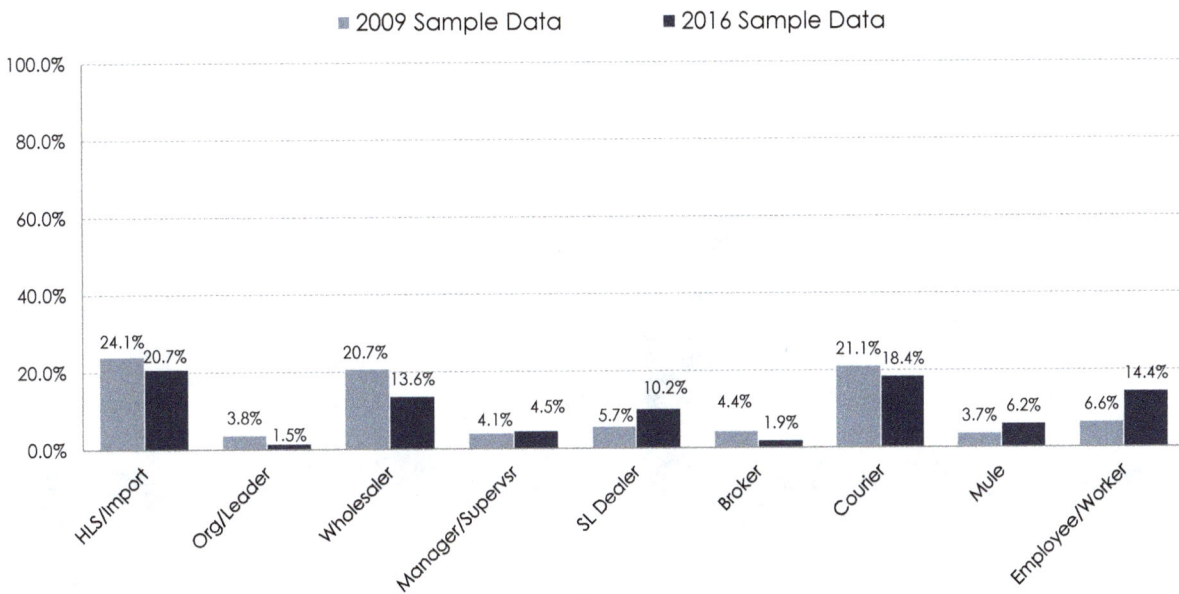

■ 2009 Sample Data   ■ 2016 Sample Data

[1] There were offenders in the samples whose function could not be determined. These offenders are not included in the overall percentages.
[2] In the fiscal year 2009 sample, 6.0 percent of powder cocaine offenders had "Other" or "Miscellaneous" functions. In the fiscal year 2016 sample, 8.5 percent of powder cocaine offenders had "Other" or "Miscellaneous" functions. These percentages are not represented in the figure above. There were no powder cocaine offenders whose function was "grower or manufacturer," therefore, this function is not depicted.

SOURCE: U.S. Sentencing Commission, 2009 and 2016 Function Datafiles, FUNCSAMPFY09 and FUNCSAMPFY16.

Figure D9. Percent of Offenders Convicted of an Offense Carrying a Drug Mandatory Minimum Penalty and Subject to a Drug Mandatory Minimum Penalty by Offender Function
Powder Cocaine Offenders[1]
Fiscal Year 2016 Sample Data

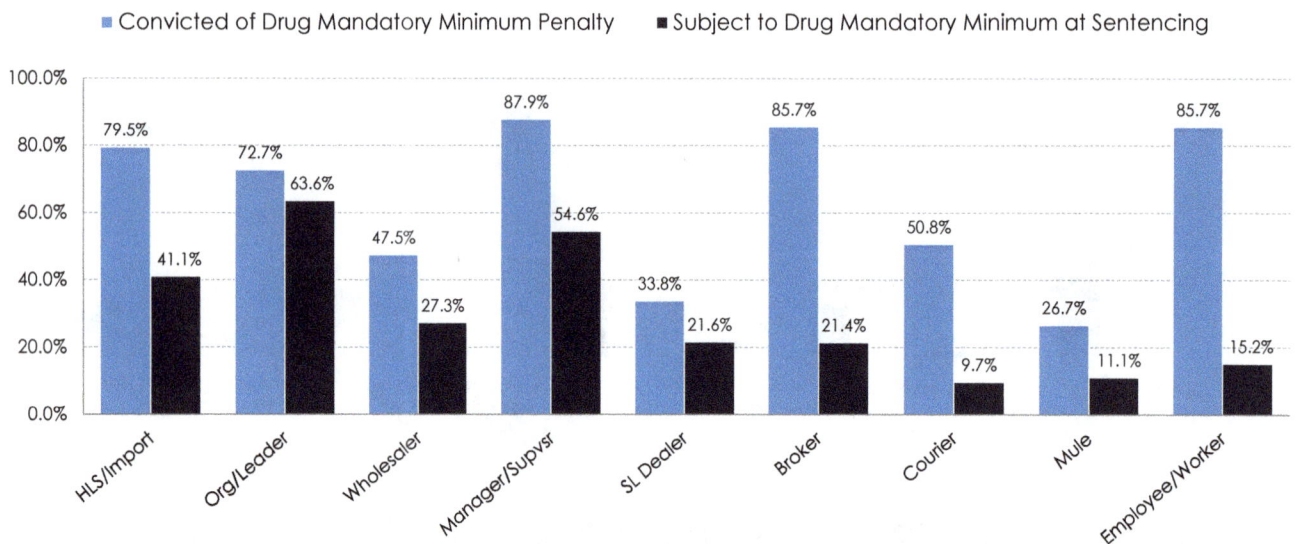

■ Convicted of Drug Mandatory Minimum Penalty   ■ Subject to Drug Mandatory Minimum at Sentencing

Function	Convicted	Subject
HLS/Import	79.5%	41.1%
Org/Leader	72.7%	63.6%
Wholesaler	47.5%	27.3%
Manager/Supvsr	87.9%	54.6%
SL Dealer	33.8%	21.6%
Broker	85.7%	21.4%
Courier	50.8%	9.7%
Mule	26.7%	11.1%
Employee/Worker	85.7%	15.2%

[1]There were no powder cocaine offenders whose function was "grower or manufacturer," therefore, this function is not depicted.

SOURCE: U.S. Sentencing Commission, 2016 Function Datafile, FUNCSAMPFY16.

Figure D10. Percent of Offenders Convicted of an Offense Carrying a Drug Mandatory
Minimum Penalty Who Were Relieved of the Penalty by Offender Function
Powder Cocaine Offenders[1]
Fiscal Year 2016 Sample Data

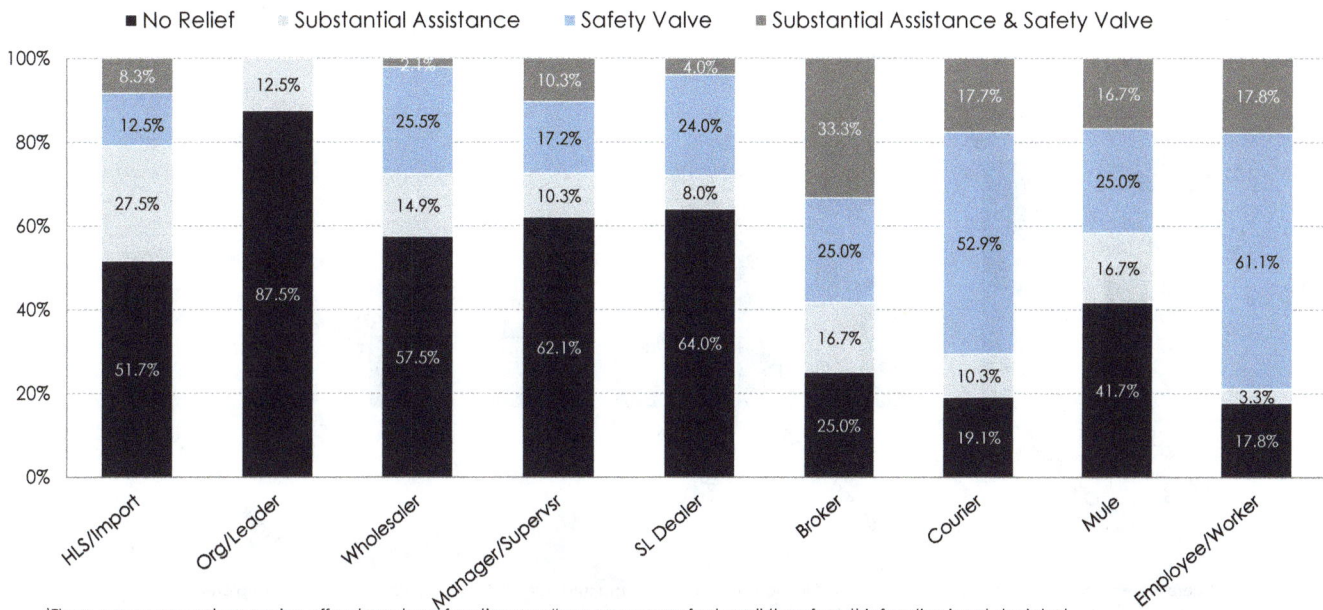

■ No Relief　　Substantial Assistance　　■ Safety Valve　　■ Substantial Assistance & Safety Valve

[1]There were no powder cocaine offenders whose function was "grower or manufacturer," therefore, this function is not depicted.

SOURCE: U.S. Sentencing Commission, 2016 Function Datafile, FUNCSAMPFY16.

Figure D11. Average Guideline Minimum and Average Sentence by Offender Function
Powder Cocaine Offenders[1]
Fiscal Year 2016 Sample Data

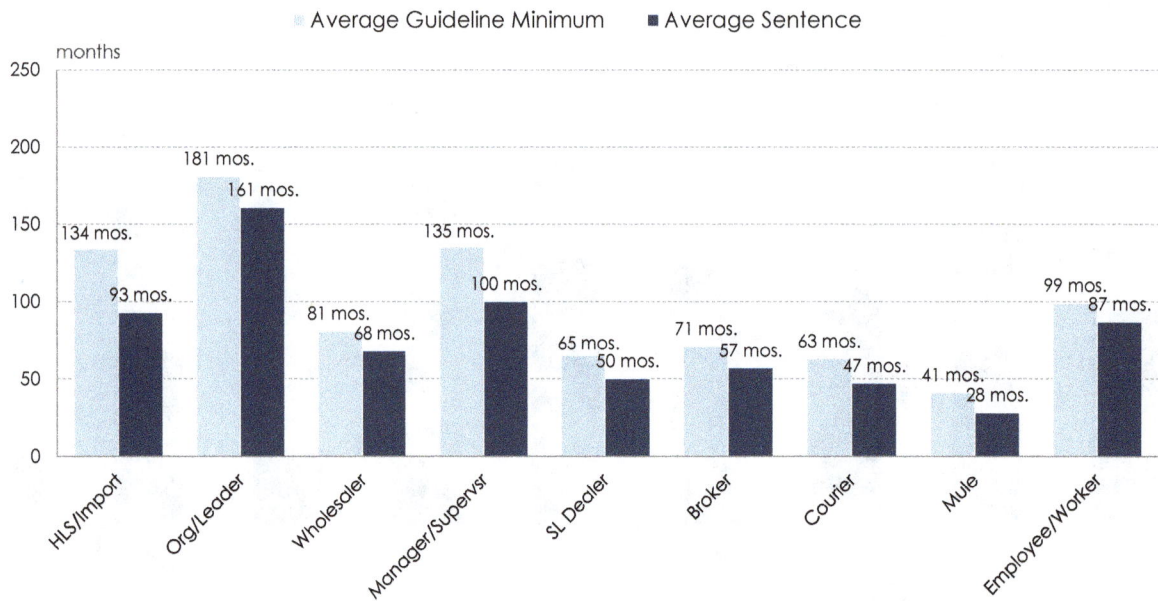

Average Guideline Minimum   ■ Average Sentence

months

Function	Average Guideline Minimum	Average Sentence
HLS/Import	134 mos.	93 mos.
Org/Leader	181 mos.	161 mos.
Wholesaler	81 mos.	68 mos.
Manager/Supervsr	135 mos.	100 mos.
SL Dealer	65 mos.	50 mos.
Broker	71 mos.	57 mos.
Courier	63 mos.	47 mos.
Mule	41 mos.	28 mos.
Employee/Worker	99 mos.	87 mos.

[1]There were no powder cocaine offenders whose function was "grower or manufacturer," therefore, this function is not depicted.

SOURCE: U.S. Sentencing Commission, 2016 Function Datafile, FUNCSAMPFY16.

A

Appendix E:
Crack Cocaine

Figure E1. Crack Cocaine Offenders Convicted of an Offense Carrying a Drug Mandatory Minimum Penalty
Fiscal Year 2016

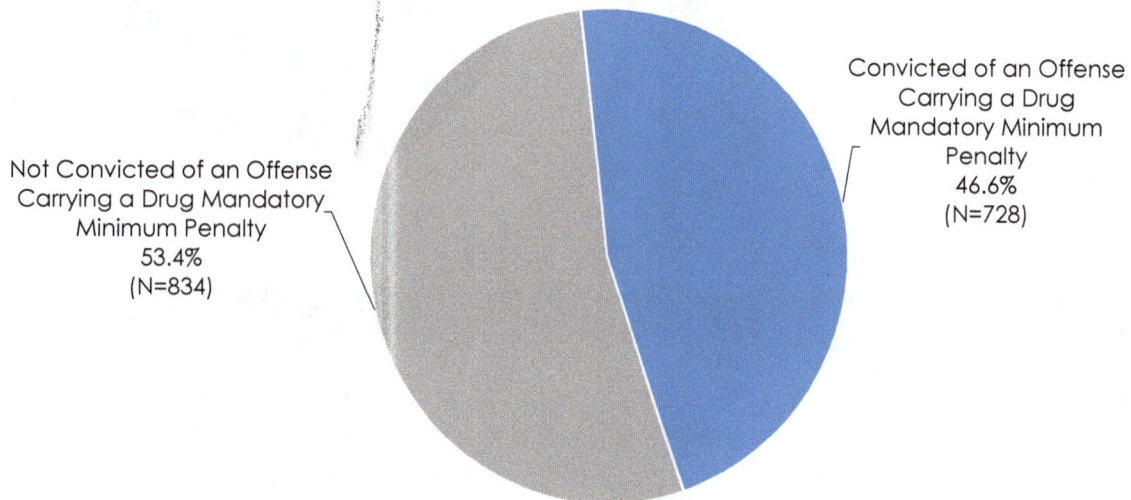

Not Convicted of an Offense Carrying a Drug Mandatory Minimum Penalty
53.4%
(N=834)

Convicted of an Offense Carrying a Drug Mandatory Minimum Penalty
46.6%
(N=728)

SOURCE: U.S. Sentencing Commission, 2016 Datafile, USSCFY16.

Figure E2. Length of Mandatory Minimum Penalty for Crack Cocaine Offenders Convicted of an Offense Carrying a Drug Mandatory Minimum Penalty
Fiscal Year 2016

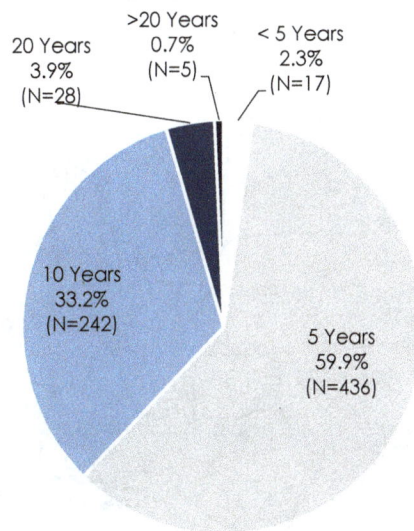

SOU RCE: U.S. Sentencing Commission, 2016 Datafiles, USSCFY16.

Figure E3. Number of Crack Cocaine Offenders Convicted of an Offense Carrying a Drug Mandatory Minimum Penalty by District
Fiscal Year 2016

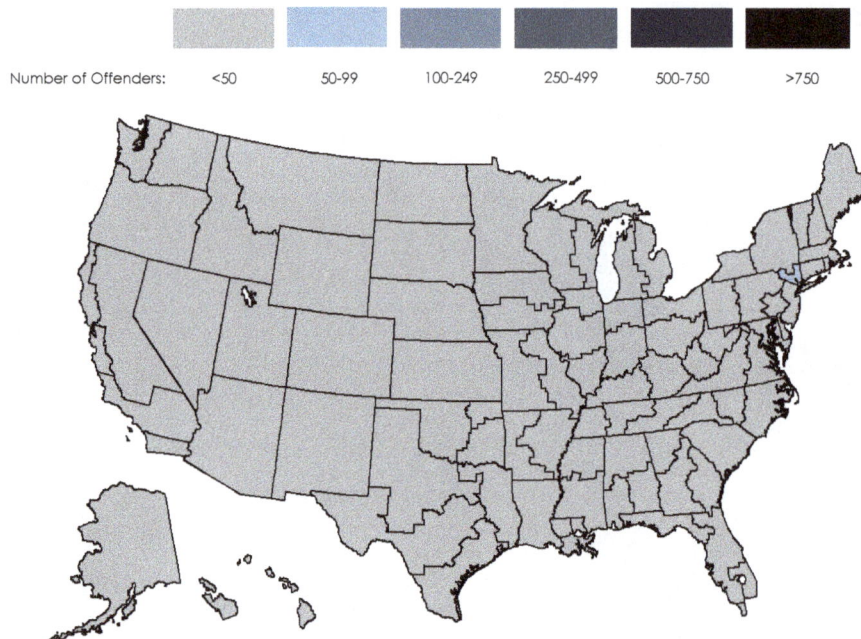

Number of Offenders: <50   50-99   100-249   250-499   500-750   >750

SOURCE: U.S. Sentencing Commission, 2016 Datafile, USSCFY16.

Table E1. Demographic Characteristics of Crack Cocaine Offenders
Fiscal Year 2016

	All Powder Crack Offenders	Convicted of an Offense Carrying a Drug Mandatory Minimum Penalty	Relieved of Mandatory Minimum Penalty	Subject to Drug Mandatory Minimum Penalty at Sentencing
Total (# of offenders)	1,562	728	220	508
RACE				
White	5.6%	3.0%	4.1%	2.6%
Black	82.6%	85.0%	79.1%	87.6%
Hispanic	11.3%	11.6%	16.8%	9.3%
Other	0.5%	0.4%	0.0%	0.6%
CITIZENSHIP				
U.S. Citizen	97.5%	96.7%	93.2%	98.2%
Non-U.S. Citizen	2.5%	3.3%	6.8%	1.8%
GENDER				
Male	90.7%	93.8%	87.7%	96.5%
Female	9.3%	6.2%	12.2%	3.5%

SOURCE: U.S. Sentencing Commission, 2016 Datafile, USSCFY16.

Table E2. Guideline Sentencing Characteristics, Role in the Offense and Criminal History of Crack Cocaine Offenders
Fiscal Year 2016

	All Crack Cocaine Offenders	Convicted of an Offense Carrying a Drug Mandatory Minimum Penalty	Relieved of Mandatory Minimum Penalty	Subject to Drug Mandatory Minimum Penalty at Sentencing
Total (# of offenders)	**1,562**	**728**	**220**	**508**
CHARACTERISTICS				
Weapon Specific Offense Characteristic	22.9%	28.6%	24.6%	30.3%
Firearms Mandatory Minimum Applied	9.7%	11.5%	14.6%	10.2%
Safety Valve Reduction	7.1%	6.9%	22.7%	0.0%
ROLE IN THE OFFENSE				
Aggravating Role	7.0%	10.9%	11.4%	10.6%
Mitigating Role	5.5%	3.3%	7.7%	1.4%
CRIMINAL HISTORY CATEGORY				
I	18.3%	17.7%	32.3%	11.4%
II	11.0%	9.8%	9.6%	9.8%
III	20.4%	22.8%	15.5%	26.0%
IV	13.3%	15.1%	13.6%	15.8%
V	8.4%	7.6%	6.8%	7.9%
VI	28.7%	27.1%	22.3%	29.1%

SOURCE: U.S. Sentencing Commission, 2016 Datafile, USSCFY16.

Figure E4. Demographics of Crack Cocaine Offenders Relieved of a Drug Mandatory
Minimum Penalty by Race of Offender
Fiscal Year 2016

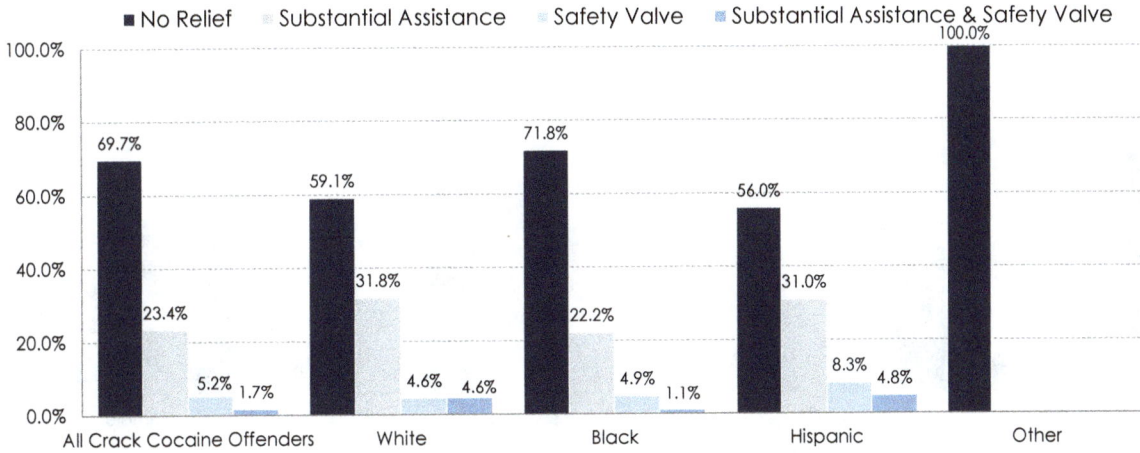

SOURCE: U.S. Sentencing Commission, 2016 Datafile, USSCFY16.

Figure E5. Demographics of Crack Cocaine Offenders Relieved of a
Drug Mandatory Minimum Penalty by Citizenship and Gender
Fiscal Year 2016

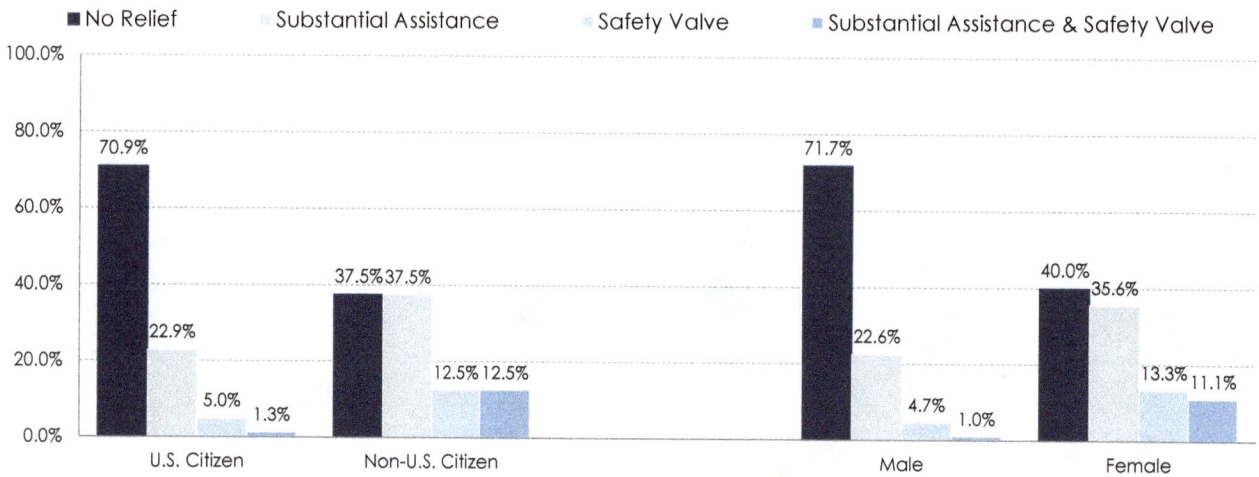

SOURCE: U.S. Sentencing Commission, 2016 Datafile, USSCFY16.

Figure E6. Average Sentence Length of Crack Cocaine Offenders
Fiscal Year 2016

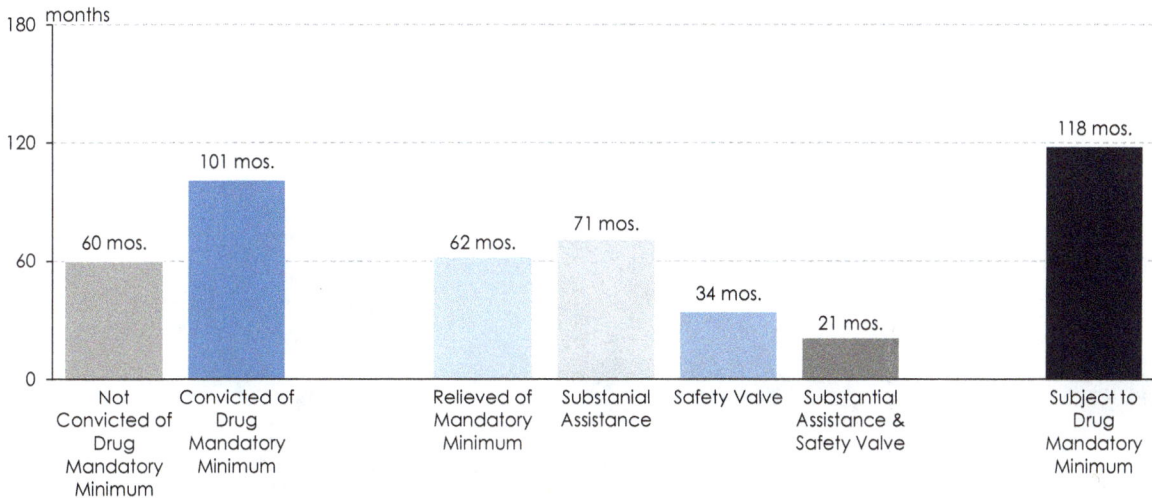

SOURCE: U.S. Sentencing Commission, 2016 Datafile, USSCFY16.

Figure E7. Average Sentence for Crack Cocaine Offenders by Demographic Characteristics
By Race
Fiscal Year 2016

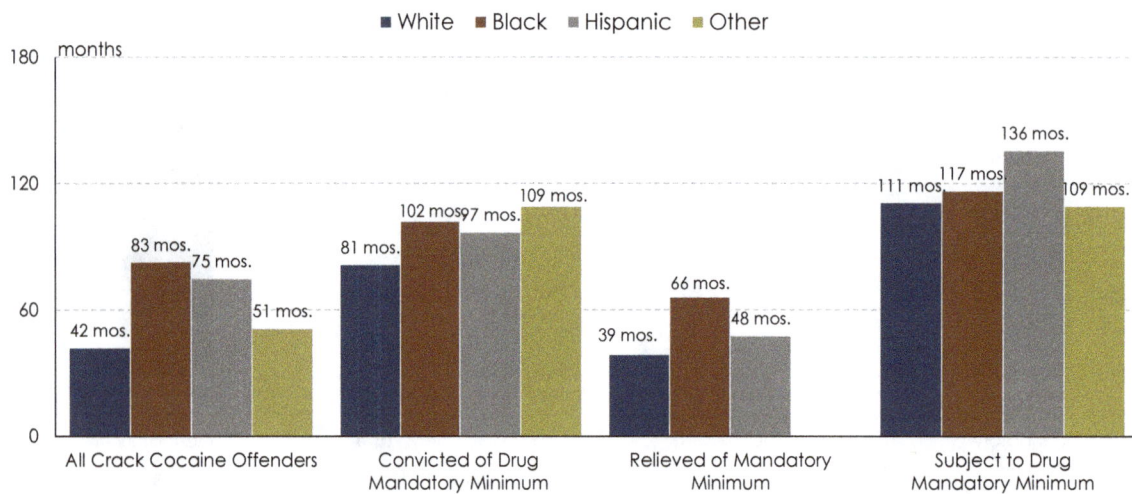

SOURCE: U.S. Sentencing Commission, 2016 Datafile, USSCFY16.

Table E3. Average Sentence for Crack Cocaine Offenders by Citizenship and Gender
Fiscal Year 2016

	All Crack Cocaine Offenders	Convicted of an Offense Carrying a Drug Mandatory Minimum Penalty	Relieved of Mandatory Minimum Penalty	Subject to Drug Mandatory Minimum Penalty at Sentencing
Total (# of offenders)	1,562	728	220	· 508
CITIZENSHIP				
U.S. Citizen	79 months	102 months	63 months	118 months
Non-U.S. Citizen	71 months	80 months	44 months	139 months
GENDER				
Male	84 months	104 months	66 months	· 119 months
Female	35 months	60 months	35 months	96 months

SOURCE: U.S. Sentencing Commission, 2016 Datafile, USSCFY16.

Table E4. Sentence Relative to the Guideline Range of Crack Cocaine Offenders
Fiscal Year 2016

	All Crack Cocaine Offenders	Convicted of an Offense Carrying a Drug Mandatory Minimum Penalty	Relieved of Mandatory Minimum Penalty	Subject to Drug Mandatory Minimum Penalty at Sentencing
Total (# of offenders)	1,562	728	220	508
SENTENCE RELATIVE TO THE GUIDELINE RANGE				
Within Range	41.0%	42.2%	7.7%	57.1%
Above Range	1.8%	1.5%	0.9%	1.8%
Substantial Assistance §5K1.1	20.7%	25.0%	82.7%	0.0%
Other Government Sponsored (no §5K1.1)	9.9%	8.7%	0.5%	12.2%
Non-Government Sponsored Below Range	26.6%	22.7%	8.2%	28.9%

SOURCE: U.S. Sentencing Commission, 2016 Datafile, USSCFY16.

Figure E8. Offender Function[1]
Crack Cocaine Offenders[2]
Fiscal Year 2009 and 2016 Sample Data

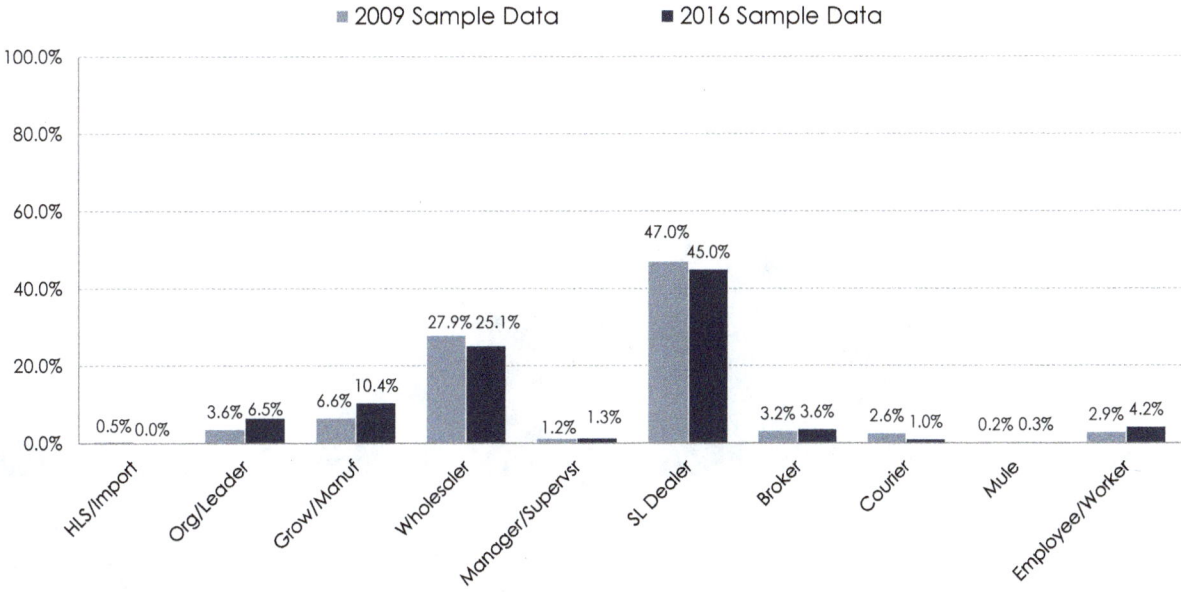

■ 2009 Sample Data   ■ 2016 Sample Data

Function	2009	2016
HLS/Import	0.5%	0.0%
Org/Leader	3.6%	6.5%
Grow/Manuf	6.6%	10.4%
Wholesaler	27.9%	25.1%
Manager/Supervsr	1.2%	1.3%
SL Dealer	47.0%	45.0%
Broker	3.2%	3.6%
Courier	2.6%	1.0%
Mule	0.2%	0.3%
Employee/Worker	2.9%	4.2%

[1] There were offenders in the samples whose function could not be determined. These offenders are not included in the overall percentages.
[2] In the fiscal year 2009 sample, 4.3 percent of crack cocaine offenders had "Other" or "Miscellaneous" functions. In the fiscal year 2016 sample, 2.6 percent of crack cocaine offenders had "Other" or "Miscellaneous" functions. These percentages are not represented in the figure above.

SOURCE: U.S. Sentencing Commission, 2009 and 2016 Function Datafiles, FUNCSAMPFY09 and FUNCSAMPFY16.

Figure E9. Percent of Offenders Convicted of an Offense Carrying a Drug Mandatory Minimum Penalty and Subject to a Drug Mandatory Minimum Penalty by Offender Function[1]
Crack Cocaine Offenders
Fiscal Year 2016 Sample Data

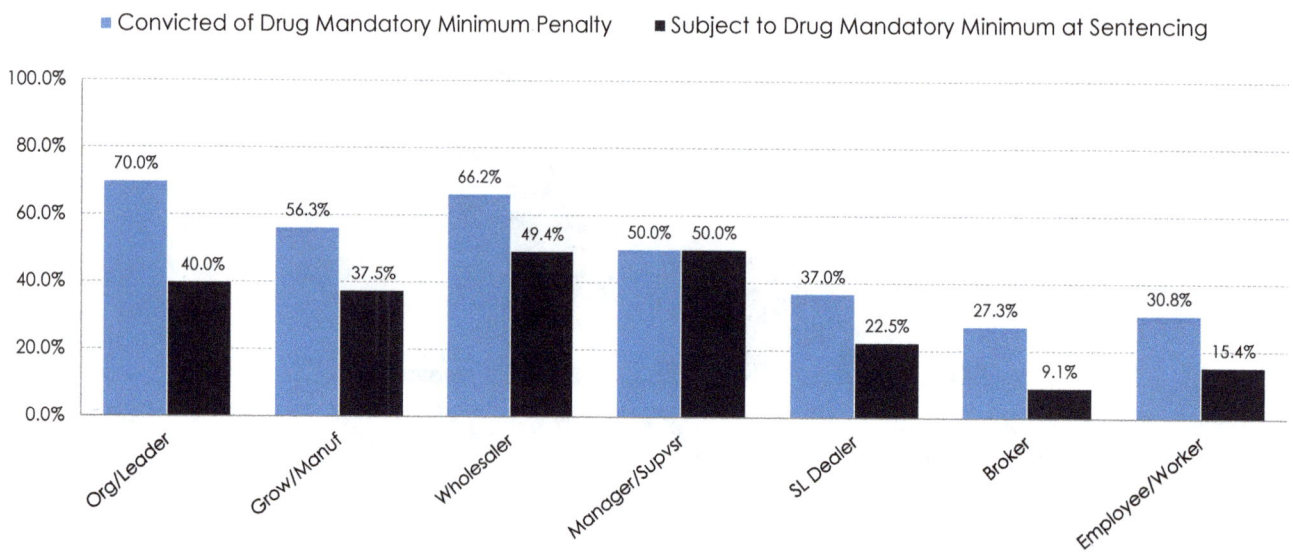

■ Convicted of Drug Mandatory Minimum Penalty ■ Subject to Drug Mandatory Minimum at Sentencing

[1]There were no crack cocaine offenders whose function was "high-level supplier/importer," therefore, this function is not depicted. Crack offenders who are mules or couriers are excluded from this analysis.

SOURCE: U.S. Sentencing Commission, 2016 Function Datafile, FUNCSAMPFY16.

Figure E10. Percent of Offenders Convicted of an Offense Carrying a Drug Mandatory Minimum Penalty Who Were Relieved of the Penalty by Offender Function[1]
Crack Cocaine Offenders
Fiscal Year 2016 Sample Data

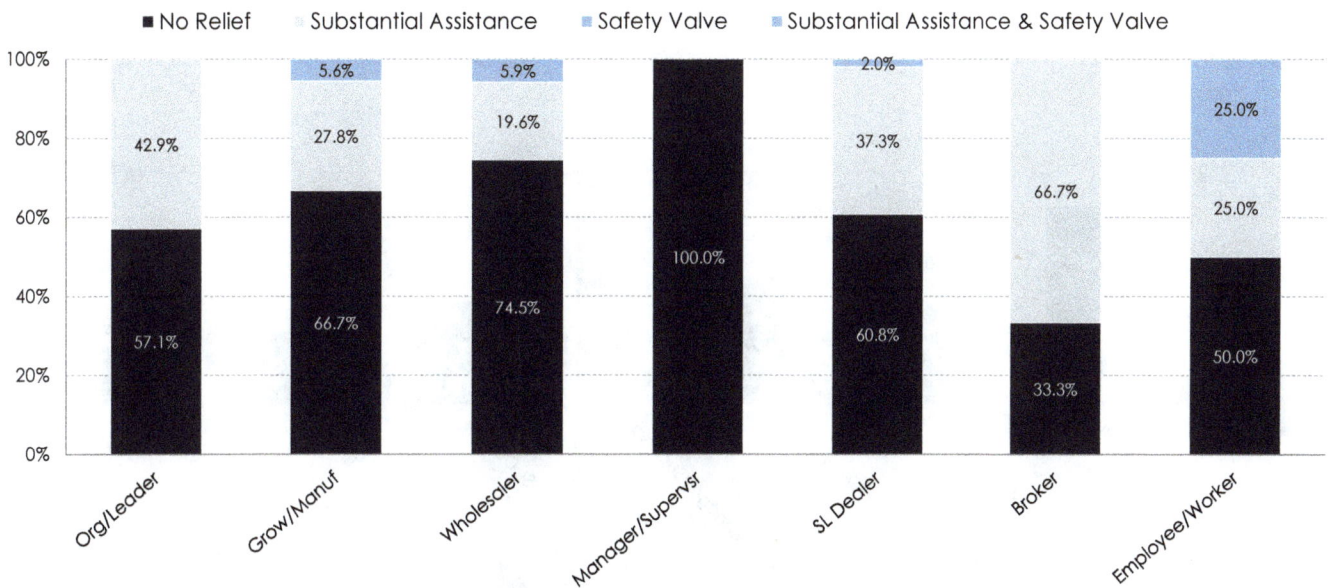

[1]There were no crack cocaine offenders whose function was "high-level supplier/importer," therefore, this function is not depicted. Crack offenders who are mules or couriers are excluded from this analysis.
SOURCE: U.S. Sentencing Commission, 2016 Function Datafile, FUNCSAMPFY16.

Figure E11. Average Guideline Minimum and Average Sentence by Offender Function[1]
Crack Cocaine Offenders
Fiscal Year 2016 Sample Data

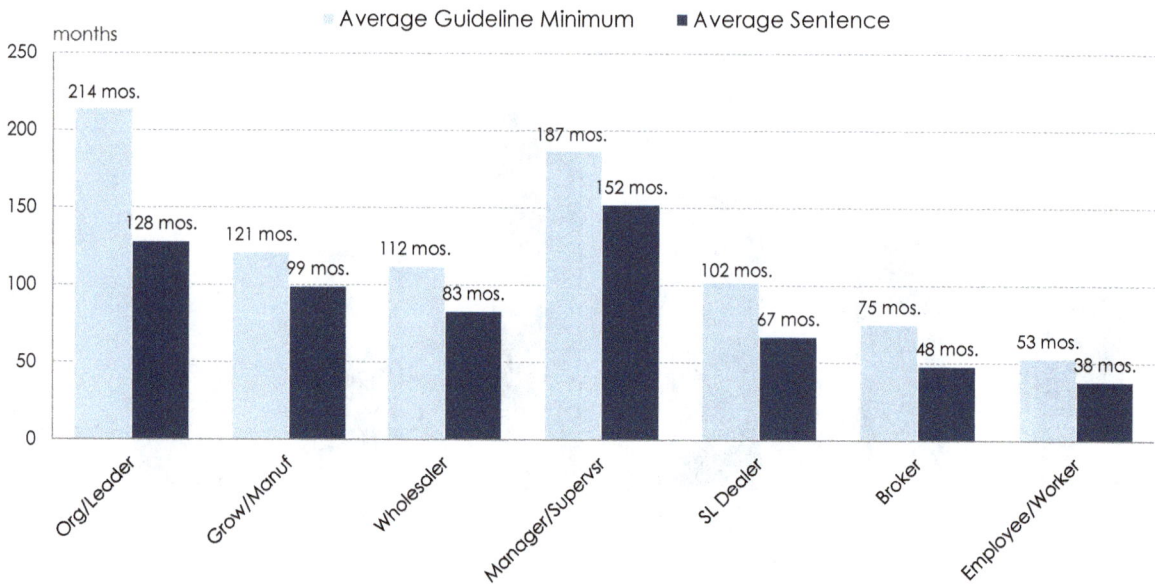

Average Guideline Minimum ■ Average Sentence

months

Offender Function	Average Guideline Minimum	Average Sentence
Org/Leader	214 mos.	128 mos.
Grow/Manuf	121 mos.	99 mos.
Wholesaler	112 mos.	83 mos.
Manager/Supervsr	187 mos.	152 mos.
SL Dealer	102 mos.	67 mos.
Broker	75 mos.	48 mos.
Employee/Worker	53 mos.	38 mos.

[1] There were no crack cocaine offenders whose function was "high-level supplier/importer," therefore, this function is not depicted. Crack offenders who are mules or couriers are excluded from this analysis.
SOURCE: U.S. Sentencing Commission, 2016 Function Datafile, FUNCSAMPFY16.

Appendix F:
Marijuana

Figure F1. Marijuana Offenders Convicted of an Offense
Carrying a Drug Mandatory Minimum Penalty
Fiscal Year 2016

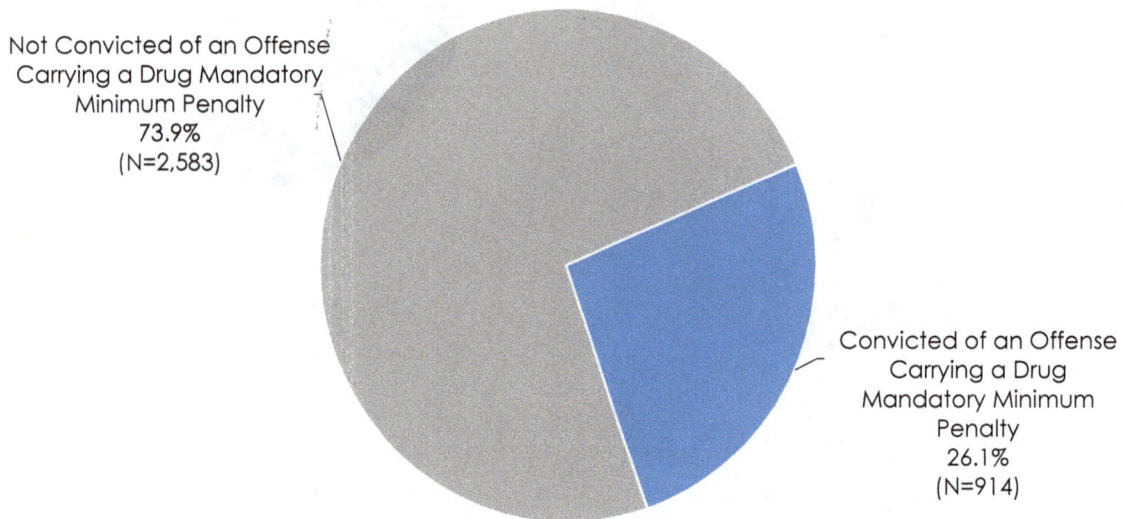

Not Convicted of an Offense
Carrying a Drug Mandatory
Minimum Penalty
73.9%
(N=2,583)

Convicted of an Offense
Carrying a Drug
Mandatory Minimum
Penalty
26.1%
(N=914)

SOURCE: U.S. Sentencing Commission, 2016 Datafile, USSCFY16.

Figure F2. Length of Mandatory Minimum Penalty
for Marijuana Offenders Convicted of an Offense
Carrying a Drug Mandatory Minimum Penalty
Fiscal Year 2016

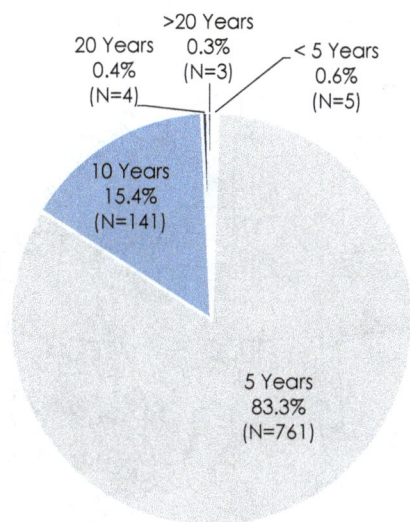

>20 Years
0.3%
(N=3)

20 Years
0.4%
(N=4)

< 5 Years
0.6%
(N=5)

10 Years
15.4%
(N=141)

5 Years
83.3%
(N=761)

SOURCE: U.S. Sentencing Commission, 2016 Datafiles, USSCFY16.

Figure F3. Number of Marijuana Offenders Convicted of an Offense
Carrying a Drug Mandatory Minimum Penalty by District
Fiscal Year 2016

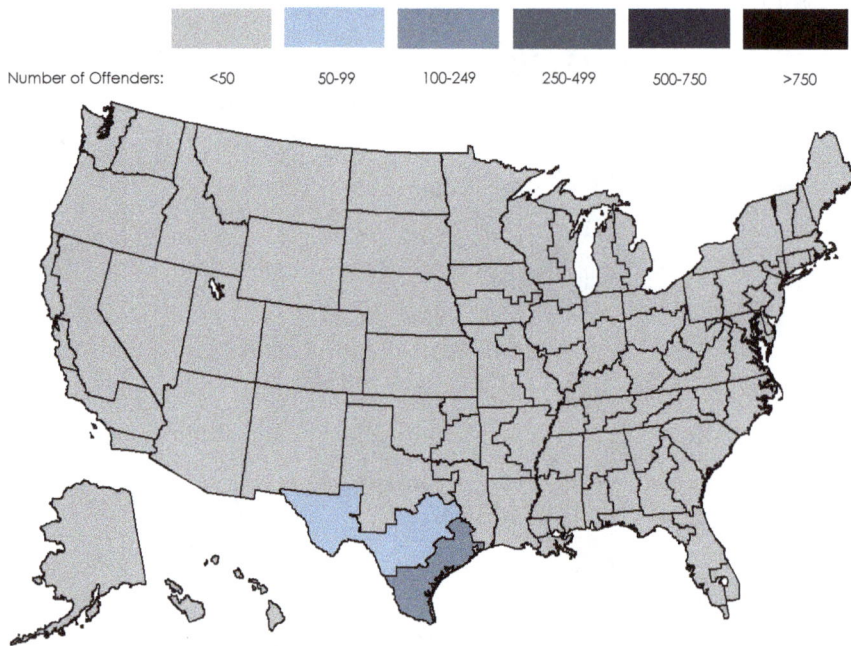

SOURCE: U.S. Sentencing Commission, 2016 Datafile, USSCFY16.

Table F1. Demographic Characteristics of Marijuana Offenders
Fiscal Year 2016

	All Marijuana Offenders	Convicted of an Offense Carrying a Drug Mandatory Minimum Penalty	Relieved of Mandatory Minimum Penalty	Subject to Drug Mandatory Minimum Penalty at Sentencing
Total (# of offenders)	**3,497**	**914**	**634**	**280**
		RACE		
White	12.0%	14.0%	14.5%	12.9%
Black	8.3%	8.4%	6.2%	13.6%
Hispanic	76.8%	73.9%	75.6%	70.3%
Other	2.8%	3.6%	3.8%	3.2%
		CITIZENSHIP		
U.S. Citizen	43.7%	44.5%	38.6%	57.7%
Non-U.S. Citizen	56.3%	55.5%	61.4%	42.3%
		GENDER		
Male	89.4%	94.3%	93.4%	96.4%
Female	10.6%	5.7%	6.6%	3.6%

SOURCE: U.S. Sentencing Commission, 2016 Datafile, USSCFY16.

Table F2. Guideline Sentencing Characteristics, Role in the Offense and Criminal History of Marijuana Offenders
Fiscal Year 2016

	All Marijuana Offenders	Convicted of an Offense Carrying a Drug Mandatory Minimum Penalty	Relieved of Mandatory Minimum Penalty	Subject to Drug Mandatory Minimum Penalty at Sentencing
Total (# of offenders)	3,497	914	634	280
CHARACTERISTICS				
Weapon Specific Offense Characteristic	4.7%	7.4%	3.6%	16.1%
Firearms Mandatory Minimum Applied	1.9%	1.1%	0.6%	2.1%
Safety Valve Reduction	53.3%	54.5%	78.4%	0.0%
ROLE IN THE OFFENSE				
Aggravating Role	4.9%	11.8%	7.6%	21.4%
Mitigating Role	37.6%	26.2%	33.3%	10.0%
CRIMINAL HISTORY CATEGORY				
I	65.9%	68.1%	85.3%	28.9%
II	13.0%	10.1%	5.2%	21.1%
III	11.3%	11.5%	5.5%	25.0%
IV	4.7%	4.6%	2.1%	10.4%
V	1.9%	1.8%	0.6%	4.3%
VI	3.2%	4.1%	1.3%	10.4%

SOURCE: U.S. Sentencing Commission, 2016 Datafile, USSCFY16.

Figure F4. Demographics of Marijuana Offenders Relieved of a Drug Mandatory Minimum Penalty by Race of Offender
Fiscal Year 2016

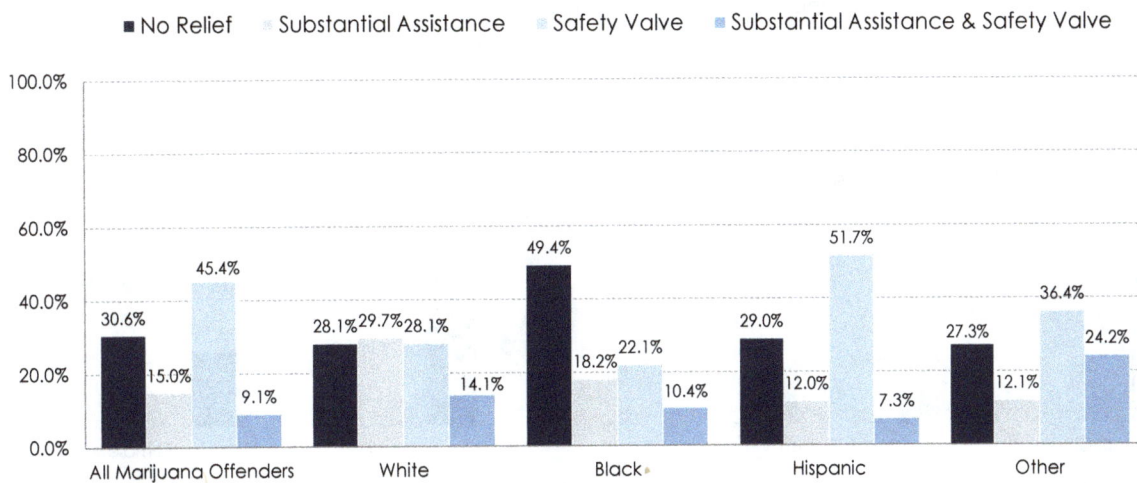

■ No Relief   Substantial Assistance   Safety Valve   ■ Substantial Assistance & Safety Valve

Group	No Relief	Substantial Assistance	Safety Valve	Substantial Assistance & Safety Valve
All Marijuana Offenders	30.6%	15.0%	45.4%	9.1%
White	28.1%	29.7%	28.1%	14.1%
Black	49.4%	18.2%	22.1%	10.4%
Hispanic	29.0%	12.0%	51.7%	7.3%
Other	27.3%	12.1%	36.4%	24.2%

SOURCE: U.S. Sentencing Commission, 2016 Datafile, USSCFY16.

Figure F5. Demographics of Marijuana Offenders Relieved of a Drug Mandatory Minimum
Penalty by Citizenship and Gender
Fiscal Year 2016

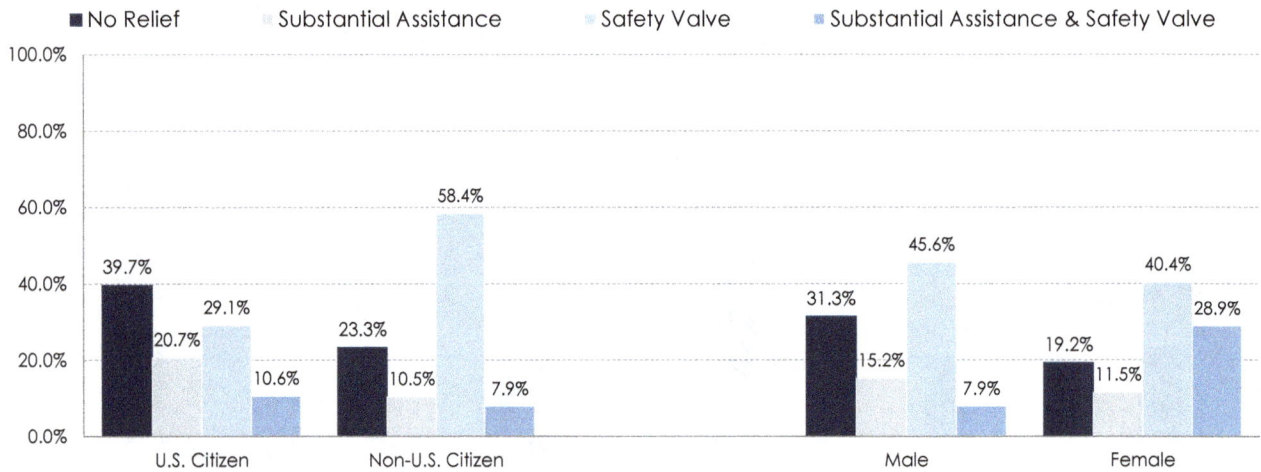

SOURCE: U.S. Sentencing Commission, 2016 Datafile, USSCFY16.

Figure F6. Average Sentence Length of Marijuana Offenders
Fiscal Year 2016

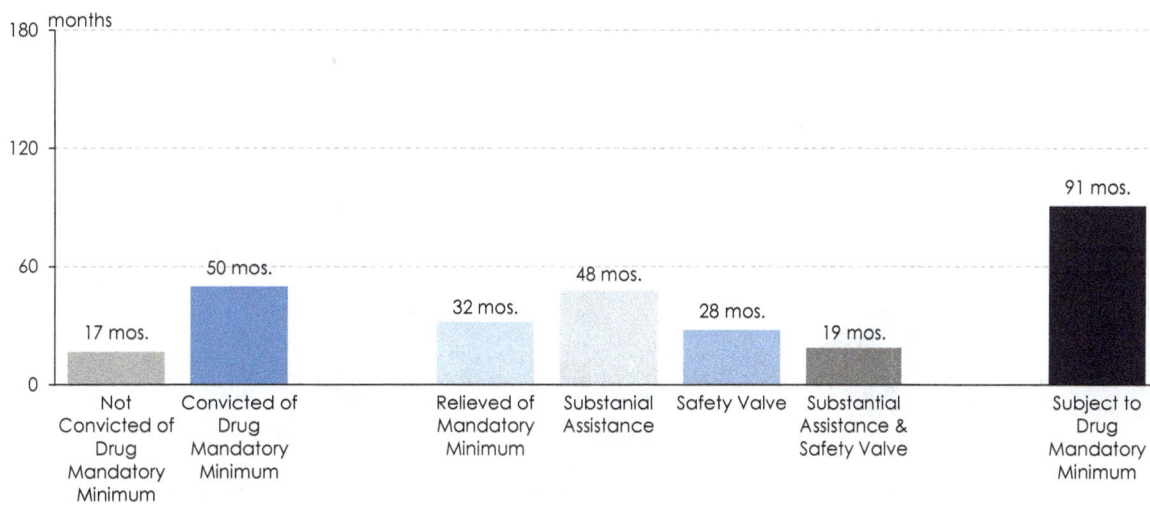

SOURCE: U.S. Sentencing Commission, 2016 Datafile, USSCFY16.

Figure F7. Average Sentence for Marijuana Offenders by Demographic Characteristics
By Race
Fiscal Year 2016

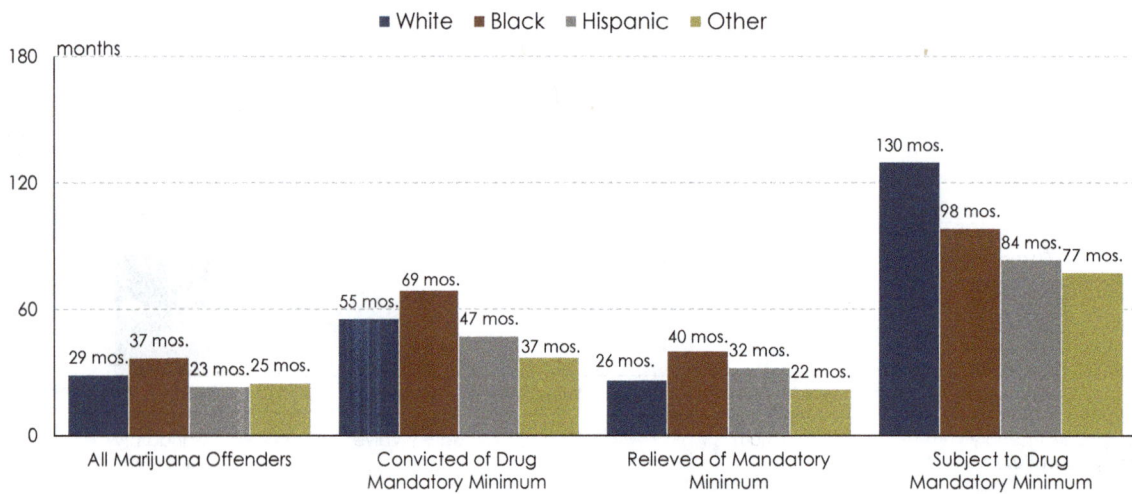

■ White ■ Black ■ Hispanic ■ Other

	White	Black	Hispanic	Other
All Marijuana Offenders	29 mos.	37 mos.	23 mos.	25 mos.
Convicted of Drug Mandatory Minimum	55 mos.	69 mos.	47 mos.	37 mos.
Relieved of Mandatory Minimum	26 mos.	40 mos.	32 mos.	22 mos.
Subject to Drug Mandatory Minimum	130 mos.	98 mos.	84 mos.	77 mos.

SOURCE: U.S. Sentencing Commission, 2016 Datafile, USSCFY16.

Table F3. Average Sentence for Marijuana Offenders by Citizenship and Gender
Fiscal Year 2016

	All Marijuana Offenders	Convicted of an Offense Carrying a Drug Mandatory Minimum Penalty	Relieved of Mandatory Minimum Penalty	Subject to Drug Mandatory Minimum Penalty at Sentencing
Total (# of offenders)	3,497	914	634	280
CITIZENSHIP				
U.S. Citizen	30 months	59 months	35 months	96 months
Non-U.S. Citizen	22 months	42 months	29 months	85 months
GENDER				
Male	27 months	51 months	32 months	92 months
Female	12 months	29 months	18 months	76 months

SOURCE: U.S. Sentencing Commission, 2016 Datafile, USSCFY16.

Table F4. Sentence Relative to the Guideline Range of Marijuana Offenders
Fiscal Year 2016

	All Marijuana Offenders	Convicted of an Offense Carrying a Drug Mandatory Minimum Penalty	Relieved of Mandatory Minimum Penalty	Subject to Drug Mandatory Minimum Penalty at Sentencing
Total (# of offenders)	3,497	914	634	280
SENTENCE RELATIVE TO THE GUIDELINE RANGE				
Within Range	47.6%	54.3%	43.7%	78.2%
Above Range	1.7%	0.8%	0.3%	1.8%
Substantial Assistance §5K1.1	12.0%	24.1%	34.7%	0.0%
Other Government Sponsored (no §5K1.1)	20.7%	6.9%	6.0%	8.9%
Non-Government Sponsored Below Range	18.0%	14.0%	15.3%	11.1%

SOURCE: U.S. Sentencing Commission, 2016 Datafile, USSCFY16.

Figure F8. Offender Function[1]
Marijuana Offenders[2]
Fiscal Year 2009 and 2016 Sample Data

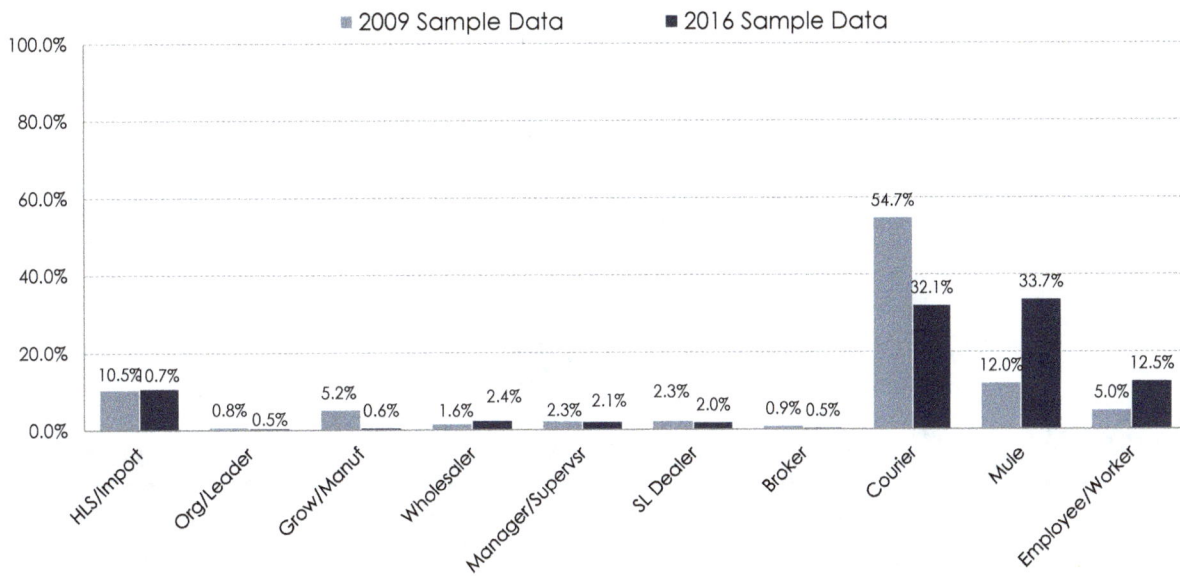

- 2009 Sample Data - 2016 Sample Data

[1] There were offenders in the samples whose function could not be determined. These offenders are not included in the overall percentages.
[2] In the fiscal year 2009 sample, 4.9 percent of marijuana offenders had "Other" or "Miscellaneous" functions. In the fiscal year 2016 sample, 3.0 percent of marijuana offenders had "Other" or "Miscellaneous" functions. These percentages are not represented in the figure above.

SOURCE: U.S. Sentencing Commission, 2009 and 2016 Function Datafiles, FUNCSAMPFY09 and FUNCSAMPFY16.

Figure F9. Percent of Offenders Convicted of an Offense Carrying a Drug Mandatory
Minimum Penalty and Subject to a Drug Mandatory Minimum Penalty
by Offender Function[1]
Marijuana Offenders
Fiscal Year 2016 Sample Data

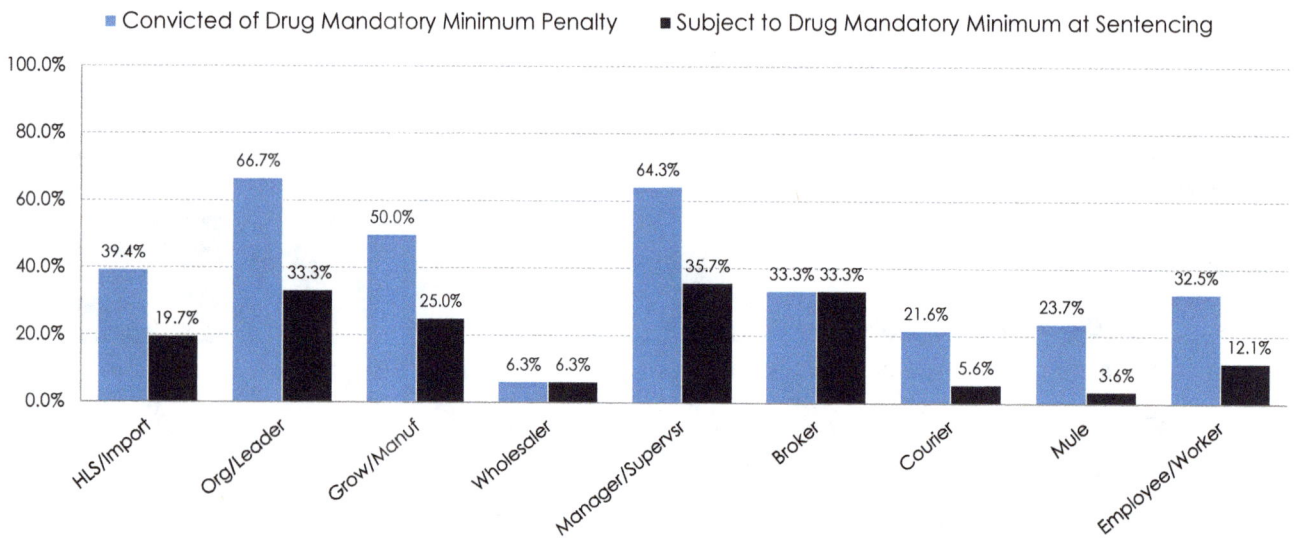

Legend: ■ Convicted of Drug Mandatory Minimum Penalty   ■ Subject to Drug Mandatory Minimum at Sentencing

Function	Convicted	Subject
HLS/Import	39.4%	19.7%
Org/Leader	66.7%	33.3%
Grow/Manuf	50.0%	25.0%
Wholesaler	6.3%	6.3%
Manager/Supervsr	64.3%	35.7%
Broker	33.3%	33.3%
Courier	21.6%	5.6%
Mule	23.7%	3.6%
Employee/Worker	32.5%	12.1%

[1] In the fiscal year 2016 sample, there were no "Street Level Dealer" marijuana offenders convicted of or subject to a drug mandatory minimum penalty, therefore, this function is not depicted.

SOURCE: U.S. Sentencing Commission, 2016 Function Datafile, FUNCSAMPFY16.

Figure F10. Percent of Offenders Convicted of an Offense Carrying a Drug Mandatory Minimum Penalty Who Were Relieved of the Penalty by Offender Function
Marijuana Offenders[1]
Fiscal Year 2016 Sample Data

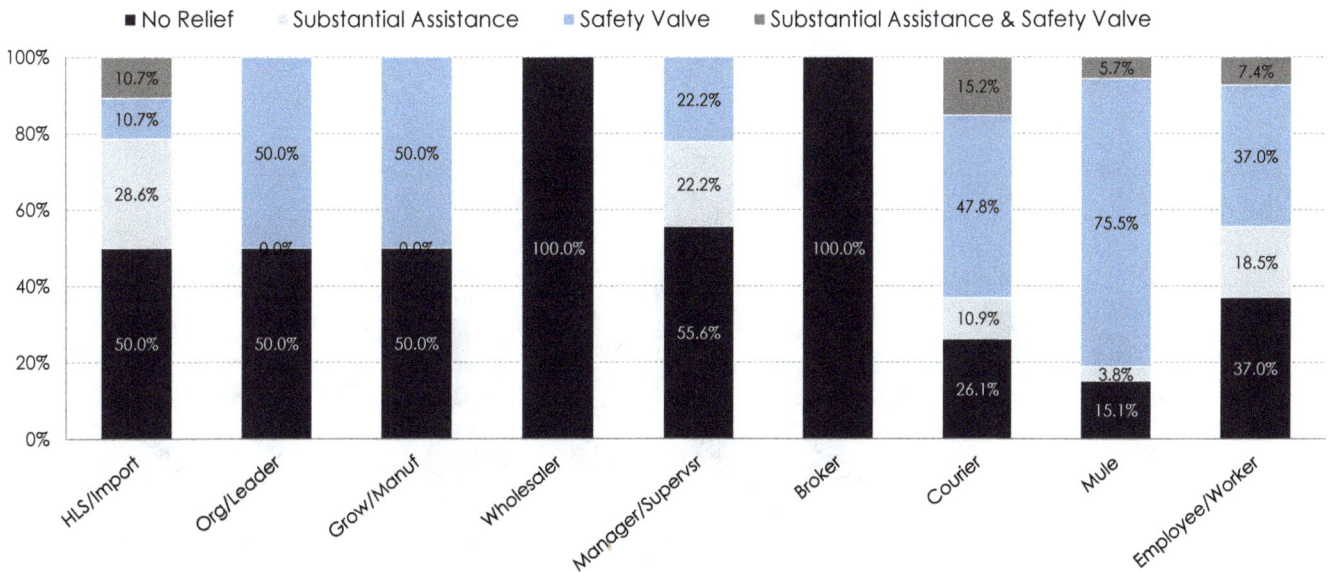

■ No Relief   Substantial Assistance   ■ Safety Valve   ■ Substantial Assistance & Safety Valve

[1]In the fiscal year 2016 sample, there were no "Street Level Dealer" marijuana offenders convicted of or subject to a drug mandatory minimum penalty, therefore, this function is not depicted.
SOURCE: U.S. Sentencing Commission, 2016 Function Datafile, FUNCSAMPFY16.

Figure F11. Average Guideline Minimum and Average Sentence by Offender Function
Marijuana Offenders
Fiscal Year 2016 Sample Data

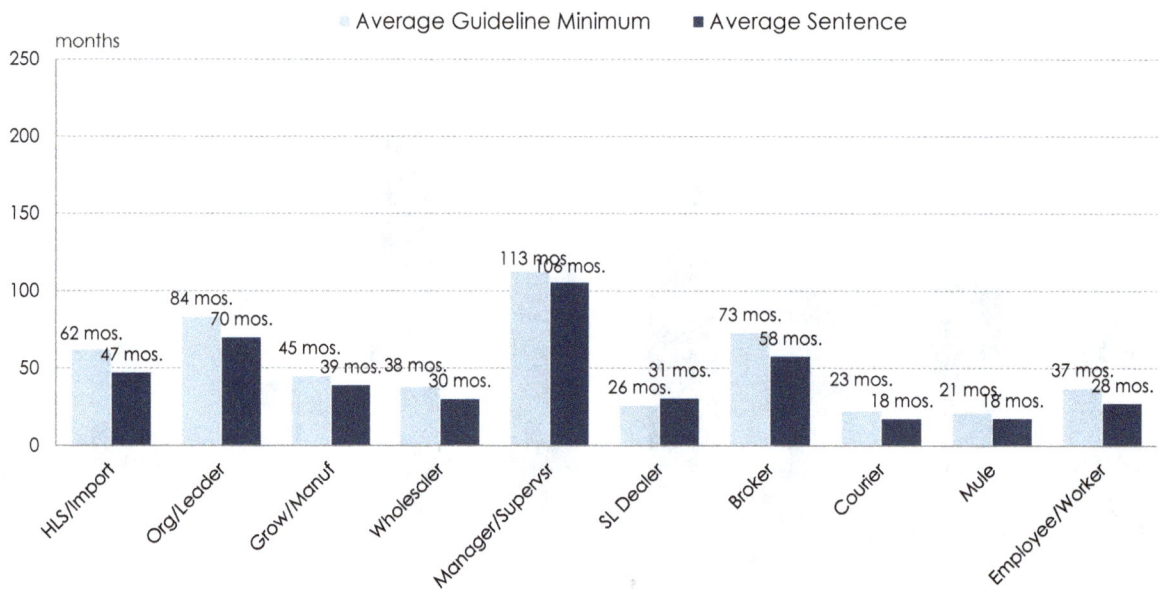

- Average Guideline Minimum ■ Average Sentence

months

- HLS/Import: 62 mos. / 47 mos.
- Org/Leader: 84 mos. / 70 mos.
- Grow/Manuf: 45 mos. / 39 mos.
- Wholesaler: 38 mos. / 30 mos.
- Manager/Supervsr: 113 mos. / 106 mos.
- SL Dealer: 26 mos. / 31 mos.
- Broker: 73 mos. / 58 mos.
- Courier: 23 mos. / 18 mos.
- Mule: 21 mos. / 18 mos.
- Employee/Worker: 37 mos. / 28 mos.

SOURCE: U.S. Sentencing Commission, 2016 Function Datafile, FUNCSAMPFY16.

A

Appendix G:
Methamphetamine

Figure G.1. Methamphetamine Offenders Convicted of an Offense Carrying a Drug Mandatory Minimum Penalty
Fiscal Year 2016

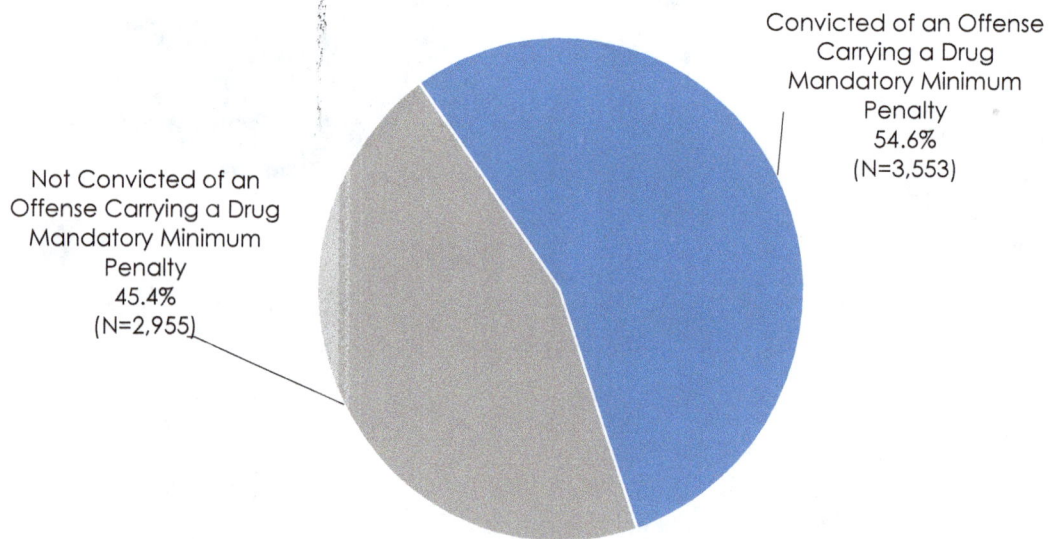

Convicted of an Offense Carrying a Drug Mandatory Minimum Penalty
54.6%
(N=3,553)

Not Convicted of an Offense Carrying a Drug Mandatory Minimum Penalty
45.4%
(N=2,955)

SOURCE: U.S. Sentencing Commission, 2016 Datafile, USSCFY16.

Figure G2. Length of Mandatory Minimum Penalty for Methamphetamine Offenders
Convicted of an Offense Carrying a Drug Mandatory Minimum Penalty
Fiscal Year 2016

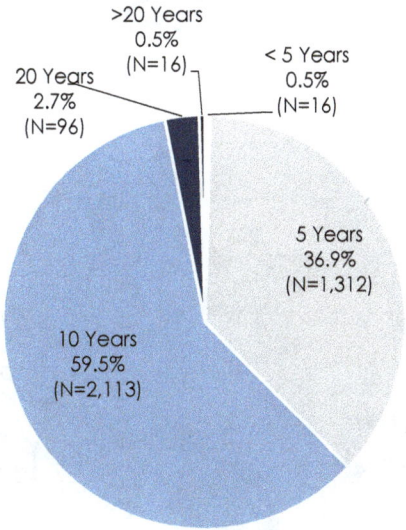

SOURCE: U.S. Sentencing Commission, 2016 Datafiles, USSCFY16.

Figure G3. Number of Methamphetamine Offenders Convicted of an Offense Carrying a Drug Mandatory Minimum Penalty by District
Fiscal Year 2016

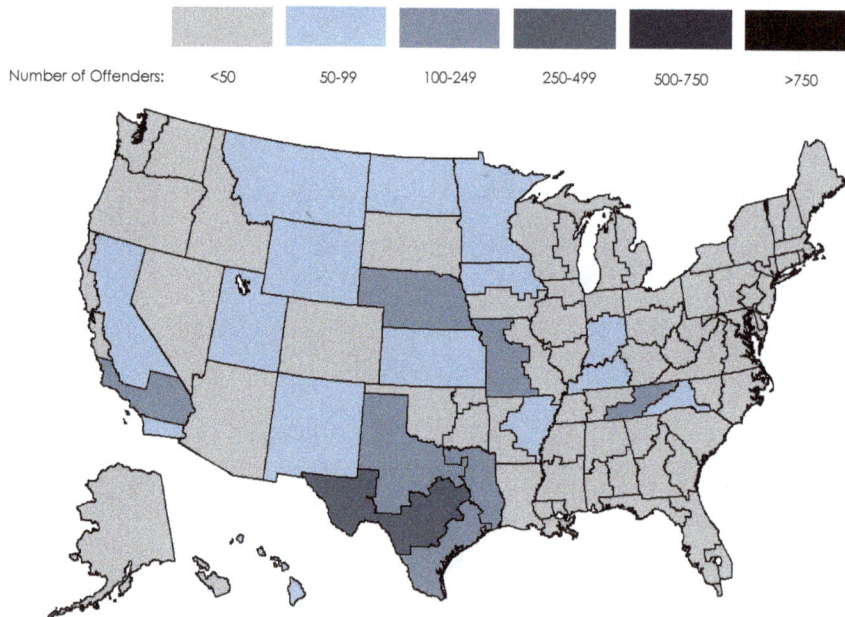

Number of Offenders: <50   50-99   100-249   250-499   500-750   >750

SOURCE: U.S. Sentencing Commission, 2016 Datafile, USSCFY16.

Table G1. Demographic Characteristics of Methamphetamine Offenders
Fiscal Year 2016

	All Methamphetamine Offenders	Convicted of an Offense Carrying a Drug Mandatory Minimum Penalty	Relieved of Mandatory Minimum Penalty	Subject to Drug Mandatory Minimum Penalty at Sentencing
Total (# of offenders)	6,508	3,553	1,707	1,846
RACE				
White	38.8%	42.7%	41.2%	44.1%
Black	6.0%	6.8%	5.3%	8.3%
Hispanic	50.4%	46.2%	49.4%	43.2%
Other	4.8%	4.2%	4.1%	4.4%
CITIZENSHIP				
U.S. Citizen	76.1%	77.6%	73.4%	81.6%
Non-U.S. Citizen	23.9%	22.4%	26.7%	18.4%
GENDER				
Male	79.6%	84.5%	79.0%	89.5%
Female	20.4%	15.5%	21.0%	10.5%

SOURCE: U.S. Sentencing Commission, 2016 Datafile, USSCFY16.

Table G2. Guideline Sentencing Characteristics, Role in the Offense and Criminal History of Methamphetamine Offenders
Fiscal Year 2016

	All Methamphetamine Offenders	Convicted of an Offense Carrying a Drug Mandatory Minimum Penalty	Relieved of Mandatory Minimum Penalty	Subject to Drug Mandatory Minimum Penalty at Sentencing
Total (# of offenders)	**6,508**	**3,553**	**1,707**	**1,846**
CHARACTERISTICS				
Weapon Specific Offense Characteristic	17.7%	21.3%	14.4%	27.6%
Firearms Mandatory Minimum Applied	3.8%	5.0%	3.7%	6.1%
Safety Valve Reduction	30.8%	22.4%	46.6%	0.0%
ROLE IN THE OFFENSE				
Aggravating Role	6.2%	9.0%	5.5%	12.2%
Mitigating Role	21.4%	11.3%	16.8%	6.3%
CRIMINAL HISTORY CATEGORY				
I	44.5%	36.3%	54.5%	19.3%
II	12.8%	12.7%	9.9%	15.3%
III	14.3%	16.3%	12.8%	19.5%
IV	8.8%	10.9%	6.9%	14.6%
V	5.3%	6.3%	4.1%	8.4%
VI	14.3%	17.6%	11.8%	22.9%

SOURCE: U.S. Sentencing Commission, 2016 Datafile, USSCFY16.

Figure G4. Demographics of Methamphetamine Offenders Relieved of a Drug Mandatory Minimum Penalty by Race of Offender
Fiscal Year 2016

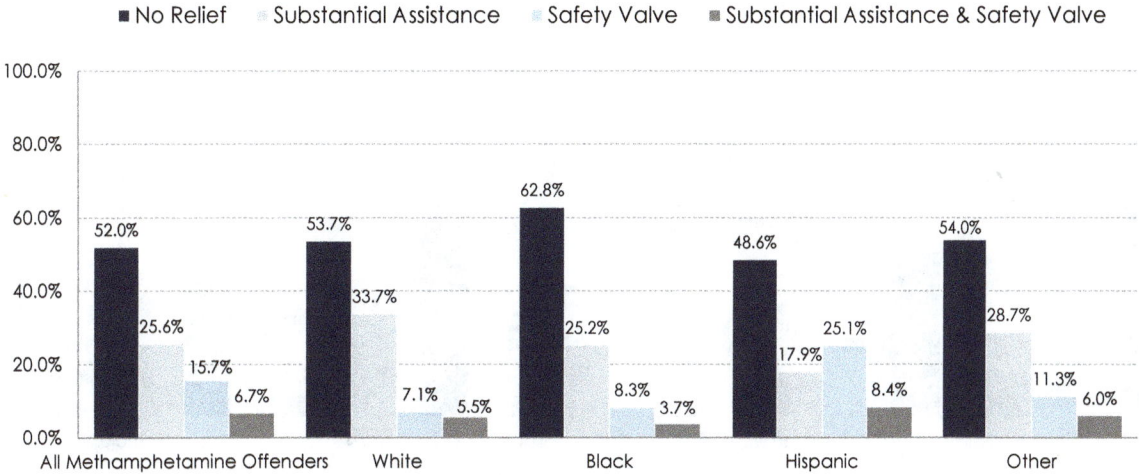

■ No Relief ■ Substantial Assistance ■ Safety Valve ■ Substantial Assistance & Safety Valve

	No Relief	Substantial Assistance	Safety Valve	Substantial Assistance & Safety Valve
All Methamphetamine Offenders	52.0%	25.6%	15.7%	6.7%
White	53.7%	33.7%	7.1%	5.5%
Black	62.8%	25.2%	8.3%	3.7%
Hispanic	48.6%	17.9%	25.1%	8.4%
Other	54.0%	28.7%	11.3%	6.0%

SOURCE: U.S. Sentencing Commission, 2016 Datafile, USSCFY16.

Figure G5. Demographics of Methamphetamine Offenders Relieved of a Drug Mandatory Minimum Penalty by Citizenship and Gender
Fiscal Year 2016

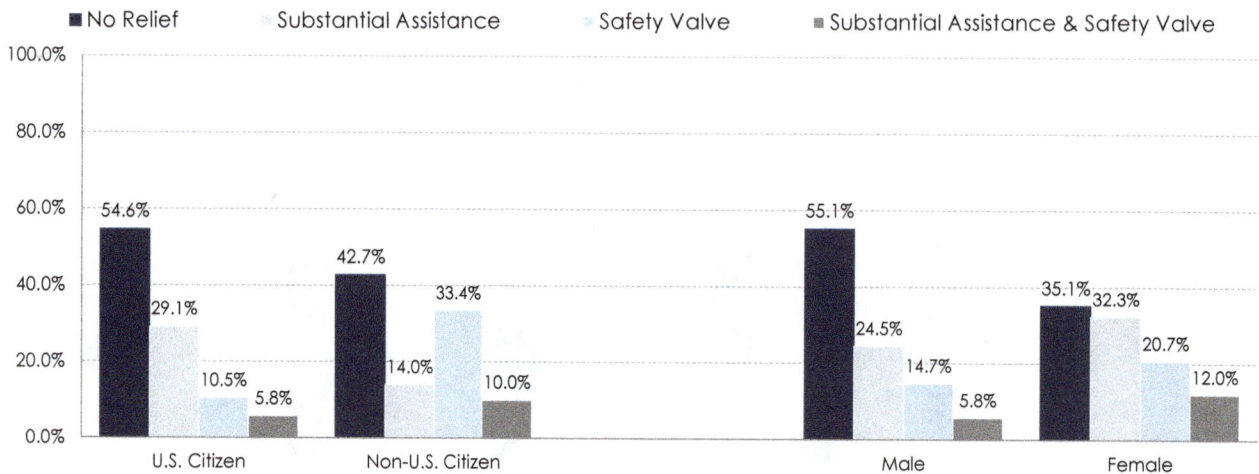

SOURCE: U.S. Sentencing Commission, 2016 Datafile, USSCFY16.

Figure G6. Average Sentence Length of Methamphetamine Offenders
Fiscal Year 2016

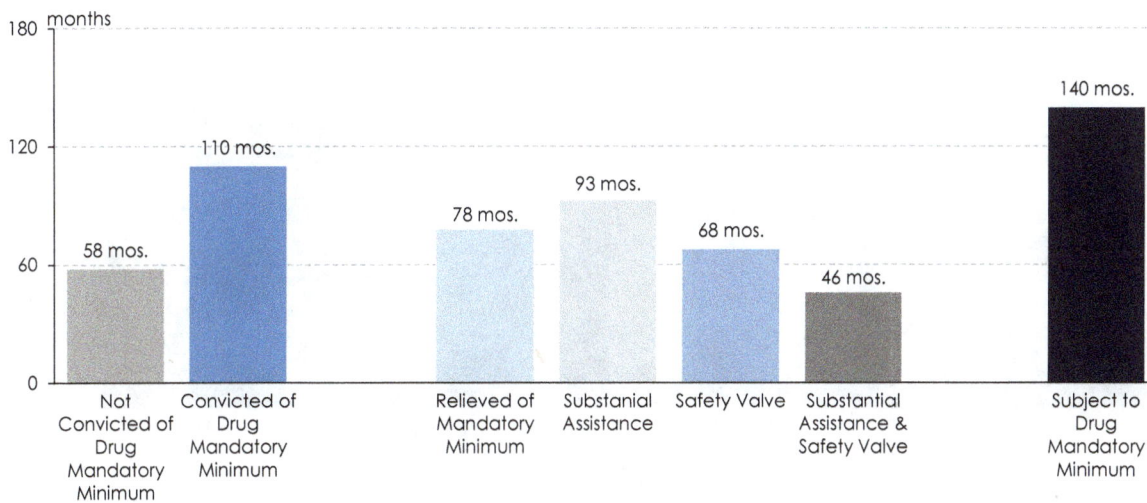

months

180

120

60

0

58 mos. (Not Convicted of Drug Mandatory Minimum)
110 mos. (Convicted of Drug Mandatory Minimum)
78 mos. (Relieved of Mandatory Minimum)
93 mos. (Substanial Assistance)
68 mos. (Safety Valve)
46 mos. (Substantial Assistance & Safety Valve)
140 mos. (Subject to Drug Mandatory Minimum)

SOURCE: U.S. Sentencing Commission, 2016 Datafile, USSCFY16.

Figure G7. Average Sentence for Methamphetamine Offenders by Demographic
Characteristics By Race
Fiscal Year 2016

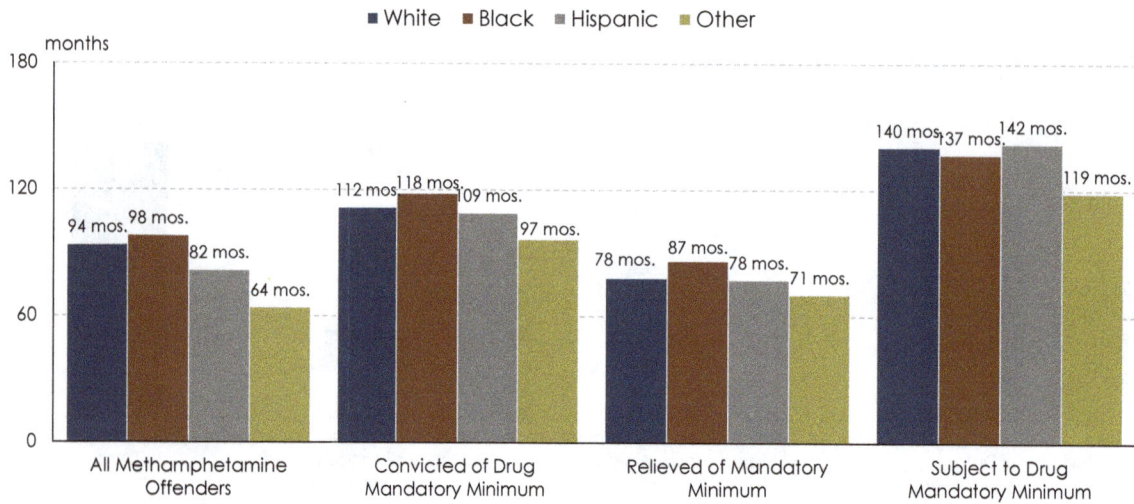

SOURCE: U.S. Sentencing Commission, 2016 Datafile, USSCFY16.

Table G3. Average Sentence for Methamphetamine Offenders by Citizenship and Gender
Fiscal Year 2016

	All Methamphetamine Offenders	Convicted of an Offense Carrying a Drug Mandatory Minimum Penalty	Relieved of Mandatory Minimum Penalty	Subject to Drug Mandatory Minimum Penalty at Sentencing
Total (# of offenders)	6,508	3,553	1,707	1,846
CITIZENSHIP				
U.S. Citizen	88 months	112 months	79 months	139 months
Non-U.S. Citizen	82 months	106 months	77 months	145 months
GENDER				
Male	94 months	115 months	81 months	143 months
Female	58 months	83 months	66 months	115 months

SOURCE: U.S. Sentencing Commission, 2016 Datafile, USSCFY16.

Table G4. Sentence Relative to the Guideline Range of Methamphetamine Offenders
Fiscal Year 2016

	All Methamphetamine Offenders	Convicted of an Offense Carrying a Drug Mandatory Minimum Penalty	Relieved of Mandatory Minimum Penalty	Subject to Drug Mandatory Minimum Penalty at Sentencing
Total (# of offenders)	**6,508**	**3,553**	**1,707**	**1,846**
SENTENCE RELATIVE TO THE GUIDELINE RANGE				
Within Range	31.1%	34.7%	15.9%	52.1%
Above Range	0.6%	0.6%	0.2%	1.0%
Substantial Assistance §5K1.1	25.9%	32.4%	67.5%	0.0%
Other Government Sponsored (no §5K1.1)	20.7%	12.1%	4.4%	19.1%
Non-Government Sponsored Below Range	21.7%	20.2%	12.0%	27.8%

SOURCE: U.S. Sentencing Commission, 2016 Datafile, USSCFY16.

Figure G8. Offender Function[1]
Methamphetamine Offenders[2]
Fiscal Year 2009 and 2016 Sample Data

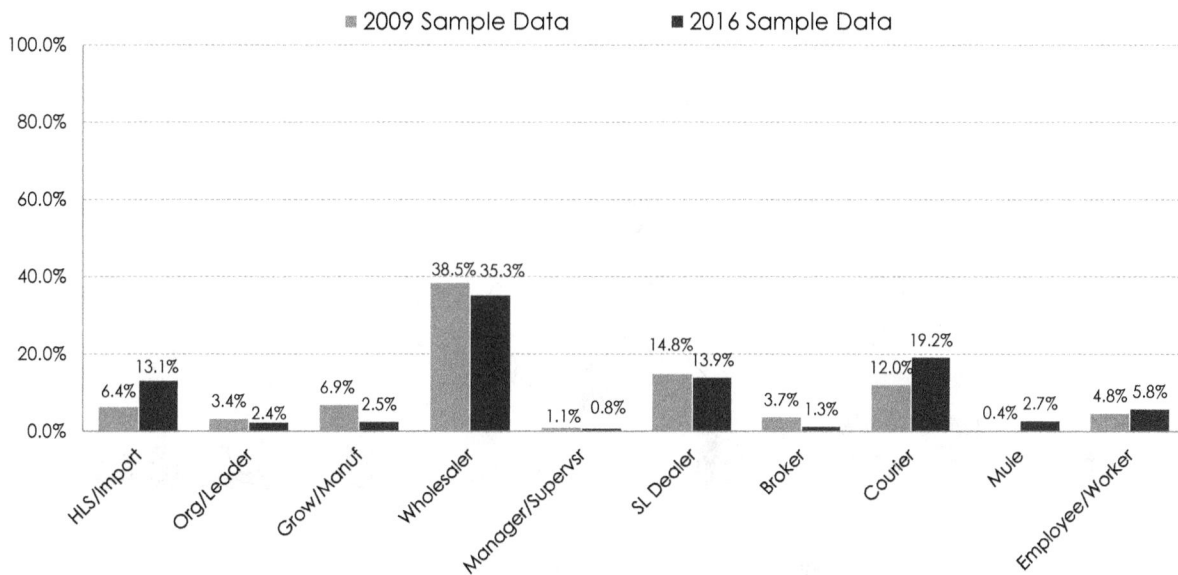

[1] There were offenders in the samples whose function could not be determined. These offenders are not included in the overall percentages.
[2] In the fiscal year 2009 sample, 8.1 percent of methamphetamine offenders had "Other" or "Miscellaneous" functions. In the fiscal year 2016 sample, 3.1 percent of methamphetamine offenders had "Other" or "Miscellaneous" functions. These percentages are not represented in the figure above.

SOURCE: U.S. Sentencing Commission, 2009 and 2016 Function Datafiles, FUNCSAMPFY09 and FUNCSAMPFY16.

Figure G9. Percent of Offenders Convicted of an Offense Carrying a Drug Mandatory Minimum Penalty and Subject to a Drug Mandatory Minimum Penalty by Offender Function
Methamphetamine Offenders
Fiscal Year 2016 Sample Data

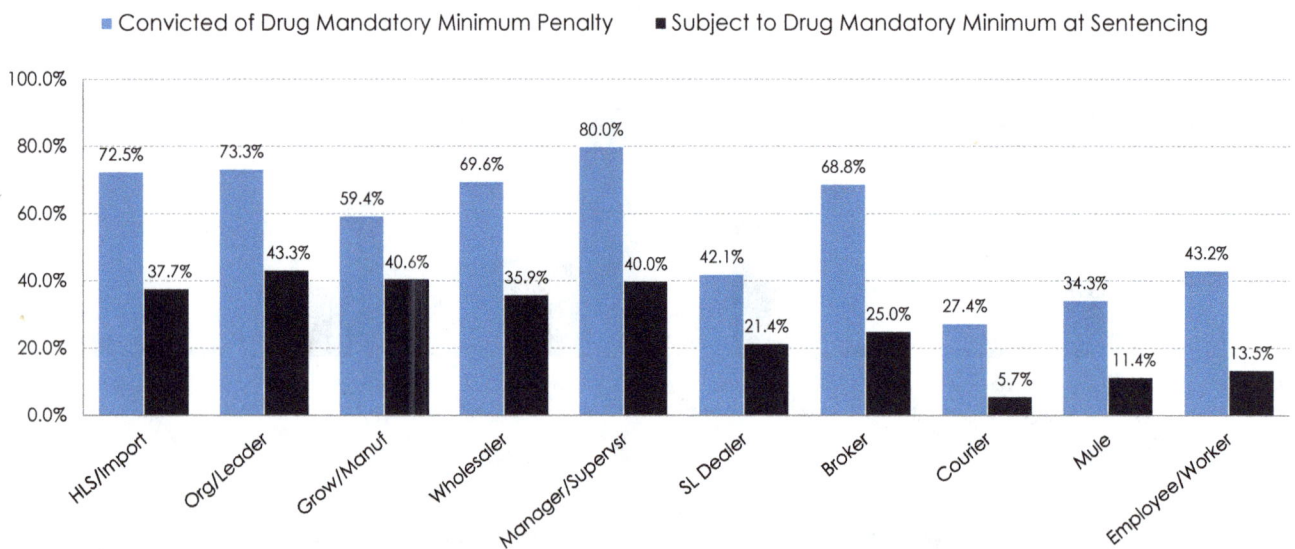

■ Convicted of Drug Mandatory Minimum Penalty   ■ Subject to Drug Mandatory Minimum at Sentencing

Function	Convicted	Subject
HLS/Import	72.5%	37.7%
Org/Leader	73.3%	43.3%
Grow/Manuf	59.4%	40.6%
Wholesaler	69.6%	35.9%
Manager/Supervsr	80.0%	40.0%
SL Dealer	42.1%	21.4%
Broker	68.8%	25.0%
Courier	27.4%	5.7%
Mule	34.3%	11.4%
Employee/Worker	43.2%	13.5%

SOURCE: U.S. Sentencing Commission, 2016 Function Datafile, FUNCSAMPFY16.

Figure G10. Percent of Offenders Convicted of an Offense Carrying a Drug Mandatory Minimum Penalty Who Were Relieved of the Penalty by Offender Function
Methamphetamine Offenders
Fiscal Year 2016 Sample Data

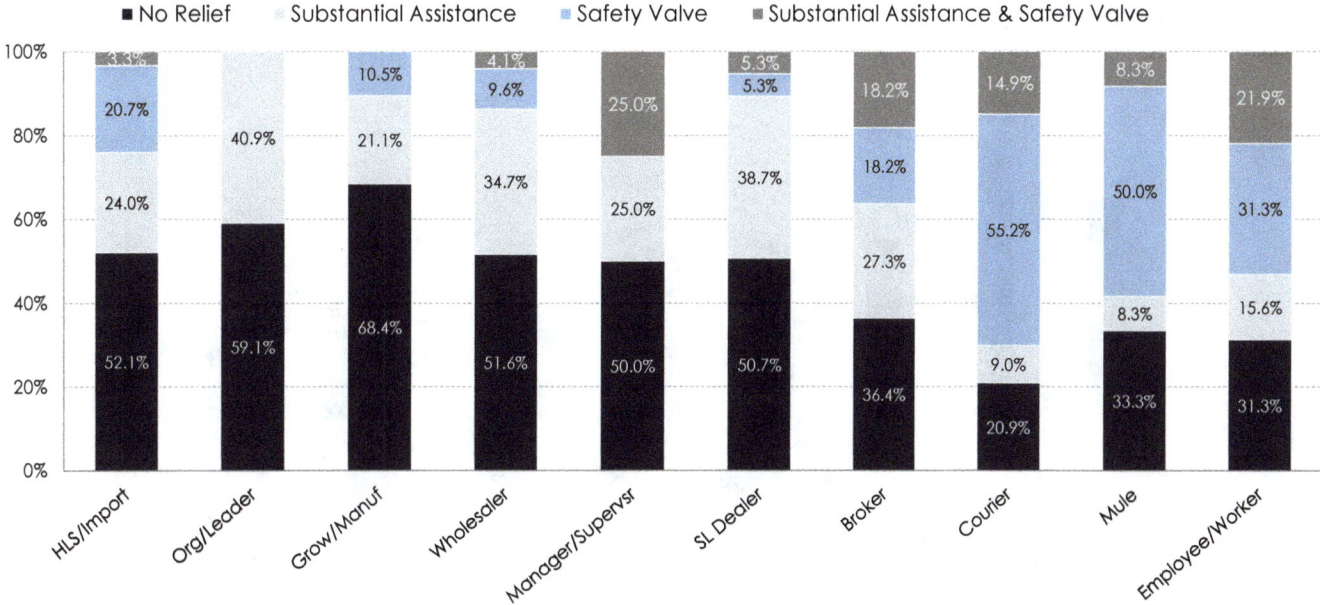

■ No Relief ▪ Substantial Assistance ▪ Safety Valve ▪ Substantial Assistance & Safety Valve

Function	No Relief	Substantial Assistance	Safety Valve	Substantial Assistance & Safety Valve
HLS/Import	52.1%	24.0%	20.7%	3.3%
Org/Leader	59.1%	40.9%		
Grow/Manuf	68.4%	21.1%	10.5%	
Wholesaler	51.6%	34.7%	9.6%	4.1%
Manager/Supervsr	50.0%	25.0%		25.0%
SL Dealer	50.7%	38.7%	5.3%	5.3%
Broker	36.4%	27.3%	18.2%	18.2%
Courier	20.9%	9.0%	55.2%	14.9%
Mule	33.3%	8.3%	50.0%	8.3%
Employee/Worker	31.3%	15.6%	31.3%	21.9%

SOURCE: U.S. Sentencing Commission, 2016 Function Datafile, FUNCSAMPFY16.

Figure G11. Average Guideline Minimum and Average Sentence by Offender Function
Methamphetamine Offenders
Fiscal Year 2016 Sample Data

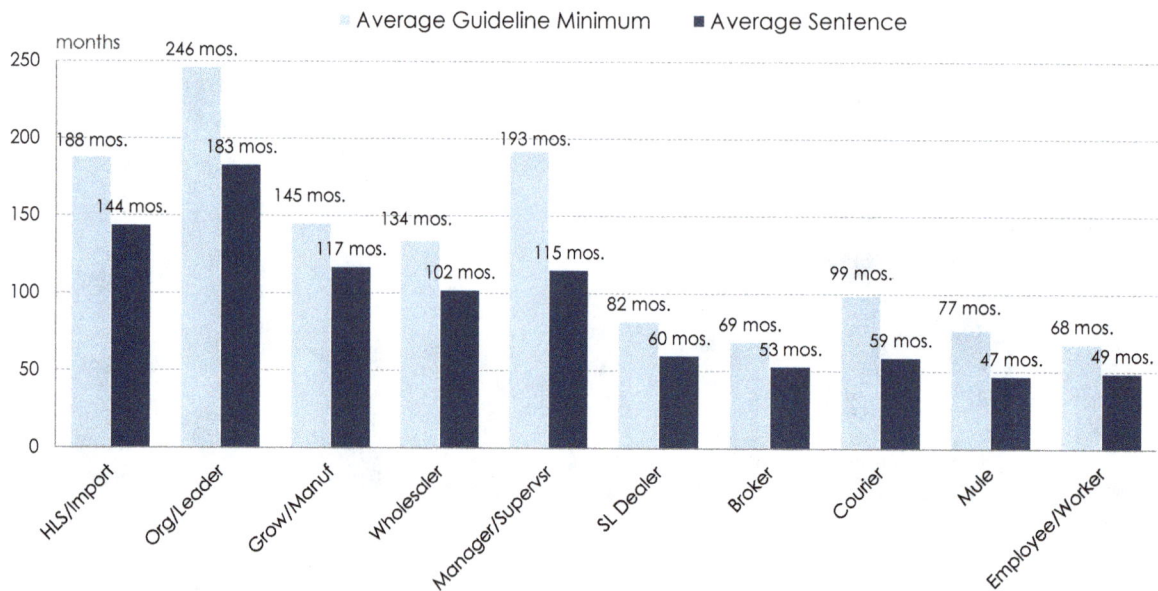

SOURCE: U.S. Sentencing Commission, 2016 Function Datafile, FUNCSAMPFY16.

Appendix H:
Heroin

Figure H1. Heroin Offenders Convicted of an Offense Carrying a Drug Mandatory Minimum Penalty
Fiscal Year 2016

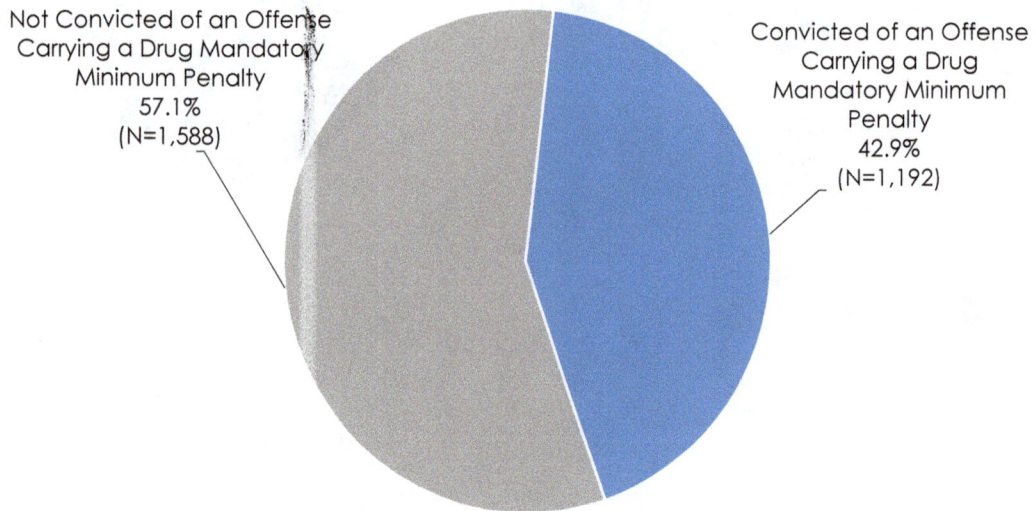

Not Convicted of an Offense Carrying a Drug Mandatory Minimum Penalty
57.1%
(N=1,588)

Convicted of an Offense Carrying a Drug Mandatory Minimum Penalty
42.9%
(N=1,192)

SOURCE: U.S. Sentencing Commission, 2016 Datafile, USSCFY16.

Figure H2. Length of Mandatory Minimum Penalty for Heroin Offenders Convicted of an Offense Carrying a Drug Mandatory Minimum Penalty
Fiscal Year 2016

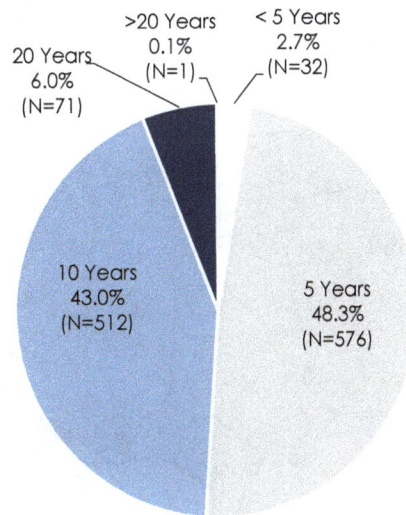

>20 Years
0.1%
(N=1)

< 5 Years
2.7%
(N=32)

20 Years
6.0%
(N=71)

10 Years
43.0%
(N=512)

5 Years
48.3%
(N=576)

SOURCE: U.S. Sentencing Commission, 2016 Datafiles, USSCFY16.

Figure H3. Number of Heroin Offenders Convicted of an Offense Carrying a Drug Mandatory Minimum Penalty by District
Fiscal Year 2016

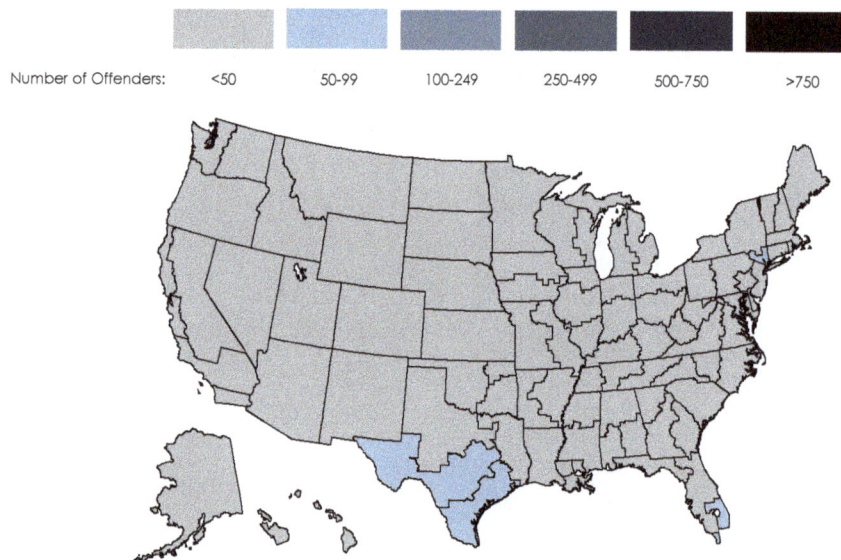

| Number of Offenders: | <50 | 50-99 | 100-249 | 250-499 | 500-750 | >750 |

SOURCE: U.S. Sentencing Commission, 2016 Datafile, USSCFY16.

Table H1. Demographic Characteristics of Heroin Offenders
Fiscal Year 2016

	All Heroin Offenders	Convicted of an Offense Carrying a Drug Mandatory Minimum Penalty	Relieved of Mandatory Minimum Penalty	Subject to Drug Mandatory Minimum Penalty at Sentencing
Total (# of offenders)	2,780	1,192	566	626
RACE				
White	16.8%	10.1%	10.6%	9.6%
Black	40.0%	41.7%	27.6%	54.4%
Hispanic	42.0%	46.7%	60.4%	34.4%
Other	1.2%	1.5%	1.4%	1.6%
CITIZENSHIP				
U.S. Citizen	81.3%	78.5%	67.3%	88.7%
Non-U.S. Citizen	18.8%	21.5%	32.7%	11.3%
GENDER				
Male	83.7%	88.7%	83.4%	93.5%
Female	16.3%	11.3%	16.6%	6.6%

SOURCE: U.S. Sentencing Commission, 2016 Datafile, USSCFY16.

Table H2. Guideline Sentencing Characteristics, Role in the Offense and Criminal History of Heroin Offenders
Fiscal Year 2016

	All Heroin Offenders	Convicted of an Offense Carrying a Drug Mandatory Minimum Penalty	Relieved of Mandatory Minimum Penalty	Subject to Drug Mandatory Minimum Penalty at Sentencing
Total (# of offenders)	2,780	1,192	566	626
CHARACTERISTICS				
Weapon Specific Offense Characteristic	13.4%	16.9%	9.5%	23.5%
Firearms Mandatory Minimum Applied	4.4%	4.8%	4.2%	5.3%
Safety Valve Reduction	25.7%	25.2%	52.8%	0.0%
ROLE IN THE OFFENSE				
Aggravating Role	9.2%	17.2%	12.2%	21.7%
Mitigating Role	14.4%	8.7%	16.1%	2.1%
CRIMINAL HISTORY CATEGORY				
I	39.8%	38.8%	60.6%	19.2%
II	12.2%	12.6%	8.5%	16.3%
III	17.6%	18.0%	11.8%	23.5%
IV	8.8%	7.6%	5.1%	9.9%
V	5.4%	5.8%	2.8%	8.5%
VI	16.3%	17.2%	11.1%	22.7%

SOURCE: U.S. Sentencing Commission, 2016 Datafile, USSCFY16.

Figure H4. Demographics of Heroin Offenders Relieved of a Drug Mandatory Minimum
Penalty by Race of Offender
Fiscal Year 2016

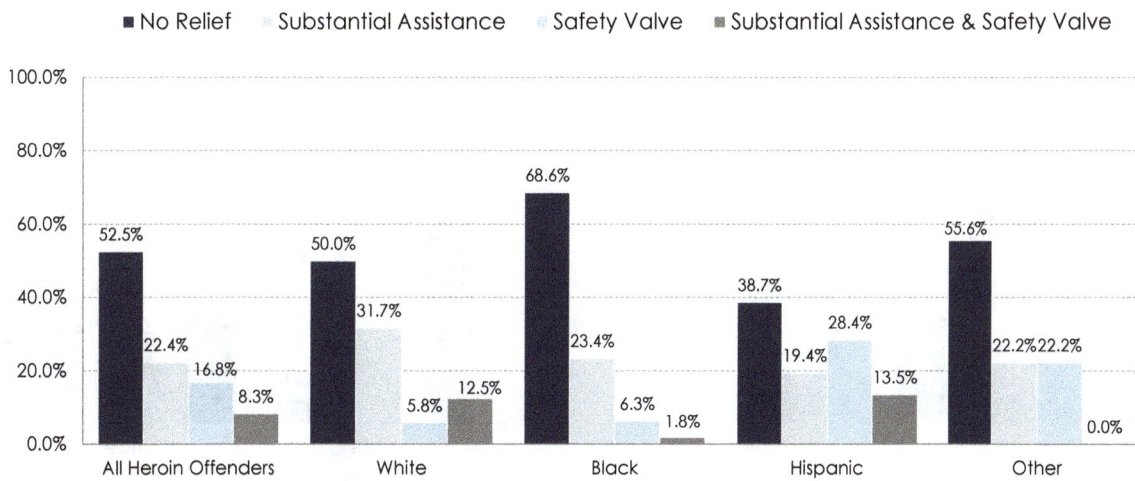

Legend: ■ No Relief Substantial Assistance Safety Valve ■ Substantial Assistance & Safety Valve

All Heroin Offenders: 52.5%, 22.4%, 16.8%, 8.3%
White: 50.0%, 31.7%, 5.8%, 12.5%
Black: 68.6%, 23.4%, 6.3%, 1.8%
Hispanic: 38.7%, 19.4%, 28.4%, 13.5%
Other: 55.6%, 22.2%, 22.2%, 0.0%

SOURCE: U.S. Sentencing Commission, 2016 Datafile, USSCFY16.

Figure H5. Demographics of Heroin Offenders Relieved of a Drug Mandatory Minimum
Penalty by Citizenship and Gender
Fiscal Year 2016

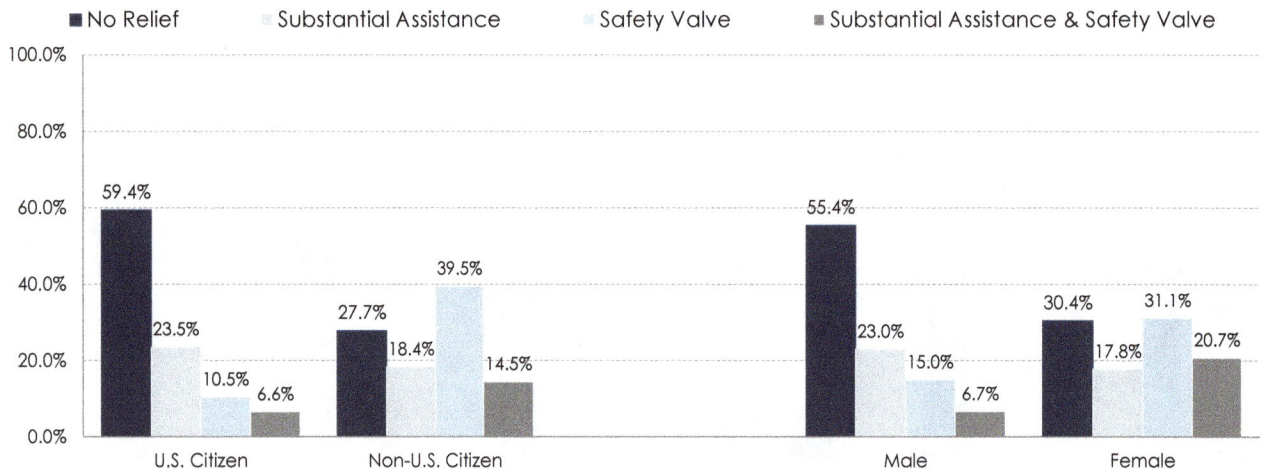

SOURCE: U.S. Sentencing Commission, 2016 Datafile, USSCFY16.

Figure H6. Average Sentence Length of Heroin Offenders
Fiscal Year 2016

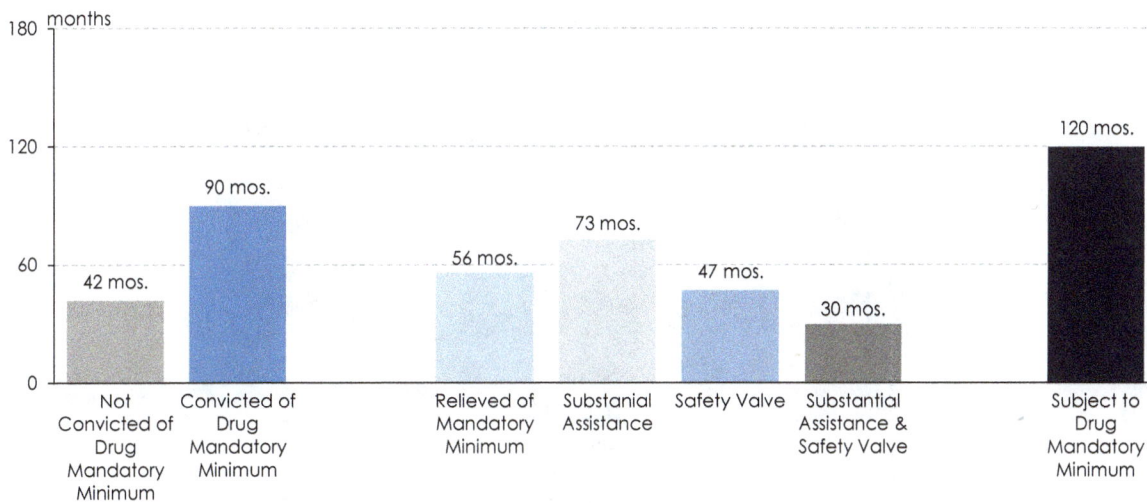

SOURCE: U.S. Sentencing Commission, 2016 Datafile, USSCFY16.

Figure H7. Average Sentence for Heroin Offenders by Demographic Characteristics
By Race
Fiscal Year 2016

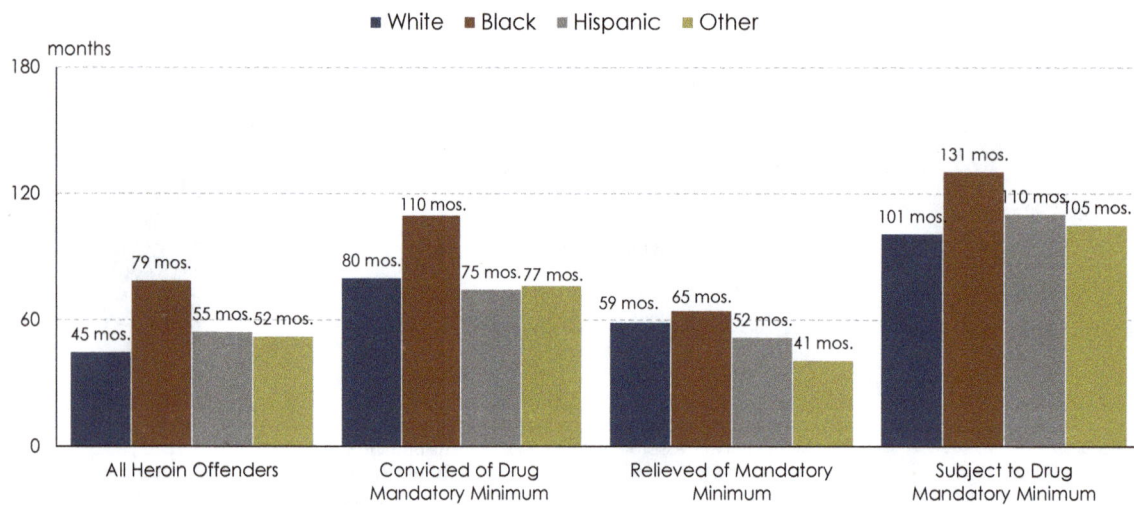

SOURCE: U.S. Sentencing Commission, 2016 Datafile, USSCFY16.

Table H3. Average Sentence for Heroin Offenders by Citizenship and Gender
Fiscal Year 2016

	All Heroin Offenders	Convicted of an Offense Carrying a Drug Mandatory Minimum Penalty	Relieved of Mandatory Minimum Penalty	Subject to Drug Mandatory Minimum Penalty at Sentencing
Total (# of offenders)	2,780	1,192	566	626
CITIZENSHIP				
U.S. Citizen	66 months	96 months	58 months	123 months
Non-U.S. Citizen	50 months	67 months	53 months	105 months
GENDER				
Male	69 months	95 months	60 months	123 months
Female	31 months	52 months	37 months	87 months

SOURCE: U.S. Sentencing Commission, 2016 Datafile, USSCFY16.

Table H4. Sentence Relative to the Guideline Range of Heroin Offenders Drug Offenders *Fiscal Year 2016*

	All Heroin Offenders	Convicted of an Offense Carrying a Drug Mandatory Minimum Penalty	Relieved of Mandatory Minimum Penalty	Subject to Drug Mandatory Minimum Penalty at Sentencing
Total (# of offenders)	2,780	1,192	566	626
SENTENCE RELATIVE TO THE GUIDELINE RANGE				
Within Range	35.5%	38.8%	16.6%	58.8%
Above Range	2.7%	1.7%	0.2%	3.0%
Substantial Assistance §5K1.1	21.6%	30.7%	64.7%	0.0%
Other Government Sponsored (no §5K1.1)	15.0%	8.9%	3.7%	13.6%
Non-Government Sponsored Below Range	25.2%	20.0%	14.8%	24.6%

SOURCE: U.S. Sentencing Commission, 2016 Datafile, USSCFY16.

Figure H8. Offender Function[1]
Heroin Offenders[2]
Fiscal Year 2009 and 2016 Sample Data

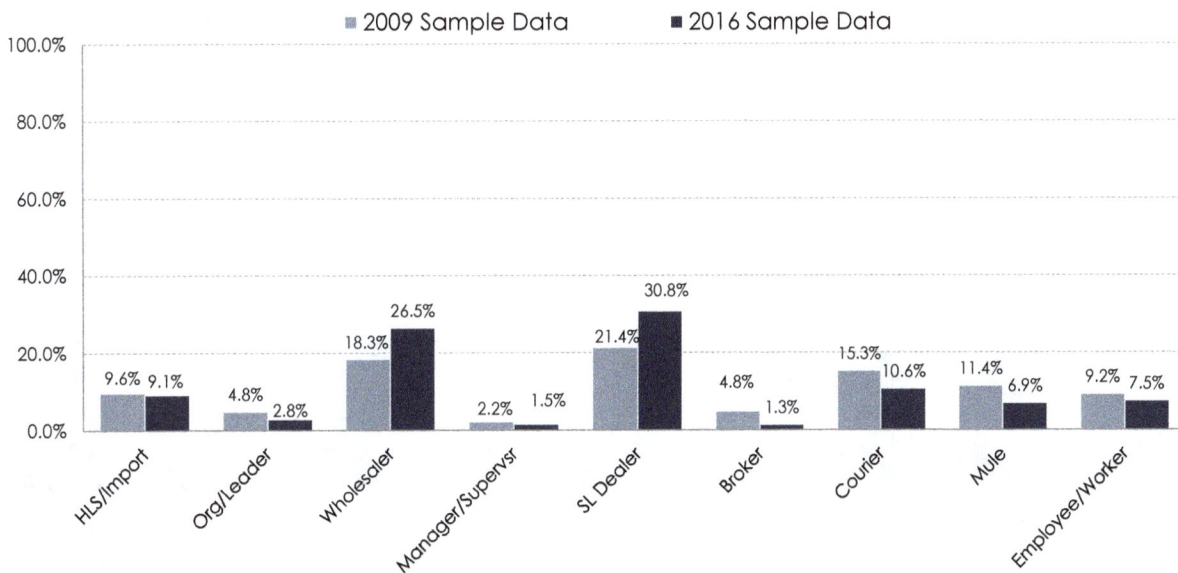

■ 2009 Sample Data   ■ 2016 Sample Data

[1] There were offenders in the samples whose function could not be determined. These offenders are not included in the overall percentages.
[2] In the fiscal year 2009 sample, 3.1 percent of heroin offenders had "Other" or "Miscellaneous" functions. In the fiscal year 2016 sample, 3.0 percent of heroin offenders had "Other" or "Miscellaneous" functions. These percentages are not represented in the figure above. There were no heroin offenders whose function was "grower or manufacturer," therefore, this function is not depicted.

SOURCE: U.S. Sentencing Commission, 2009 and 2016 Function Datafiles, FUNCSAMPFY09 and FUNCSAMPFY16.

Figure H9. Percent of Offenders Convicted of an Offense Carrying a Drug Mandatory Minimum Penalty and Subject to a Drug Mandatory Minimum Penalty by Offender Function Heroin Offenders[1]
Fiscal Year 2016 Sample Data

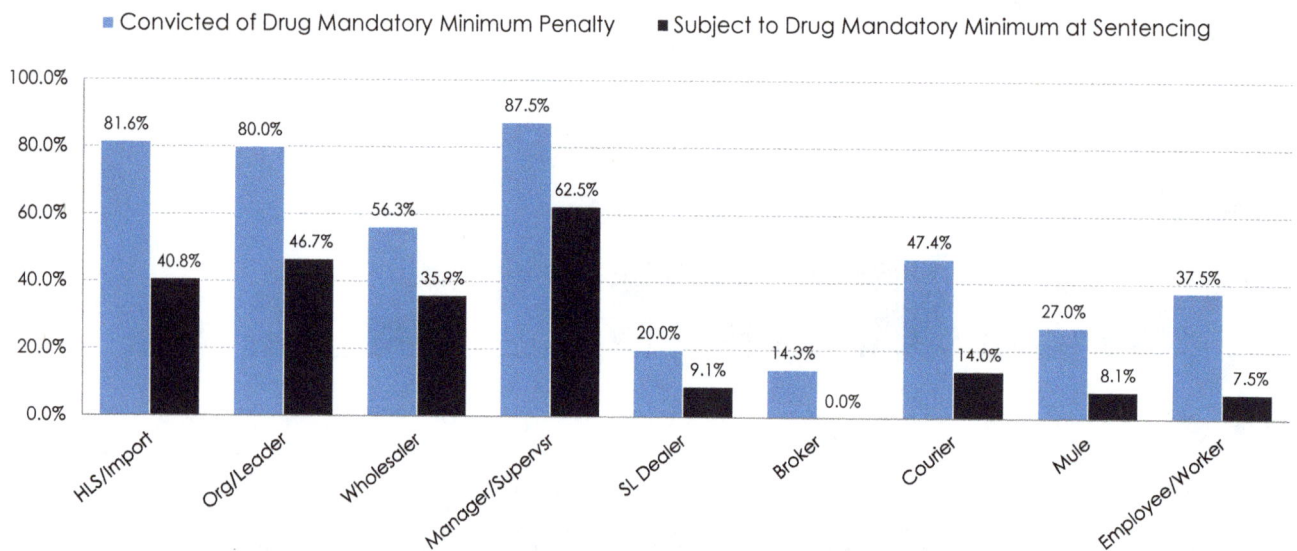

- Convicted of Drug Mandatory Minimum Penalty
- Subject to Drug Mandatory Minimum at Sentencing

Function	Convicted	Subject
HLS/Import	81.6%	40.8%
Org/Leader	80.0%	46.7%
Wholesaler	56.3%	35.9%
Manager/Supervsr	87.5%	62.5%
SL Dealer	20.0%	9.1%
Broker	14.3%	0.0%
Courier	47.4%	14.0%
Mule	27.0%	8.1%
Employee/Worker	37.5%	7.5%

[1] There were no heroin offenders whose function was "grower or manufacturer," therefore, this function is not depicted.

SOURCE: U.S. Sentencing Commission, 2016 Function Datafile, FUNCSAMPFY16.

Figure H10. Percent of Offenders Convicted of an Offense Carrying a Drug Mandatory Minimum Penalty Who Were Relieved of the Penalty by Offender Function
Heroin Offenders[1]
Fiscal Year 2016 Sample Data

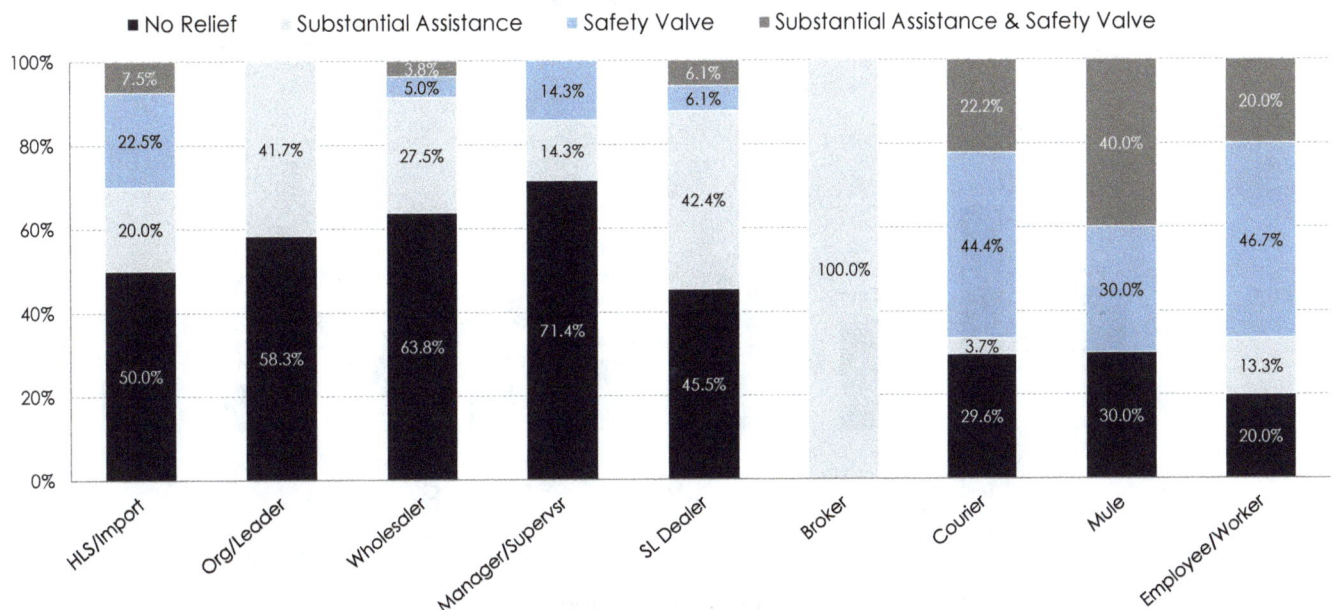

■ No Relief   Substantial Assistance   ■ Safety Valve   ■ Substantial Assistance & Safety Valve

	HLS/Import	Org/Leader	Wholesaler	Manager/Supervsr	SL Dealer	Broker	Courier	Mule	Employee/Worker
Substantial Assistance & Safety Valve	7.5%		3.8%		6.1%		22.2%	40.0%	20.0%
Safety Valve	22.5%		5.0%	14.3%	6.1%		44.4%	30.0%	46.7%
Substantial Assistance	20.0%	41.7%	27.5%	14.3%	42.4%	100.0%	3.7%		13.3%
No Relief	50.0%	58.3%	63.8%	71.4%	45.5%		29.6%	30.0%	20.0%

[1]There were no heroin offenders whose function was "grower or manufacturer," therefore, this function is not depicted.

SOURCE: U.S. Sentencing Commission, 2016 Function Datafile, FUNCSAMPFY16.

Figure H11. Average Guideline Minimum and Average Sentence by Offender Function Heroin Offenders[1]
Fiscal Year 2016 Sample Data

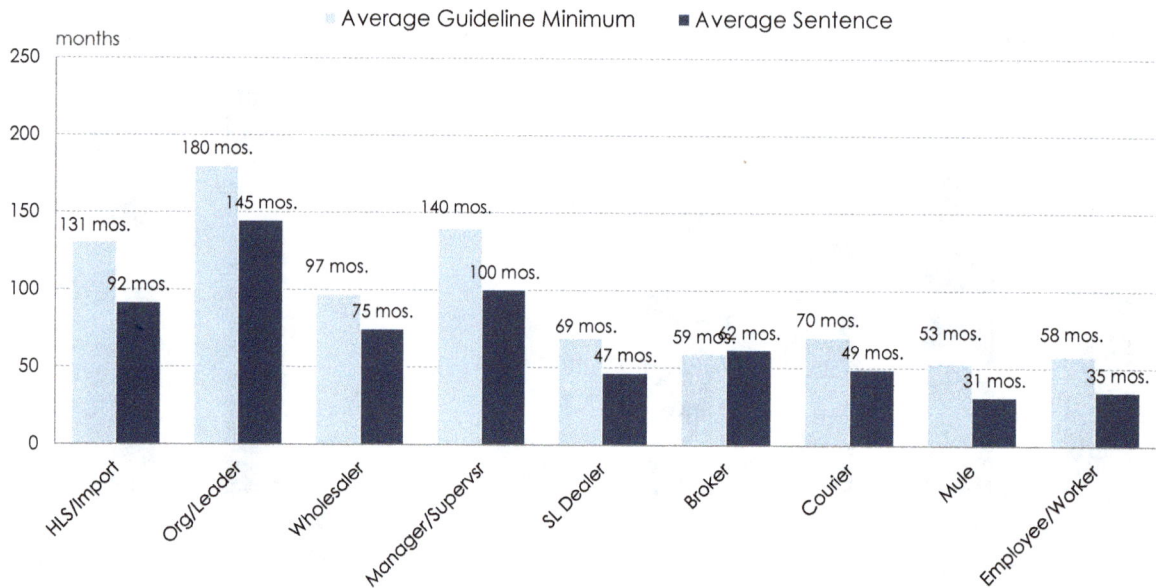

[1]There were no heroin offenders whose function was "grower or manufacturer," therefore, this function is not depicted.

SOURCE: U.S. Sentencing Commission, 2016 Function Datafile, FUNCSAMPFY16.